BRIEF LIVES

By the same author

The Civilization of Ancient Egypt
A History of Christianity
A History of the Jews
A History of the English People
A History of the American People
A New History of Art
Modern Times
The Birth of the Modern: World Society 1815–1830
Elizabeth I: A Study in Power and Intellect
Edward III
Pope John XXIII
Pope John Paul
Napoleon
George Washington
The Renaissance
Churchill

BRIEF LIVES

Paul Johnson

Hutchinson
London

Published by Hutchinson 2010

4 6 8 10 9 7 5 3

Copyright © Paul Johnson 2010

First published in Great Britain in 2010 by
Hutchinson
Random House, 20 Vauxhall Bridge Road,
London SW1V 2SA

www.rbooks.co.uk

Addresses for companies within The Random House Group Limited can be found at:
www.randomhouse.co.uk/offices.htm

The Random House Group Limited Reg. No. 954009

A CIP catalogue record for this book
is available from the British Library

ISBN 9780091936792

The Random House Group Limited supports The Forest Stewardship
Council (FSC), the leading international forest certification organisation. All our titles that are
printed on Greenpeace approved FSC certified paper carry the FSC logo. Our paper procurement
policy can be found at www.rbooks.co.uk/environment

Mixed Sources

Typeset in Fairfield

Printed

To Marigold, whose life with me has been very far from brief

THE ART OF WRITING LIVES

We all like to hear about famous men and women. The more particular and personal the information, the better. That is why, instead of putting together an autobiography, mainly about myself, I have chosen to produce these sketches, varying greatly in length according to the material I possess, of the remarkable people I have known during a long life, which has brought me at times near the centres of power, and has often enabled me to see at close quarters those who form public opinion, shape taste and set trends, or simply add to the gaiety of existence.

Biography is a very ancient art, one of the oldest, indeed, which probably had its origins in the funeral dirge, and was prescriptive. I don't, of course, mean the word itself, which comes from the Latin *dirige*, and is taken from the Old Testament psalms, *Dirige, Domine, Deus meus, in conspectu tuo viam meam*: 'Direct, O Lord, my God, my way in thy sight'. Long before Latin, or even Greek, became a written language, dirges, recited by poets, accompanied the bodies of the dead to their last resting places. The dirge survived in some societies, such as the west of Ireland, until the nineteenth century. But it had meantime reached written form, probably first in ancient Egypt, where stelae inscribed in primitive hieroglyphs go back to the fourth millennium BC. By that time the dirge had already taken the form of the funeral oration in the case of prominent men and women. That is an art form in itself, practised by Demosthenes, Pericles and Cicero, and reaching its apogee in the funeral sermons of John Donne, Dean of St Paul's, in the early seventeenth century. We all know Antonio's provocative tribute to Caesar, which Shakespeare gives us in his play, and there was a time when I could recite it in full. I have since practised the modern form of the art, which is the tribute to a departed friend given at the public 'celebrations' of his or her life, which have now taken the place of requiems in church funerals.

The earliest biographies date from the first century AD and emerge almost simultaneously in Hebrew, Greek and Latin. Actually, the four lives of Jesus Christ, which we call the Gospels, were first composed for verbal transmission, in Aramaic, the language which Jesus and his disciples spoke, but quickly reached written form in Greek. The father of Greek biography, Plutarch (c. AD 50–120), also had a religious background since he spent the latter part of his life as a priest at Delphi. Of his 227 known works, fifty-six biographies have survived, including twenty-three pairs of 'parallel lives', which he compiled to bring out the psychology of famous subjects. These *Lives* remained popular for two millennia, and as late as the 1880s Professor Jowett, Master of Balliol College, Oxford, was recommending them to young people to be read 'over and over again', alongside Bunyan's *Pilgrim's Progress* and *Robinson Crusoe* by Daniel Defoe. Plutarch's Latin equivalent and contemporary Suetonius was much read too, until the twentieth century, not least because, though lacking analytical perception, he had a taste for scandalous gossip which makes up a good part of his most famous work, *The Twelve Caesars*.

In the ancient literature there are good biographical sketches provided by historians, notably Herodotus and Thucydides in Greek, and Tacitus in Latin, the latter also providing a full biography of his father-in-law, Agricola. Thus there were plenty of models for medieval writers, from the Venerable Bede in the early eighth century, to sixteenth-century authors who had one foot in the medieval world and the other in the Renaissance – I am thinking, in England, of Thomas More, who gave us a remarkable *Life* of Richard III, which Shakespeare found useful, and Francis Bacon, who did the same for Henry VII, the first a demonisation, the second a hagiography.

This brings us to the seventeenth century, and to two outstanding compilers of multiple biographies. The first, Thomas Fuller, was an irenic clergyman who did his best to compose the differences between the crown and parliament, and was made a chaplain to Charles II after his restoration. His *History of the Worthies of England* was published in 1662, the year after his death. It has been a favourite of mine since my youth.

Far more delectable, however, is the volume compiled from the scattered notes of his younger contemporary John Aubrey (1626–97). He was not a systematic writer, and made a mess of his financial and emotional life, but he was a great digger into ancient documents and monuments, and showed skill in tapping the memories of people who had known the personages of the sixteenth and seventeenth centuries. He had an eye for the fascinating detail and a superb choice of words. He sums people up with memorable brevity. Thus, of the hyperactive Sir Walter Ralegh, he writes: 'He was no slug.' And Charles Chester, who never stopped talking, he epitomised by 'He made a noise like a drum in a room.' His lives vary enormously in length: the great philosopher Thomas Hobbes who, like Aubrey, came from Wiltshire, and was a friend for many years, gets thousands of words; others, such as Shakespeare, only a few sentences, though nonetheless of great interest and value. The work put together from his jottings is known as *Brief Lives* and to some extent is a model for this volume. I would happily have refrained from pinching the title, particularly as it has already been used by one or two modern writers of biographical essays. But, despite much cogitation, I have been unable to come up with a better.

One of Aubrey's merits was his persistent efforts not just to record what people did but what they thought. He loved psychology. So do many clever people. The attempt to enter into the minds of famous men and women had its roots in autobiography, and in particular two works from late antiquity, the *Meditations* (as it is generally known) of Marcus Aurelius, written in the second century AD, and the *Confession* of St Augustine, which dates from the early fifth century. Both had immense influence, over a long period, on the practice of describing states of mind, and the skill with which it is done. Aubrey was familiar with both these noble works, and made excellent use of them. He also had an admirable liking for listening carefully to, memorising and recording direct speech. Nothing brings a historical person to life more vividly than his ejaculations – William II (Rufus) being a prime example. Thus, on being informed of the death of the Pope: 'God rot him! Who cares a damn for that?' Or, when his chamberlain brought him a three-shilling pair of shoes: 'Three shillings? You son of a whore, since when has the king worn such a cheap pair. Go and bring me a pair worth a silver mark!'

James Boswell's *Life of Samuel Johnson* is the first, and exemplary, modern biography because it includes a large number of Johnson's sayings, which Boswell recorded verbatim in his diaries, often written the same evening after a session with the great man, and usually within a few days. I have tried to do the same in these vignettes, sometimes using as a source my own diaries. Whenever possible, I have used direct, rather than indirect, speech. I have also tried to convey verbal mannerisms, accents, and facial expressions while talking. J. B. Priestley, for instance, used to screw his face up into the most extraordinary grimaces when making a forceful conversational point. We also like to know about people's personal possessions. An inventory, made ten days after the death of King Edward I, records that his baggage contained fifty-nine gold rings, which he liked to give to visitors, especially pretty ladies, a pair of table knives with crystal handles, a gold cup given to him by his second young wife, Margaret, and a chest of relics, including an arm of St David, milk from the Virgin Mary and a thorn from Christ's crown. One of the relics, a saint's tooth, was specifically recorded as efficacious in warding off thunderstorms.

Clothes are another biographical detail of importance. One of my favourite volumes is *Essays in Biography* by J. M. Keynes, who besides being a notable economist was a writer of distinction, capable of what Cyril Asquith called 'limpid, satanic fluency'. As a Treasury representative he had a privileged position during the negotiations over the Treaty of Versailles, and his portraits of the leaders of the Allies are memorable. Thus he pictured Clemenceau: 'At the Council of Four he wore a square-tailed coat of very good, thick black broadcloth, and on his hands, which were never uncovered, grey suede gloves. His boots were of thick black leather, very good, but of a country style, and sometimes fastened in front, curiously, by a buckle instead of laces.' Keynes also had a gift for biographical metaphysics. His portrait of Lloyd George begins, 'How can I convey to the reader, who does not know him, any first impressions of this extraordinary figure of our time, this siren, this goat-footed bard, this half-human visitor to our age from the hag-ridden magic and enchanted woods of Celtic antiquity?' It continues: 'Mr Lloyd George is rooted in nothing; he is void and without content; he lives and feeds on his immediate surroundings; he is an instrument and a player at the same time which plays on the company and plays on them too; he is a prism which collects light and distorts it and is most brilliant if the light comes from many quarters at once; a vampire and a medium in one.'

I am very interested, as is right, in the intellect of the people I describe. But I make a distinction between rationality and what I call intuition. Princess Diana, in my conversations with her, and my observations of her in action with people of all kinds, struck me as the most intuitive person I have ever met, with an almost uncanny gift for striking up a relationship with a person the moment they met. Her intellect was commonplace – 'Thick as two planks' was the way she described herself – but her intuition was of the genius class, and the secret of her success. Yet it is clear there are different kinds of intuition. Hers was primitive, untutored, almost animal-like, a psychological apparatus of great power but adjusted entirely to work on the personal level, incapable of dealing with anything abstract. Keynes, in the volume I have described, gives a remarkable portrait of Isaac Newton in which he shows him to possess an intuition as powerful as Diana's, but of a different kind, capable of solving the most difficult scientific and philosophical problems:

> His peculiar gift was the power of holding continuously in his mind a purely mental problem until he had seen straight through it. I fancy his pre-eminence is due to his muscles of intuition being the strongest and most enduring with which a man has ever been gifted . . . I believe that Newton could hold a problem in his mind for hours and days and weeks until it surrendered to him its secret. Then being a supreme mathematical technician he could dress it up, how you will, for purposes of exposition, but it was his intuition which was pre-eminently extraordinary.

The use of the word 'muscles' in this context is worth noting. They can also be important, actually or metaphorically, in a sexual context. Take the case of Wallis Simpson, Duchess of Windsor. At the time of the Abdication in 1936, people often asked, 'What is her hold over the King?' Evelyn Waugh would reply: 'Oriental tricks, old man, Oriental tricks.' What he meant was a muscular practice known as 'the Baltimore clinch'. For historical reasons connected with the China trade, many people from Baltimore had Oriental blood, and Wallis Simpson was one of them. And many Baltimore ladies possessed or acquired Chinese accomplishments in the bedroom. Here, then, was another instance of muscular intuition, though of a radically different kind. I find it illuminating, and of great interest. As Dr Johnson said, 'I like a little secret history.'

Writing the lives of people called to high office and the centre of great events has always attracted me, fascinated as I am by the interaction between brains and politics. My one full-scale biography, of Queen Elizabeth I, had as its subtitle 'A Study in Power and Intellect'. It is a fact that very clever people seldom make good rulers, whereas men and women of moderate intelligence often occupy the highest executive positions with great distinction. Among the many short biographies I have written, two gave me particular satisfaction, on Napoleon and Washington. They were near-contemporaries, living in a revolutionary age, and both were military commanders who became statesmen. Napoleon was a man of astonishing brilliance, whose life ended in failure, and whose example has been disastrous to subsequent generations of power-seekers. Washington was a plodder whom many thought obtuse, but his career in war and in peace was one of almost unqualified success: the constitution he interpreted and the republic he fought for and founded have lasted for a quarter of a millennium, in unrivalled prosperity and benevolence. The moral character of a ruler is more important, in the end, than other qualities, essential though they may be to initial success.

But in judging people's performance, one should beware of generalisations. I have written four volumes of biographical essays, grouping together those I have categorised as intellectuals, creators, heroes and humorists, making a total of nearly sixty men and women. I loved doing these books, for human beings are infinitely worth studying if one has a curious mind, especially those who develop outstanding gifts, and the many peculiarities which go along with them. I now present for the reader some 250 sketches of people I have come across during more than sixty years as a writer, editor, historian, broadcaster and lecturer, all over the world. Some are mere glimpses, others attempts to pluck out the mystery. I have been obliged to exclude a number of interesting people who are still living, and I present my findings more for diversion and amusement than for edification. I simply raise the curtain on the human comedy I have witnessed, and present what I have seen, and heard, and learned, often in whispers and asides.

Paul Johnson

BRIEF LIVES

Konrad Adenauer (1876–1967) held a press conference I attended in Bonn in 1956. He was by far the greatest German statesman of modern times, for the Reich he created was more durable than Bismarck's and Hitler's and practised peace, not war. It also made the Germans really rich for the first time. He was a citizen of Cologne, and looked it, through and through – tall like the cathedral, knobbly and indented, well-dressed, elegant, clean-shaven, high cheekbones, huge ears, strong hair which took a long time to go grey, let alone white. He was very fond of champagne, and usually had a glass in or near his hand. He said he drank German champagne, but he liked French, too. His house, at the foot of the Drachenfels, opposite Bonn, was surrounded by vineyards, except for his garden leading down to the Rhine. There were sixty steps from the road up to his front door. He told me: 'Germany is a big country and there are a lot of Germans. They are hard-working and productive, clever and purposeful. It is a matter of opinion whether Germany should be united or not. She should certainly *not* be united and centralised, because then she becomes too powerful and is tempted to dominate Europe. So the answer is a federal Germany, and preferably a federal Germany within a federal Europe.'

That was true in the fifties, but today the German birth rate is so low there is a danger of a human vacuum at the heart of Europe. And the federal Europe, whose foundation Adenauer did much to lay, is secular and, if anything, anti-Christian. This would have broken his old heart.

Salvador Allende (1908–73), killed in the Pinochet takeover – though whether by his own hand, or by his Communist 'supporters', or by the army is unclear – was a nice man, who looked rather like a lecturer at the London School of Economics. I met him in Santiago some years before he became president. He took me to the races, and warned me not to bet on the last race, as he thought there was something fishy about the set-up. Sure enough, the winning horse was 'pulled' and there was a minor riot. He took me to a sumptuous tea in the Senate, of which he was a member. He told me: 'I shall never, I think, be president. The right-wing vote is too big. But they might possibly split, and then I will slip in between them.' That is exactly what happened. He was elected on a minority vote. But once he was in office, the far left took over, he was too weak to control them, and the result was a revolution, a counter-revolution, and his death.

Kingsley Amis (1922–95) was not a great or even a major novelist, but was an influential literary figure for thirty years. With *Lucky Jim*, he not only wrote a superb comic novel but also invented a new kind of writing (like Hemingway), combining the demotic with a brilliantly ironic and pseudo-academic insistence on correct syntax. Nobody had thought of this before, and nobody since has been able to exploit it so ingeniously for comic effect. He often failed to do it himself in his later novels. Kingsley Amis could not have done this without being a teacher of English, at which he was very thorough and knowledgeable. Like Waugh, he was devoted to words and their meaning. He always had by him the *Concise OED* (he thought the *Shorter* in two volumes too long, and the *Pocket* too short), and ransacked it daily. He told me he got through a copy every three years, when it fell to bits and he bought another.

Amis wrote only two other novels of any merit, *Ending Up* and *The Old Devils*, though of the rest some have brilliant passages. But he kept up a great literary act which was the delight of his friends. No other writer except Waugh generated more gossip and stories. He was the greatest living mimic, Jeremy Thorpe alone excepted. In some ways he was better than Thorpe for, like Kipling, he saw machines as fictional characters and did the noises they made in an anthropomorphic fantasy style. The best of all was his imitation of trying to start up an antique Renault four-ton lorry in Belgium during the Ardennes offensive of 1944–5. This was an amazing performance, and took it out of Amis. He needed a lot of persuasion to do it – I used triple Scotches as bribes. He could also do to perfection the *twonnnggg* noise made by the door to the kitchen of the *pension* in *M. Hulot's Holiday*. Eccentric gearboxes, the way an Old Etonian Cabinet Minister clears his throat before speaking at the Dispatch Box, pre-war steam engines, the begging yelping of the King Charles spaniel of his second wife, French telephone operators and their equipment, American radio ads, Stuka 87s diving, and lavatory noises in an old-fashioned Italian hotel were other items I remember. Amis's set pieces included a virtuoso Lord David Cecil, distinguishing carefully between Cecil lecturing, Cecil in a tutorial and Cecil at a sherry party. Then there was a cruel double act, Mary McCarthy and Edmund Wilson, both drunk after giving a party, quarrelling about taking out the rubbish, ending in threats, thumps, squeals, groans and bumps. Ernest Bevin embracing Diana Cooper in the British Embassy lift, a Cabinet meeting in Leopoldville, c. 1960, White's Bar conversations, sometimes contrasted with Brendan Behan in the Oyster Bar, Dublin – noisy, that – Henry Kissinger arguing about Vietnam with Richard Nixon, George Brown trying to kiss Princess Margaret, and the Queen holding an investiture, especially if Noel Annan, Leavis or Empson were recipients. He loved to do a peculiarly silly Bishop of Durham discussing progressive theology and President Kennedy seducing a hat-check girl. Ken Tynan's stutter during an S&M session, LBJ on how underlings should 'Kiss my ass', and Khrushchev hammering with his shoe at the UN were other prize titbits. But, properly rewarded, he would try anything. He was at his best when George Gale was there to detonate him with rasping ejaculations, and I put in a few ideas: we made a happy trio.

Amis's private life tended to become public and was much talked about. He was a negligent parent. When he left Hilly for Elizabeth Jane Howard, she was horrified to discover how their three children were being brought up. She rescued Martin, the cleverest of them, and saw that he got some schooling. They had a big house, Lemmons, at Barnet, with a six-acre garden which Jane made a paradise. Kingsley did a deal with Sanderson, the wallpaper firm, to redecorate the house and advertise their wares – 'Very Kingsley Amis, Very Sanderson' – and he was also, at this time, doing a column about restaurants, whiskys, wines, etc. There were crates of wine and spirits all over the ground floor. For a time Amis was perhaps the best-known literary figure in the country and got a knighthood plus other marks of celebrity. He and Jane entertained a lot, and we often stayed at Lemmons. But life there was precarious. Amis was not a normal man. He had countless phobias, some of them really serious. He never flew. He did not like trains much. He was afraid of the dark, and might scream horribly if left alone. Drink augmented these terrors, yet he never made any serious effort to give it up. On the contrary, it steadily increased as an element in his life until it dominated his exist- ence, though it never stopped him working. There were very few days in his entire adult life when he did not spend the morning at the typewriter. But he was often a bit tight when writing. As an experienced editor, used to handling copy from the bohemians, I could usually detect anything written even slightly under the influence. One of Amis's novels, *Jake's Thing*, struck me as largely so composed. Amis began to hate Lemmons because it was too far from the nearest pub for him to walk there. Jane had to make elaborate taxi arrangements. That dictated his move to Flask Walk, Hampstead, and even before the move he told me exactly how many steps it was from the pub. I knew then that the end of the marriage with Jane was near. Apart from the drink, he had developed an increasing phobia about women. He began to hate them and their ways (especially upper-middle-class ways) increasingly. Soon after they set up in Flask Walk, Jane left for good. Amis found it too difficult to live alone – he was often so drunk that he climbed up to bed on his hands and knees – and moved out. When the books which had filled a bookcase occupying an entire wall were removed, the wall fell down, to the dismay of the people who had bought the house.

Amis's last phase began when he did a deal with Hilly, who had married as her third husband a landless Scotch peer called Lord Kilmarnock (a second marriage to the weird Cambridge don Shackleton Bailey, an expert on Tibetan and obscure Latin poets, did not last long). This fellow tried to set up a business in Spain, but it failed, and when they came back to England they were penniless. Amis bought a house in Primrose Hill. He lived in the middle storey, and the Kilmarnocks had the top and ground floors. They both agreed, in return for free accommodation, to look after Amis, she as cook-housekeeper, he as butler-handyman. Amis worked in the morning, had a long session at the Garrick, came back and often worked a bit more, then went to the pub. The system functioned reasonably well, though Hilly found looking after him increasingly tiring and needed an annual holiday, at which time Amis went to stay with the Old Devils in Swansea. On one such vacation, he fell down, backwards, cracked his nut and died after a short illness. The month before, he had had his last *tête-à-tête* lunch with me. I have a full record of it in my diary. Among other things we discussed the precise daily duties of a butler, and whether Lord Kilmarnock was performing them satisfactorily.

We attended his simple funeral, held a few days after, which was perfectly suitable – not many there, but nice prayers and hymns. The elaborate memorial service arranged by Martin Amis at St Martin-in-the-Fields was a travesty. His father's closest friends, like George Gale and Philip Larkin, were mostly dead. The only one left was Bob Conquest. He lived in California at Stanford University. He told me he would willingly have come, but he was not asked to speak so assumed he was not wanted and did not come. The speakers were all left-wing cronies of Martin's, whose friendship with Amis was not as close as they claimed. Some were more interested in using the opportunity of the crowded church and media coverage to do some self-advertisement than in paying a proper tribute to the old boy. As I said afterwards, outside the church, to anyone listening, 'This is the worst case of body-snatching since Burke and Hare.'

Those interested in Amis should also beware of the official biography. A life was written by one of Amis's Garrick Club cronies, who knew him well. It is undistinguished but faithful. Martin Amis commissioned an American, called Zachary Leader, to do a thorough job. He produced a thousand pages, well researched and including a lot of information new to me. But it was done under the close supervision of Amis Jr, and contains a mass of stuff about him and his friends which pad out the book horribly. There are many errors of fact and nuance, due to Leader's ignorance of Amis, his generation's England, and those times, now long ago, when the old boy was in his prime. So a real life remains to be written, and probably now never will be.

Much better, and more valuable, is Leader's excellent edition of Amis's *Letters*. This reveals him as, at times, a superb letter-writer. Unfortunately, Amis, being incorrigibly selfish and self-centred, failed to keep most of the letters written to him; in particular, he kept only four from his most constant and interesting correspondent, Philip Larkin. He, by contrast, being a librarian, kept all of Amis's, which are fascinating. If Amis had been conscientious, this correspondence would have formed the finest of the twentieth century. As it is, there are only one or two minor masterpieces, especially Amis's sardonic letter to Henry Fairlie, upbraiding him for seducing Hilly.

Oh, how I miss Amis! And George Gale! If I could suddenly have them both back, forming one of the joyful trios, how happy I would be!

Noel Annan (1916–2000) was clever, but sacrificed a life of scholarship for one of academic and public careerism, collecting many glittering prizes but ending up dissatisfied. At the beginning of his life he wrote a promising biography of Leslie Stephen. At the end of his life he wrote it again. In between – nothing. His other writing was scrappy gossip. I used to see him at the Porchester Baths, swimming furiously up and down, half submerged, wearing a snorkel. He pretended he was a Second World War U-boat commander, and would say, half aloud, 'British Cruiser, NNW, bearing Six! Prepare forward torpedoes!' *'Ja, mein Kommandant!'* etc. The other interesting thing about him was that, when he was angry or excited, steam would rise from his enormous pink bald head.

Clement Attlee, Earl Attlee (1883–1967) was by no means as mild as he sometimes seemed. He could be snappish. In 1965, after the Wilson government had been in office for a year, I asked him to write an article for the *New Statesman* giving his view about how well the Labour government was doing. He wrote to me saying, 'Your suggestion is most improper. You are obviously trying to make trouble and I will not be a party to it.' Usually, however, he tried to avoid arguments by being non-committal. His wife was very fierce and bossy. When Attlee was ill and in hospital, Marigold had the next room. The nurses were terrified of Mrs Attlee and dreaded her visits. So, she thought, did Attlee. He never drove a car and, except when he had a government driver, she was always his chauffeur. She was known to the police as 'the worst driver in the Home Counties'.

When the Labour government was formed in 1964, Douglas Jay was made President of the Board of Trade. His driver, Longfellow, had driven Attlee when he was PM; Jay asked Longfellow: 'What was Mr Attlee like to drive?' 'Very nice gentleman, sir. Never talked. Each day he would say, "Good morning, Longfellow." And in the evening he would say, "Good night, Longfellow." Nothing else. Except once. We were driving to Chequers on a Friday evening, dusk like, and a car overtaking us nearly put us into the ditch. Mr Attlee was rattled, and he said, "Who was that bloody fool?" I said, "That was Mrs Attlee, Prime Minister!" So he said, "Best say no more about it."'

After his retirement, Attlee gave the Godkin Lectures at Harvard. His theme was the end of the Empire, and the subsequent book was called *From Empire to Commonwealth*. It was, characteristically, a slim volume. I was asked to interview him about it on the books programme of ABC TV at Teddington. We only had about three minutes but I prepared twenty questions, knowing he always replied briefly. I had been trained never to ask questions to which the answer was 'yes' or 'no', but to ask 'how' or 'what' questions. But that did not do for Attlee. If he didn't wish to answer a question, he simply said: 'What's your next question?' He did this two or three times; very disconcerting. So we got through most of the questions on my list. Afterwards, I asked Attlee if he would sign my copy of his book. 'Oh no, you don't want my signature. It has no value. I am a person of no significance now.' 'Yes, Lord Attlee, I do want your signature. Please do as I ask.' 'Oh, very well.' He took the book away, and stood in a corner with it, writing for what seemed a very long time. Then he came back and handed me the book, shut. As there were others talking to us, I didn't like to look until I was alone. But I might have guessed. All he wrote was: 'Attlee'.

I gave him a lift back to central London in my studio car. He, with characteristic modesty, had not asked for one. We got on to the subject of the sing-songs politicians used to have up to the 1920s, or thereabouts, after dinner. He said, 'There were a lot of topical songs about events in those days. None now.' 'Sing one.' 'Oh, very well.' He sang several, about the Boer War, in a small but tuneful voice. As we got into London, I asked him where he wanted to be dropped. 'Army and Navy Stores. Going off to India next week. Must get kitted up.' The last I saw of him he was striding purposefully through the swing doors, to a small salute from the commissionaire.

W. H. Auden (1907–73) I know about mainly from stories told me by Spender, who hero-worshipped him. When I met him I was so fascinated by the lines on his face I did not listen to what he said. Similar networks of lines on Lord Kitchener's face were described by the political journalist, Harry Massingham, as 'like a map of the Polish Railway System'. Auden's were even more intricate, the furrows deeper. The only question was: did Auden have more lines on his face than Leonard Woolf? All these corrugations were caused by excessive smoking.

A. J. Ayer (1910–89), as a young philosopher, published a book, *Language, Truth and Logic*, in the thirties, which made him famous. But he never thereafter did anything else of note. He just became more famous, and seduced young women. In 1947 I was talking to Gilbert Ryle, our philosophy tutor, standing at the railings of Magdalen Deer Park, when a spritely figure pranced rapidly across the close-cut lawns in front of New Buildings, and then vanished into the Cloisters. 'Know who that was?' asked Ryle. 'No.' 'Freddie Ayer.' Pause. 'Might have been a great philosopher. *Ruined by sex*. As of today, let that be a warning to you.' But at that stage of my life I would have happily taken the risk of ruin by having a great deal more sex than I was getting.

Later, in 1953, I was in London, arranging an article on Great Living Philosophers for *Réalités*, the French magazine I worked on. Freddie then had a chair at London University and lived in a smart mews flat. I rang the bell. To my surprise, no professor opened the door but a voluptuous young woman, in trousers. Confused, I said: 'Am I addressing Mrs Freddie Ayer?' She said: 'I wish you were.'

When I got to know Freddie, in the 1960s, he struck me as essentially frivolous, not willing, for instance, to have a serious discussion about God, in whom (he said) he emphatically did not believe, but happy to spend hours playing parlour games at which he was brilliant. His wife, Dee Wells, was much more intelligent, as well as wonderfully witty, and could give many striking examples of Freddie's incompetence and stupidity. He was often at Tom Stoppard's house in Iver Heath, and supplied material for the leading character in *Jumpers*. Later he had a near-death experience, and came to believe there might be a God, and an afterlife, after all. But when I talked to him about this possibility, he showed himself confused, and in articles he wrote on the subject was no clearer. I said to Dee: 'What's the matter with Freddie?' 'Oh, the usual problem – lack of brain-power.'

One thing I did admire about Freddie. He papered the front hall of his house with the honorary degrees he had received from universities. The elaborate black penmanship and bright red seals made a delightful decorative scheme.

Lauren Bacall (b. 1924) was born in New York and as a teenager became a movie addict. She got a job as an usherette to be close to her passion. That is how she secured tiny roles in Hollywood, subsequently becoming a star and making twenty-six movies. The one that made her was *The Big Sleep*, from the novel written by Raymond Chandler, when she met and married Humphrey Bogart (1945), the love of her life. She was often in London, and some-times came to the summer parties we had in the garden. She was a beautiful woman, who read poetry and prose well, in her fine, deep voice. Not at all actressy, let alone film-starry; a lady, rather. She told me: 'One great thing in life is always to give people, visually, a little bit less than they want of you.'

James Baldwin (1924–87), black American novelist, author of *The Fire Next Time* and other controversial works. I met him at a big party in the London Savoy. He complained to me about what he called 'rabid discrimination' and the persecution of him in particular. I gathered it was worse in Britain than in his own country. He was an interesting physical specimen. He was black but he also seemed, as it were, pale, as though sickening for something. He looked weak, wasted, thin. His features seemed too big for his face or head. His eyes in particular were enor-mous. I would have felt sorry for him, had he not gone on, and on, whining. Finally I said: 'Look, Mr Baldwin, I know how you have suffered. Why do I know? Because if, like me, you were born in England red-haired, left-handed and a Roman Catholic, there is nothing you do not know about discrimination.' This set off another bout of caterwauling. So I left him to his woes.

Thomas Balogh (1905–85) was fundamentally a good man. I liked him, though most people did not and some hated him. When I joined the staff of the *New Statesman* in 1955, he was the paper's economic correspondent, and one of my tasks was to turn his articles into English. This was no easy job but I worked hard at it, did it well, and he was duly grateful. He came from a well-to-do Budapest Jewish family (his father head of public transport, his mother daughter of a professor) and went to the famous city Gymnasium, 'the Eton of Hungarian Youth'. In 1928 he got a two-year research job at Harvard, then went into banking, in Paris, Berlin and Washington, before coming to England. He knew what he was talking about. Keynes, who published his first article in English in the *Economic Review*, said: 'Thomas tells me more about the economic situation in the world in an afternoon than I can learn in London in a week.' Balogh got British citizenship in 1938 and the next year joined Balliol, to which he remained connected nearly all his life. He was both hated and loved at Balliol. Indeed, wherever he went and in whatever circles he moved – academic, political, social – he aroused strong feelings. 'Nobody is neutral about Thomas,' said Hugh Dalton, who also said: 'I would like to kick his bloody Hungarian arse.'

Tommy's interest in statistics brought him into close contact with Harold Wilson, who was primarily a statistician rather than an economist, and when Wilson formed his government in 1964 Tommy became economic adviser to the Cabinet office. He devised all kinds of mad statistical projections for Labour's first year in office – they made my hair stand on end – and he also had a major hand in devising the strategy for 'creative tension' in the Cabinet with the Exchequer balanced by a Ministry of Economic Affairs, under George Brown, of all crazy people. This fundamental error was one reason why the Wilson government was doomed from the start. And, of course, with Balogh a prominent member of Wilson's Kitchen Cabinet, rowing with Marcia Falkender and Colonel Wigg, both of whom loathed him for different reasons as well as hating each other, there was bound to be trouble. Looking back on it, it amazes me there was not more. Gerald Kaufman, my political correspondent when I first took over the *New Statesman*, whom I persuaded to accept Wilson's invitation to join his private office, used to provide me with hilarious accounts of the rows. Both Balogh and Wigg had loud voices, and used them generously, and their *bassos profundos* were punctuated by Marcia's indignant squeaks and squawks. And if the Secretary of State for Economic Affairs tottered in on a tipsy foray, there was 'Brown murder', as Balogh put it. One of the delights of listening to his tirades was his torturing of the English language and his extraordinary skill in getting the wrong end of the metaphorical stick. He it was – and I know because I heard him say it – who came out with the splendid piece of invective (directed at Dick Crossman and *à propos* of statute law, I think): 'You think I know fuck nothing, but in fact I know *fuck all!*'

Balogh was a kind man. He knew I had a growing family and not much money, and that I loved the Lake District. So he lent me, rent-free, the Balliol-owned cottage he leased, overlooking Buttermere, for holidays. This was the most magically placed house I have ever had the privilege of occupying. He later lent us the house owned by his wife, near Loweswater. Of course he was grateful for all the help I gave him with his articles. I also, I must say, gave him a lot of advice about not making more enemies than was absolutely necessary – I was fond of him, in an exasperated way. But I slowly reached the conclusion that his judgement on economics and politics was hopeless.

Unlike Kaldor, Balogh was a good-looking man, tall and impressive. He could appear dignified too, so long as he kept his mouth shut. He had a high colour, and doubtless high blood pressure. When roused, angry and vociferating, as with Noel Annan the steam used to rise from his bald head in the most alarming manner. I often wanted to get the two of them together, and see who could raise more steam. But they hated each other too much for that. Being good-looking and a talker, Balogh caught the eye of Pam Berry, who had him to her lunches. She had a soft spot for him, and loved filling him up with rich food and strong drink. Two days before his sudden death from apoplexy, he had come to one of our big Sunday lunches where he did himself well. When I heard of his death I blamed myself for not restraining his appetite. Then Pam told me he had lunched with her on the Monday 'and gorged, darling, simply gorged'. So I felt less responsible. Anyway, as Pam said: 'Not a bad way to go.'

Natalie Barney (1876–1972) still ran her weekly salon in the rue Jacob when I lived in Paris in the early fifties. She went back to France before the First World War. A notorious lesbian, she had entertained Gide, Proust, Gertrude Stein, Hemingway, Anatole France, André Siegfried, André Maurois – the lot. She told me: 'I am pre-Proust, you know.' You went into a big room, dimly lit from stained-glass windows. There was a big table in the middle, sparsely provided with sticky biscuits and glasses of sweet vermouth to drink – not exactly Babylonian luxury. You sat on chairs round the periphery of the table, or went out into the little garden at the back, with white-painted cast-iron chairs and benches, and a melancholy statue or two. Once you had been properly introduced, you could come every week – it was always on the same day, about 5 p.m. – Tuesday, I think. I once saw Cocteau there, and once François Mauriac. He came, albeit a Catholic, because he was left-wing. Paul Claudel would not come because it was atheist and sinful in atmosphere. But I never heard anything indecorous said there. It struck me as *dull*, though in a Parisian way, of course.

David Basnett (1924–89) was General Secretary of the General and Municipal Workers' Union (GMWU). He was typical of the union officials who brought Britain to its knees in the 1970s and tried to set up a trades union state ruled by themselves. Not that Basnett was an extremist like Arthur Scargill. He was what the media called a 'leading moderate'. I got to know him well as I sat on the Royal Commission on the Press, which Harold Wilson set up to spite the newspapers and which was a notable waste of (our, or at any rate my) time and public money. I found him slippery, mendacious and quite untrustworthy. In that he was quite typical of the union bosses I met (usually on TV interviews or debates) during the 1960s and 1970s. They felt that the interests of 'the workers' (whom they claimed to speak for) were so overwhelming morally that a few lies and exaggerations were entirely permissible. In due course he retired and was given a peerage. What for? A good question. Bosses of important unions were always offered peerages in those days. Some, like Jack Jones, turned them down. Basnett was delighted with his and loved to be called 'My Lord' and referred to as 'His Lordship'. His *DNB* notice says he 'derived considerable satisfaction from his contributions to the House of Lords'. He was a self-satisfied man altogether.

Donald Baverstock (1924–95). The most brilliant TV producer I ever came across. He made *Tonight* the best regular programme ever on British TV. He would put two chairs almost touching, sit you in one, take the other himself, and grill you, nose to nose. Somehow, this worked. I found him horrible but was fascinated by his skill and method. He was married to a daughter of Enid Blyton, with plenty of money. The world appeared at his feet. But the Goddess of TV success is notoriously fickle. The endless strain of producing a topical TV newsmagazine five nights a week took its toll, he became a drunk and disappeared without trace in Yorkshire.

The Beatles were the subject of my most successful article in the *New Statesman*, 1955–64, before I became its editor. I wrote it when they first made the headlines and were praised by a Conservative Cabinet Minister for 'representing all that is best in the youth of modern Britain'. My piece was called 'The Menace of Beatleism' and dealt with the coming downfall of high culture and its replacement by populist pandemonium. We had more than a thousand letters, the most I have ever received as a result of an article. Two-thirds were against me, but the remaining one-third was notably better written and argued. I got a number of death threats, too. I don't repent one word of what I wrote half a century ago. Indeed, I underestimated the menace.

The Duke of Beaufort (1900–84) invited me to the annual lunch of the Masters of Foxhounds in 1959. His name was Henry and he was the 10th Duke but everyone called him Master. He was an Etonian, often beaten for 'pride and obstinacy'. 'I still have scars on my arse,' he told me (I didn't believe him but other OEs say it's possible). When he passed out of Sandhurst into the Horse Guards he was given 'equestrian leave' to hunt two days a week in the season. 'Well, of course I took three, but if you are to take hunting seriously it ought to be four.' He told me: 'I was called Master or Little Master as a boy because my father gave me a pack of hounds when I was twelve.' Hunting was his 'trade', as he called it. 'I know a bit about it. That is, I know a hell of a lot about it. It's the only thing I know. You may think I'm a stupid, wasteful fellow, but running a pack of hounds provides work and gives pleasure to a lot of people, as well as the hounds who, let's face it, are more important than people. Well, nicer, anyway.' 'Why are they nicer, Duke?' 'Because hounds are al-al-al-altruistic. Whereas the people who hunt have mixed motives, often bad ones.' He ran his pack for nearly fifty years, a record.

The Master married into the Royal Family. When war came in 1939 he invited the widowed Queen Mary to take refuge at Badminton, his vast house in Gloucestershire. 'She told me she had cut her staff to the bone. But when she arrived she brought fifty-three people with her, in a long convoy of Daimlers. It stretched like in that play – *Macbeth*, was it? – "to the crack of doom". I couldn't believe my eyes. My family had to move out of the house. She was very determined. Once dug in, she set about the ivy – she hated ivy – tearing it down from the house and the park walls. She had everybody at it – her own servants, ours, the estate staff and the soldiers who guarded her. When I came back from leave it was all gone. I rather liked the ivy. But at least she didn't steal our furniture.' 'How do you mean, Duke?' 'Well, she had this trick of saying, "You have our permission to present us with that", pointing to a pretty object. And you had to hand it over. But she didn't do that to us – wartime, you know. Anyway, the best things had been put away.' After his death the anti-blood-sports people tried to dig up his body, but they did themselves nothing but harm. As Trollope used to say, 'Let sleeping dukes lie is a good motto'.

Lord Beaverbrook (1879–1964) was a generous man. He had a magnificent cellar, containing many bottles, including magnums and jeroboams of vintage champagne, some going back to before the First World War. When I dined with him at his country house,

Cherkley Court, he gave me some of this nectar, a Krug from the early 1920s. I praised it, saying quite truthfully that I had never drunk such fine wine. The next day, his driver delivered at my house two magnums of it.

At the same dinner he did a pantomime act with his old friend and wartime assistant at the Ministry of Aircraft Production, Sir Patrick Hennessy, by now Chairman of Ford (UK). When the cigars were handed round, this man took two, lighting one and putting the other in his top pocket. Beaverbrook remonstrated: 'No, Sir Patrick, that is rude. You should take only one cigar. Put the other back in the box.' 'No, Max. These are good cigars and you can afford to give me two. I will not put the other back in the box.' Beaverbrook said nothing more but, a minute later, he crept up behind Sir Patrick's chair and tried to snatch the cigar out of his top pocket. But he was not fast enough. Sir Patrick grabbed his hand and, after a struggle, prised the cigar out of it. The Beaver had to go back to his seat empty-handed. He muttered: 'Force has triumphed over justice.' The table watched this scene aghast. Was it all a joke, or were they serious? Afterwards, George Malcolm Thomson, who was close to the Beaver, said to me: 'They always do that sort of thing. It could have been worse.'

The Beaver had a farm in Somerset which provided the fruit and vegetables for his table. There is a photograph of him, walking near the farm in a Somerset lane with very high hedges, an enormous Rolls-Royce following respectfully behind. He was particularly proud of his pears. Henry Fairlie told me that when he lunched with Beaverbrook at Arlington House, in St James's, the meal concluded with a great bowl of Somerset pears being placed on the table. As he stretched out his hand for one, Beaverbrook interposed. 'Now, now, Mistah Fairlie, let me choose you a good one.' He took a pear, sliced it in two with a knife, prodded both halves, then pushed them aside. 'Not good enough.'

He did it again, with the same results. And again. And again. Eventually there was only one pear left. But that would not do either. So Beaverbrook pushed the entire lot of detritus to one side, and said: 'Pears no good today.'

Beaverbrook said to me: 'Mistah Johnson. Let me give you some good advice. Don't be in a hurry to buy yourself an expensive steam yacht' (pronounced 'yat'). 'I made that mistake once.' He explained that he had been persuaded by the 2nd Lord Rothermere to buy his yacht, at a bargain price. 'Now listen here, Mistah Johnson. There is no such thing as a bargain price for a yat. Unless they give you money to take it off their hands. Yats were invented by the Devil to take your money from you.

'I bought this yat and boarded it near Washington, DC. We set off down the Chesapeake, heading for the sea. I was on the bridge next to the Captain. Suddenly there was an almighty *ker-lunk*. I said, "Captain, what was that *klunk*?" He said, "I don't know, Lord Beaverbrook. I will find out." I said: "It sounded a very expensive klunk to me." And so it proved. We had to go straight back to harbour, and that klunk cost me thirty thousand bucks.

'And that was just the beginning. So my advice to you, Mistah Johnson, is, hesitate a long time before you buy yourself an expensive steam yat!'

Brendan Behan (1923–64) was educated by the Sisters of Charity in Dublin before becoming a member of the IRA, aged fourteen. Arrested in Liverpool in 1939, he got three years in Borstal. In 1942 he was arrested again in Dublin and sentenced to fourteen years by an Irish military court. His riveting play *The Quare Fellow* was put on in 1956 and filmed. He did other things in London and New York, and wrote other things, but mostly he drank and talked. He was sometimes in London in the late fifties and early sixties. But whenever I saw him he was drunk or about to become so.

At the pub, which no longer exists, near the Royal Court Theatre I once saw him do something I have never seen any other drunken man do: he attempted to pour whisky not into his mouth but into his ear.

Muriel Belcher (1908–79) was the owner-manager for thirty years of the Colony Room in Dean Street, Soho, during its period of greatest success and notoriety. She would sit for hours on a stool, just inside the door, and when it opened would stretch out a claw-like arm, draw in the person entering, inspect him and decide whether he could stay or not. She was fat and horrible to look at, but not disagreeable if you were in her good books. Next to her sat her lady friend, a dame as gruesome as she was herself. Muriel would allow Francis Bacon unlimited credit, and at one time his champagne bill stood at over £2,000, an immense sum in the fifties. The Colony Room was unique in that ravenous queers, ferocious lesbians and perfectly normal sex maniacs mixed in friendly promiscuity. She imposed strict discipline, especially on drunks. She had a talent for creating an atmosphere in which gifted and famous, but lonely, people could be happy, and the place was never the same after she died.

David Ben-Gurion (1886–1973) was one of the three creators of Israel. Herzl thought of it and founded the Zionist movement. Weitzman did the behind-the-scenes work which made it an immediate diplomatic and political possibility, and Ben-Gurion did the work on the ground and led the new nation through its triumphant baptism of fire.

I met Ben-Gurion in 1957, being taken to see him by his *chef de cabinet*, Shimon Perez. There was much talk, some argument, chiefly exposition by the great man. He was a wonderful talker, brief but eloquent, but forceful, epigrammatic, and full of drama.

It was like talking to one of the prophets – Elijah. He was wild-haired, bronzed, muscular, in open-necked shirt – *de rigueur* in those days, suits being forbidden and worn only by 'Begin and his gang' – short cotton trousers, short socks and sandals. His office was the Defence Ministry, the only one in Tel Aviv, not Jerusalem, for security reasons, the Holy City being too near the Arab lines (they then still occupied East Jerusalem).

Ben-Gurion had a big Torah in front of him on his desk. He banged it with his fist, repeatedly. 'There,' he said. 'It's all there, the past, the present and the future of the Jewish people.' He looked at me with eyes that both blazed and pierced. 'God? Who knows God? Can you believe in someone you don't know? But I believe in the Bible. [Bang, bang.] The Bible is a fact. [Bang.] A record and a prophecy. [Bang.] It is all there, Mr Johnson. Read your Bible, understand your Bible and you won't go wrong about the Jews. [Final bang.]'

Arnold Bennett (1867–1931). Of course I never met him but when I was a boy in the Potteries he was still very much remembered. The house in Waterloo Road where he had lived was pointed out. I went there to do a drawing of it. In those days, the thirties, there was always an unemployed man hanging around a place of interest, rich in information, true or false, and hoping to earn a penny. So when I stopped to draw, a lounging man immediately accosted me. 'Art drawing Mr Bennett's house, lad?' Then, after a pause, 'I knew Mr Bennett and his mother before 'im.' 'What was he like?' I asked politely. 'Ard. 'Ee was an 'ard man.' More followed. 'As soon as 'ee became a book-writer, 'ee upped and went. They all do. 'Eed'd say, what's in Potteries for the likes of me? Nowt. So 'ee goes to London and – what's it called? Parees. Ar. 'Ee comes back at times, but 'ad nowt to say. And 'ee 'ad that luke about 'im. As if ter say, Ah doan't know what tha' wants, but whatever it is, Ah'm not giving it thee. Ee, 'ee was an 'ard man, was Mr Bennett.'

Many years later, oddly enough, Lord Beaverbrook told me: 'Mr Bennett, when he wrote for my *Evening Standard*, negotiated a very good deal for himself. I said: "You're a hard man, Arnold." He said: "Coming from you, Max, that's the best compliment I have ever been paid."'

Lady Pamela Berry (1914–82) had a passionate devotion to her father, the famous and notorious 'FE', Earl of Birkenhead. Before I met her, I had antagonised her by writing something critical about him in the *New Statesman*. Then, in 1960, Will Camp published a short, very hostile biography of FE, which was sent to me for review. I took it with me to a party at Colin Welch's house in Putney, and put it on a chair in the hall. Unknown to me, Pam Berry had agreed to come to the party, since Colin was number two on the *Telegraph*, her husband's chief paper, 'Provided you ensure I am not in the same room as that unspeakable friend of yours, Paul Johnson.' The party was crowded and we did not meet, but on leaving she spotted the offending volume in the hall, and said, 'I know who brought that disgusting book here. Well, I shall burn it!' So she took the book and carried out her threat. Shortly afterwards, we met, and instantly became friends, remaining so until her death from cancer nearly twenty years later.

She was dark, almost gypsy, pretty, vivacious, brilliant with words both in speech and in letters, very warm and affectionate and fiercely loyal, but could also be hot-tempered and totally un-reasonable. She was a first-class hater and infinitely obstinate in her vendettas. A superb letter-writer – the best. She loved to dress in gold – gold moiré frocks, masses of gold jewellery, chunky and solid, heavy make-up, jet-black hair. Flashes of red, and rubies. She carried fire with and around her as though she had just stepped out of Hell, where she had been attending a high-powered party of senior devils. She was pandemonium personified.

She was the best hostess in Europe, not just London. Her lunches at Cowley Street, her bijou home in Westminster, were wonderful. Her rules as hostess were (1) Never more than twelve or less than eight guests. (2) Don't bother about husbands or wives. (3) Superb food, served swiftly. (4) Good vintage claret or burgundy, not served in bottles but in individual carafes by each person's plate. (5) Parlourmaids not waiters, being more efficient, less trouble and quicker. (6) People invited for their personality, wit and achievement, not ex officio. (7) Always have a troublemaker. (8) No drunks or heavy drinkers. (9) No party preferences; mix pols and writers, with a Yank or two if quick and full of Transatlantic gusto and gossip, occasionally an Anglophone Frog; a woman or two but must pull her intellectual weight without talking too much. And if possible pretty or alluring; worthwhile people being busy, lunch must start promptly at one and break up at 2.30 on weekdays. (But I often stayed behind for a *tête-à-tête*.)

Pam also gave weekend lunches at her house in Oving, overlooking the Vale of Aylesbury – these lasted much longer and might be followed by a walk and tea; dinner in London, and really big parties at the Savoy on election nights and for special occasions. Pam never to my knowledge gave an unsuccessful party, a lunch that did not work or even a tiny drinks party for close friends which failed to entertain hugely. All this involved careful preparation, a fanatical attention to detail and sheer hard work. 'And no bloody thanks, on the whole', as she complained to me. I have written an essay about her (and other hostesses) in my collection, *Heroes*. I wanted her to do an autobiography and promised I would help her, but she would not agree. Her letters ought to be collected and published – they were much better than Nancy Mitford's, Annie Fleming's, Diana

Cooper's, etc., all of which are in print – but my efforts to bring this about have failed.

I suspect many of them have already been lost or destroyed. There is no entry for her in the *DNB*. But maybe, in the fullness of time, a clever, industrious young person will collect the material for a really good biography (with letters), the least this adorable and useful woman deserves.

John Betjeman (1906–84) I used to listen to at the Beefsteak Club. Gossip and stories about schoolgirls. He liked panamas, velour hats, pigtails, gymslips, black stockings and navy-blue serge bloomers. He was also fascinated by the case involving a disgraced vicar who seduced a married parishioner and used to enjoy her on the table in his Gothic study. She was called Mrs Brandy. 'Which gives a real zest to the business', as he put it. He was an ugly man for a poet but when he smiled his whole face lit up and became seraphic.

Aneurin Bevan (1897–1960) told me that his extraordinary command of the spoken word came from his stammer. As a child, with an overwhelming urge to express himself, he found there were many words he could not pronounce. So, with the help of a dictionary and Roget's *Thesaurus* he contrived to find alternatives he could say. Hence his knowledge of words and their meanings, the width of his vocabulary and the freshness of his verbal choices, which gave his speeches a special tone of novelty. He came from a family of miners, had been a miner himself and, though big, had a miner's build – strong thighs, powerful upper-back and neck muscles. Thick biceps. His head was notable and he had a habit of flourishing it by angry and impatient thrusts of his neck muscles when roused. His silver hair was thick and floppy, like a cockscomb, and that too formed part of his oratorical action-man image. He was in every way an aristocrat of the valleys, almost regal by instinct, who challenged the world to commit *lèse-majesté* at its peril, and warned even his friends *noli me tangere*. Whenever he stood, a natural court formed around him.

I was never part of his court, which consisted mainly of MPs. Having met Howard Samuel in Paris, he invited me, the next time I was in London, to a big lunch he gave for *Tribune* supporters, and put me next to Nye, to my delight. We got on well, I pressing the buttons, he performing with genial charm and considerable power. The sheer excitement of his conversation is not easy to describe because so much of its electricity lay in his voice, modulations of volume and mannerisms. (Lloyd George was the same.) So Boswellisation would not have worked, just as reading his speeches in *Hansard*, you are aware of the sinewy force of his arguments but not of the tingling ecstasy they could produce among hearers. Beside each plate was a fine cigar in an aluminium case. At the end of lunch, Nye took his out, lit it and puffed luxuriously. He noticed I did not touch mine. 'Not smoking your cigar, boy?' I explained awkwardly that, as a new member of the Labour Party, I had given up cigars and other ostentatious luxuries. 'Oh, you're one of those, are you?' he said contemptuously. 'Well, give it here, then.' He took my cigar and put it into his top pocket for future consumption. He said: 'I feel entitled to take the good things which come, in respect for my forebears, who were denied them.'

Not being part of his court, I stood on equal terms with him, and argued, often furiously, when he pushed things too far. He liked this. He always liked an argument with someone who could thrust skilfully and with knowledge. As a middle-class intellectual I did not belong to his approved categories but I had no subservience, never tried to flatter him and was always ready for a bout of conversational fisticuffs. So we got on, and in 1956 he generously wrote an introduction to my first book, *The Suez War*, which helped to speed it on its way. We disagreed about the Middle East, he being pretty contemptuous of the Arab nationalists and their pseudo-socialism (as contrasted with the genuine socialism of the Israeli kibbutzim) and we had a slam-bang argument the evening before he was seized by his fatal illness in 1960. Our acquaintance thus was short – four years or so – but I relished and valued every second I spent in his company.

His court was the top echelon of the Bevanites, as they were called from 1957. It consisted of Michael Foot, Dick Crossman, Barbara Castle and a dozen others, all MPs, mainly clever people with middle-class backgrounds. He did not attract working-class MPs, union leaders or their representatives in parliament, or Labour voters in the big industrial centres. At meetings of the Parliamentary Labour Party, where working-class MPs were well drilled and loyal to the leadership, he was invariably defeated, and his middle-class followers were liable to be shouted down. On the other hand, among the middle-class party activists of the local Labour parties he had an overwhelming majority. Hence from October 1957, Bevan and his followers held all the constituency seats in the National Executive. It was a position of influence rather than power. Bevan could not hope to dominate the party that way. The result was deadlock, and intense frustration on Bevan's side. He was not loyal to his court followers, and did not bother to consult them before changing his policy decisions or giving voice to inflammatory remarks which got the Bevanites into trouble. He was, in short, unfit to be leader of a faction. But he could have led the party, with panache and success. He was moving back towards a central position, having repudiated unilateral nuclear disarmament in 1957, and would have made a satisfactory number two to Gaitskell if Labour had won the 1959 election and formed a government. Indeed, if he had outlived Gaitskell, he could have succeeded him and, in my view, would have made a fine party leader and a great Prime Minister.

Except in small matters sometimes, there was nothing petty about Nye. He was big in spirit, magnanimous, broad-minded, patriotic (in the widest sense), undogmatic and nourished a love of jokes and fun. He was the best speaker in the House by far, the only one whose arguments could visibly induce opponents to change their minds. A speech by Nye, whether in the House, at a public meeting or a Party Conference, was always a great occasion, and an exciting one, for you could never be sure what would happen, what he would say or how he would say it. He *rehearsed* his speeches but did not have much in the way of notes and never a prepared text. He embodied political theatre at its highest level and, so long as he lived, the House of Commons lived, too – throbbed with life, indeed.

Bevan left little in the way of letters or papers, and Michael Foot, who wrote the official two-volume biography, had a hard time of it. Indeed, there was no real Bevan legacy of thought or anything else. He was a magus, and he lingers on in the minds and hearts of those who knew him and are still alive, a rapidly dwindling band. I consider myself extremely fortunate to have known him as well as I did.

Tony Blair (b. 1953) had become leader of the Labour Party before I met him. When that happened I wrote to him and said I had known all his predecessors from Clem Attlee on, but had never even shaken his hand. Could he come to lunch? He did, and we became friends. I never thought of him as a socialist, or even as a politician. He had the nicest manners of any Prime Minister I have come across, in Britain or anywhere else. They were natural good manners, but cultivated, too. If I ever did anything for him, however trivial, he would always send me a sweet, hand-written letter from Number Ten. I have a thick folder of such letters, none typewritten, all holographs. The letter he wrote to Marigold and myself for our Golden Wedding is delightful and touching.

Like many successful politicians, Tony Blair climbed the greasy pole because he could present himself, as an affable, well-meaning, sympathetic and sensitive person who enjoyed life and wanted everyone else to enjoy it, too. He was a born actor. Eric Anderson, who was his housemaster at Fettes, and his wife Poppy, used to say that Tony's political destiny was settled by Shakespeare. They were both involved in a production of *Julius Caesar*, that hardy fixture in schoolboy drama because it provides so many good parts for teenage boys, and puts few demands on them if they have to dress up as girls. The production was held up because no adequate Antony could be found, and that is the key point. 'I knew Tony Blair could act but he was only fifteen and I wanted an older boy to do it. However, we tried several in succession, and none was any good. So I said: "It will have to be young Blair after all." And it was. And he was brilliant.' Eric continued: 'Poppy dressed Brutus and his followers in blue, and Antony and his followers in red – and that is why Tony Blair became Labour.'

But it was not only that, of course. Tony has a big heart. Nye Bevan always used to say that a big heart was the one really essential prerequisite for a Labour person. 'You have to feel here,' he said, thumping his chest. I told Tony all about Nye, who was just a name to him – indeed, I gave him a lesson in Labour history, dwelling on the personalities: old George Lansbury, Ernest Bevin, Stafford Cripps, Morrison, Attlee, Gaitskell, Brown, Wilson, Callaghan. He had not actually met any of them. His weakness was that he rarely read. He went through his papers, as Prime Minister, conscientiously. But books were not to his taste. Rebuked for not reading, he said, 'I have got a book.' 'On what?' 'On the slave trade.' 'How far have you got.' 'Oh, a long way. I have finished Chapter One. I'm thinking of starting Chapter Two.'

He was remarkably lacking in malice. He never volunteered criticism of anyone. You could not get him to say a word against Gordon Brown, for instance. 'I really know Gordon, and he is a good fellow.' He was very loyal. I told him: 'The first requisite for a British Prime Minister is to stick close to the Americans. Make the American president not just your ally but your friend. Believe in him, and make him believe in you.' Tony Blair followed this advice to the letter and the Anglo-American alliance flourished mightily in his decade at Number Ten, just as it had in the days of Thatcher and Reagan. He had a high opinion of George Bush Jr and often said (as I knew from my own experience) that he was a much more intelligent man than his critics would admit, and very well informed in anything that mattered. Bush told me he had the highest possible opinion of Blair: 'A good man to be with in times of trouble.' Both insisted the other always stuck by his promises and never let you down. I hope our relationship with the most important ally – our only one of consequence – is always as firm and fruitful as in Blair's day.

Blair had a high opinion of Margaret Thatcher, and valued her approval more than that of anyone else. But he was not, in general, a good judge of character. How he could place so much trust in people like Peter Mandelson, Alastair Campbell and Lord Levy was and is beyond my understanding. Therein lay the source of his weakness – he could not sort out the good from the mediocre and the plain bad.

T. S. R. Boase (1898–1974). He was President of Magdalen most of the time I was up, in succession to Tizard. He took a great interest in my painting but always seemed to me muzzy about art, though he held endless top jobs – Director of the Courtauld,

Professor of History of Art at London University, Editor-in-Chief of the *Oxford History of Art*, etc. He was in hush-hush work in the Second World War (he was an MC in the First), both at Bletchley Park and in MI6 in the Middle East. The fact that he was a close friend of Blunt made him suspect. But he never pounced. His Christianity prevented him from being an active queer. He said to me: 'Magdalen is full of proselytising homosexuals. When you are going around the college, always keep your arse to the wall.'

Lady Violet Bonham Carter (1887–1969) was a regular figure at the Anglo-German gathering of notabilities held every year at Königswinter on the Rhine. That is where I got to know her. I valued her because she had an astounding memory – instant recall of details of events which took place half a century before. Her father, H. H. Asquith, had become Chancellor of the Exchequer in 1905 and Prime Minister in 1908, a post he held until Lloyd George ousted him at the end of 1916. She had been in love with Churchill, and wrote one of the two really good books about him, *Winston Churchill as I Knew Him*, which reflected her prodigious memory bank. She married an insignificant official (she was no beauty, and never had been) but really she was in love with her father all her life, made herself keeper of his shrine after his death, and when given a life peerage by Wilson ('very generous of him, I must say', she told me) called herself 'Lady Asquith'. Even as a little girl she was in the thick of politics. A letter to her from Asquith survives in which he describes Cabinet rows and battles, ending: 'So glad you are now able to button up your gaiters yourself.' She told me wonderful tales of those days before the First World War; arranging the flowers and the *placement* cards of a Cabinet dinner; the way the butler at Number Ten announced the guests – it was always 'Mr George', never 'Lloyd George'; the youthful Winston telling her: 'We are all worms, but I really think

I may be a glow-worm'; the smell of Edward VII: 'Cigars – and a touch of scent. But whose?' As she spoke you could hear the clip-clop of a hansom cab taking her up to Hampstead or along Park Lane.

She stood for the Commons, but never got in. She was, however, a wonderful speaker, the best woman orator I ever heard. She could be, suitably provoked, splendid on the box. A programme I did with her and Bob Boothby, in which they had a sparkling row, with me as ringmaster, was the finest TV show I ever did. Henry Fairlie called her 'the uncrowned queen of the English Establishment'. In those days – I am talking about the fifties – before the meretricious sixties revolution ruined everything – London was full of dragons: powerful, outspoken ladies who ticked young men off, put them in their place, laid down the law. There was Pamela Hansford Johnson, Norah Smallwood, Annie Fleming, Rose Macaulay, Lady Violet Powell. But Lady V was chief of them all, and many a rocket I got from her. Even when I was an editor in the mid-sixties, she used to phone me up to deliver a broadside whenever I published an article attacking liberalism by Malcolm Muggeridge, whom she detested. She always called me by my full name: 'Mr Paul Johnson'. She did the same to 'Mr Roy Jenkins' who wrote the authorised life of her father.

Bob Boothby (1900–86) was universally popular, despite his enormities, because he was always willing to do you a service. He was immensely kind to me. He never did anything mean. It always made me laugh that he was the only child of the manager of the Scottish Provident Institution. No one was less provident in any sense. Eton, Magdalen and White's, he always mixed with the elite but his seat in Aberdeenshire, which he held for thirty-four years, kept him earthbound. He was a wonderful speaker. His voice, deep, resonant and mellow, was magic, his command of words overpowering. His arguments were sinewy. He was well read and kept up to date (he was one of the earliest Keynesians). But he was never a serious candidate for high office. Harold Macmillan said: 'Poor Bob. He always had his hand in the till.' He seemed to have an imperfect understanding of the difference between right and wrong (rather like Dick Crossman). He was PPS to Churchill when Churchill was Chancellor of the Exchequer, and did a lot of city stock-gambling to support his extravagant way of living. That was bad enough. Worse, he began an affair with Lady Dorothy Macmillan, wife of an MP colleague, in 1929, and it continued in one form or another until her death. He may have begun the affair in his usual good-natured way, but she became the dominant figure in the partnership and would never let him go. In Churchill's wartime coalition, Boothby was made Under-Secretary of Food, a key job since the minister, Woolton, was in the Lords. But in October, a Commons committee found him guilty of improper behaviour – in effect, failing to declare an interest. There is argument about the degree of his guilt but Churchill dropped him, and he never got office again.

Churchill grudgingly gave him a knighthood in the 1953 Coronation honours. But not office. Eden and Macmillan threw him over, too. But he became a huge TV star. He was a delight to do TV with as he was courteous, witty, fun, outrageous, laughed at your jokes and applauded your thrusts. He was a gentleman rogue. That year, I think, he had a sort of heart attack and gave up his seat. Macmillan gave him a life peerage, which he enjoyed as much as TV, treating it as more or less the same thing. 'Only better,' he said to me. 'They pay you just for turning up. It's the best racket I've ever been involved in. You go there, make sure they've checked you in, have a drink in the bar with chums, and then just bugger off, if you feel like it. And all kinds of perks.'

He was definitely dodgy. He was always getting involved in schemes for making money fast. He loved the criminal fringe of Soho and the West End. He was bisexual. Lady Dorothy did her best to keep him straight, and to keep wicked men and boys out of his delightful but disreputable flat in Eaton Square. In 1967 the *Sunday Mirror* ran a story about his homosexual involvement with the gangsters known as the Kray twins (plus photo). Boothby replied with a letter to *The Times* denying he was a homosexual but admitting business talks with the Krays. The *Mirror* paid him £40,000. This tax-free capital sum, a fortune in those days, came as a blessing and enabled him to make a defensive marriage to a Sardinian lady, who turned out to be a very good wife. (He had earlier had a two-year marriage to another Cavendish.) When Boothby died it was shown he was certainly a lifelong homosexual. Of his two volumes of memoirs, the second (1978), *Boothby: Recollections of a Rebel*, is good for a laugh, and I gave it a splendid review (which he acknowledged in a delightful letter) but not all of it is true. On the big issues of the day, economic and international, he was nearly always right, and spoke out bravely. But his character made any progress in the direction of high politics impossible. Poor old Bob! But he had a jolly life, didn't he? As the Queen Mother said: 'Bob's not your uncle. But he's my favourite nephew.'

Maurice Bowra (1898–1971). The most overrated don of his generation, Warden of Wadham 'for what seemed like eternity', to quote Hugh Trevor-Roper. He had a very loud voice, needed in those days of the 'Academic Shout', the *aawacoaawah* noise dons made to be heard over the hubbub of high table. Bowra was supposed to be witty but I never heard him say anything remotely funny. His books are hopeless. When I ran the *NS* he asked if he could write columns from Oxford. The results were unpublishable. But Evelyn

Waugh spoke well of him and said he had done many good deeds, unknown to most.

Mark Boxer (1931–88) was having an epileptic fit at a party the first time I saw him in 1955. It was a spectacular incident. By art or accident he was always the centre of attention. At Cambridge (King's) he published in *Granta* the lines:

> *You drunken gluttonous seedy God*
> *You son of a bitch, you snotty old sod.*

He was sent down and turned his departure into a hugely successful publicity stunt. That was the pattern of his life in journalism, where he had two successes, *Queen* and the *Sunday Times Magazine*. His pocket cartoons were his best contribution to life and laughter. He could sometimes get a surprisingly good likeness but, unlike Osbert Lancaster and Max Beerbohm, his captions were poor, and he got details of dress wrong. He drew me with a velvet-collared overcoat, which I have never worn, and carrying a riding crop, which I have never possessed. 'Why don't you ask me for the original, Paul?' 'Don't want it.' But I have several originals of his of other people.

Edward Boyle (1923–81) was a privileged fellow who showed the futility of privilege. His grandfather, a Tory MP for Taunton, was made a baronet. We went up to Oxford the same year as I did, 1945, already a celebrity. He had inherited the baronetcy the previous year, and a lot of money and property, too. He had been captain of the Oppidans at Eton, editor of the *Eton Chronicle* and President of Pop. He was a scholar of Christ Church. Though a poor speaker, he was elected President of the Union. He did not ride but he belonged to the Bullingdon. He was the first name on the list of guests for every smart party. He did not 'dine at Blenheim' once a week – but often. Before coming up, he had had a privileged spell at the FO, so he knew the wider world, the embassy circuit and the London hostesses. The mantelpiece in his rooms was thick with enviable London invitations.

But – the girls didn't fancy him. At Miss Sprule's Typing Academy he was a joke. 'Ugh! That Edward Boyle! So fat and soft and flabby. I don't fancy that lying on top of me.' Those debs, or ex-debs, did not mince their words. 'I hear he has a tiny you-know-what.' 'How do you know?' 'How does anyone know?' 'Who's seen it?' 'I have.' 'No you haven't.' Well, I've looked at his hands. Those nails.' He was the worst nail-biter I've come across. Bitten down to the quick. Sometimes bleeding. It was said he was sure of a first, and pretty certain to get an All Souls fellowship. Instead, in the History Finals of 1949 he was a victim of 'the Massacre of the Innocents'. So was I but at least I was viva-ed for a first, and got a second. Boyle, like so many others, got a third. But in due course he got a safe Tory seat in Birmingham, was, at twenty-seven, the youngest MP, was made a PPS a year later and in 1954 given office. He resigned over Suez, but was soon back under Supermac and a member of the Cabinet in 1962.

I had a curious experience with Boyle on *Any Questions?* Margaret Thatcher was also one of the panel. She had just been made Conservative spokesman for education, to much criticism, as being 'right-wing'. Boyle joined in the left-liberal whining, echoed by the studio audience. Mrs T looked pretty and vulnerable, so I came to the rescue. I said: 'Politics is about choices. If you have Boyle speaking for the Tories on education, and a Labour person, you have no choice, for both produce the same wishy-washy liberal clichés. On the other hand, if Margaret Thatcher speaks for the Tories, you do have a choice because she stands for the genuine article of Conservative education policy. So I welcome her appointment and wish her well. Let's give her a round of applause.' So they did, and she was delighted, and gave me a big kiss afterwards.

Boyle died youngish (fifty-eight) of some sad disease, covered in honours and plaudits, still biting his fingernails to the quick.

Willi Brandt (1913–92) was a success as Mayor of Berlin but a failure as German Chancellor. Why? Perhaps because in Berlin politics didn't matter, only patriotism, and Brandt was the epitome of the Good German. I really warmed to him. So did most people. He used to say, 'God gave the Germans all the virtues except a sense of proportion. Lack of it has led them into all their disasters.' He always lunched at his desk on beef sandwiches and a bottle of beer, and I shared this modest repast with him, listening to his racy stories. He said of Adenauer: 'A bit too grand for me. Makes me feel like his butler.' 'But he looks like a butler himself.' 'I know. That's what hurts.'

George Brown (1914–85). I first met him at a left-wing garden party in Hampstead in 1954 when I was still living in Paris, but known for my writings in the *New Statesman*. He came up to me and said: 'I know about you. You are middle-class, an intellectual and a Roman Catholic. Three things I hate.' This was my introduction to the soft underbelly of the Labour Party. Brown often boasted about being born in Peabody Buildings and having genuine working-class credentials. But in fact he was East End commercial middle-class Jewish. His father was a fur salesman. George knew about fur, and if a lady at a party was wearing one he would stroke it and comment on its quality, often disparagingly. He was rude when cold sober, and ruder when drunk. He had a horrid habit, when tipsy at parties, of going up to a woman and kissing her, saying, 'One on each cheek, and one in the middle.'

He did this once too often, and to Princess Margaret. But she was also liquored up, and gave him a terrific box on the ears. He had very large, liquid, dark brown eyes, was short, plump and energetic in a disorganised way. He could be a very effective speaker in the Commons, and had a large following among right-wing back-benchers. Otherwise there was no point to him and he was infinitely more trouble than he was worth. He would have late-night irrational tantrums when in liquor and go around the lobbies abusing the Prime Minister. Harold Wilson had no choice but to give him high office when he formed his government in 1964. But the actual office, Secretary of State for Economic Affairs, was a silly novelty, and its supposed object – to promote 'creative tension' with the Exchequer – made no sense. It was bound to lead to rows, and did. Wilson should have sacked Brown after his first midnight tantrum. Then we would have heard little more of him. Instead he was allowed to go on misbehaving, and bringing Labour, and Britain, into disrepute, especially after he was moved to the Foreign Office. He was a nasty joke, never anything more. I had to deal with him several times on TV and was brutal: 'George, if you misbehave I shall simply tell the viewers you are too ill-bred and drunk for me to continue the interview.' Strangely, he did not object to this treatment. Out of office, and in the Lords, he slowly fizzled out. His final act of wickedness was to abandon his long-suffering wife, Sophie. I last saw him outside the Palace of Westminster, looking dead or dazed, like an old oil lamp with just the wick feebly glowing.

Evangeline Bruce (1910–95) was the wife of America's most famous ambassador in London in the post-war period, David Bruce. After his retirement and death she kept a flat in Albany, and entertained there. It was the discreet, gracious and elegant hospitality which went out for good in the destructive sixties. David Bruce, a hereditary democrat from Virginia, had left the party in protest at FDR's scandalous treatment of Bruce's father-in-law, Andrew Mellon. Mrs Bruce told me all about it, and many good stories of old Washington before it was mucked about by the Kennedys. She was a beautiful woman, who in old age suddenly woke up blind.

William F. Buckley (1925–2008) was the driving force behind the revival of the Intellectual Right in the United States. He created the magazine *National Review* as the voice of the new trend, and gave it clarity, wit and cerebral responsibility. He also for many years ran a top-class interview programme on TV. It would be hard to think of any other individual in the US who exerted so much influence on the political scene from outside Congress or high office. He did all this without even once departing from his high standards of moral probity and superb manners. He was an old-style gentleman, the archetype WASP of the best kind. He interviewed me twice for TV, once at my home in Iver, and I have nothing but savoury memories of these occasions. He used traditional English public-school diction, as modified by Groton and the Ivy League. When his beautiful but boisterous and outspoken wife went over the top, he would say: 'Cut it out, Pat! *Cut it out!*'

George Bush, Sr (b. 1924) was a poor speaker. When he was vice-president both of us attended a conference in Aspen, I think. He made a deplorable speech. I spoke too, and afterwards he congratulated me: 'By God, you certainly know how to do these things.' I said: 'I hope you won't mind me giving you a bit of advice, Mr Vice-President. You should either read from a text, or ad-lib from notes. Trying to combine the two is fatal. And if you decide to ad-lib, never begin a sentence without knowing what your main verb is to be.' He thought about this carefully, and said: 'I'll try to remember that.' He struck me as an unusually modest man. But then, as Churchill said of Attlee, 'He has a lot to be modest about.'

Rab Butler (1902–82) was an awkward fellow, physically. He generated unease. He had withered fingers on his right hand but still used it to shake hands with you. He walked in a kind of awkward dance step, and was once photographed doing this, entering Number Ten, with hat and cane like a song-and-dance comic, or Laurence Olivier playing Archie Rice in *The Entertainer*. He married not one but two Courtauld heiresses, and so got a lot of Impressionists. I examined them carefully when I stayed with him once, in the lodge at Trinity, Cambridge, where he had become Master in his retirement. There was not one I would have specially liked to possess.

Butler was not so much accident-prone (though he was) as a coiner of awkward phrases. He said of Eden, for example, 'He is the best Prime Minister we have got.' What was this supposed to mean? When, during the war, he was made Minister of Education, he said: 'I feel the honour deeply.' Churchill said: 'Well, it was intended as an insult.' Butler said: 'I know. I feel that deeply too.' He told me: 'I was brought up to serve. Politics is the opportunity to serve, and office the reality of service. I never refused jobs the Prime Minister asked me to do. I loved being Chancellor of the Exchequer, but I took on the Home Office and the leadership of the House, both jobs I hated, because I was asked. I took on the African job because I was asked. I took on the FO because I was asked.' In 1963 he could have torpedoed the Home government by refusing to serve (as Powell and Macleod refused), but he told me, 'It would have been against my nature.' I suppose it is true, as he argued, that the existence of people like Butler, without the ultimate aggressive ambition to get to the very top, enables the system to work. So we ought to value him. But, somehow, his self-abnegation, or self-sacrifice, or whatever you might call it, seemed puny, mean-minded, even cowardly. 'You would not want to share a slit-trench with Rab', as Nigel Birch put it.

Antonia Byatt (b. 1936). The first thing I learned when I moved in literary London was that if you talked to Margaret Drabble you were never to mention her sister, A. S. Byatt, or vice versa. 'You mean, they hate each other?' 'Oh, I wouldn't go so far as that.' Once, in the London Library Reading Room, I saw Toni Byatt at work. She was sitting at a desk piled high with books. There must have been fifty at least, and she sat among these towers like a garrison inside a castle. I whispered, 'What are you doing?' 'Writing a novel.' I thought this a curious way to write a novel. Then I remembered that Flaubert, writing *Bouvard et Pécuchet*, his last, not quite finished, novel, had *boasted* he studied more than 1,500 books in order to create it.

Ritchie Calder (1906–82). He came from Angus and had a thick Scotch accent, hard to understand. His parents were humble, though upwardly mobile (his father a linen worker, who became works manager) and he left school at sixteen, became a reporter, attending police court cases. Then, by a stroke of luck, he got involved in a science story and was hooked. He became Britain's leading science writer (through the *News Chronicle*), the first to be a celebrity. He had a rubicund dog face and longish hair plastered down with Brilliantine and parted in the middle. During the war he was taken up by Boyd Orr, the great food expert, and mixed in high political circles. By 1955 he had joined the *New Statesman* and attended our Monday morning conferences. He had many ways of irritating Kingsley Martin, two in particular. One was his accent. Thus, he would interject into a discussion of African poverty, 'What they need, really, is sometha' like Boyd Orr's food board.' Kingsley: 'I've known John Boyd Orr many years and he's never shown any interest in football. 'Not *fute ball*, Kingsley, *fude budds.*' 'Yes, yes, my dear fellow, I heard you the first time. Foot ball, indeed!' The second source of irritation was Ritchie's pipe. This was bad enough when he smoked it, but he reserved the editorial conference as a convenient time for its weekly clean. It was complicated, with thin steel sections; Ritchie spread a dirty hanky over his knees, took the thing to bits, then used a pipe cleaner to get the coagulated burnt tobacco out. This disgusting process was watched with distaste by other members of the editorial board, Kingsley in particular. But the process and then the reconstruction of the pipe took time, and we gradually lost interest and forgot about it. The topics droned on: nuclear weapons, legislation to remove homosexuality as a criminal offence, corporal punishment in schools (Kingsley's favourite topic), the outrageous behaviour of the Beaverbrook press – all the usuals. Suddenly, Ritchie, having completed his cleaning, made a triumphant *peeeeep* noise through his now burnished pipe, producing a high-pitched sound that took everyone by surprise. It always made Kingsley jump, and he would turn on Ritchie furiously. 'Do you have to make that horrible noise?' 'Ah du, Kingsley, but I weel not make it again to please ye.' He did, however. The last straw came in 1966 when Ritchie was made a peer, something Harold Wilson denied to Kingsley despite many hints. I always thought of Ritchie as a music-hall comic, in a dull way. He reached the summit of his ambition when Wilson made him Chairman of the Metrification Board, a quango which might have been invented by Trollope.

Cardinal Nicola Canali (1874–1961) was the last genuinely reactionary prelate of the Roman Catholic Church. He was probably the most important cardinal during the last years of old Pope Pius XII (d. 1958), but, once John XXIII was on St Peter's Throne, Canali's day was over. He told me that the world was now so wicked, and growing steadily more so, that he thought God would shortly end it, 'as he once destroyed Sodom and Gomorrah'. 'When will that be, Eminence?' 'Early in the twenty-first century.' But many thought Canali himself wicked. He is the villain of Roger Peyrefitte's novel *Les Chevaliers de Malte*, which is about Canali's attempt to get his hands on the vast treasures of the Knights of Malta. Many years later I asked a senior official of the Order if the novel were true. 'Every word,' he said.

E. H. Carr (1892–1982) was a sinister, behind-the-scenes supporter of Stalinist Russia for nearly half a century. He had twenty years in the Foreign Office, followed by long spells in the University of Wales, Oxford and Cambridge, plus a senior job on *The Times*, and in all three spheres he did his best to put the Soviet case, push forward those who supported it and damage its critics. He was enormously energetic and full of venom. What he liked about Lenin, and still more about Stalin, was their authoritarianism and ruthlessness. Between 1950 and 1978 he published his *History of Soviet Russia*, a detailed whitewash but which also, despite himself, serves as a mine of information (usually accurate) which can be used against Sovietism. I made good use of it in my *Modern Times*. Although he wrote a nasty and dangerous book on the writing of history, *What Is History?* (1961), he was not really a historian but a chronicler with an instinct to write propaganda. He wrote a vast amount in leaden prose, not caring how badly he wrote (like G. D. H. Cole). It is amazing, looking back on it, how he took people in. A. J. P. Taylor repeatedly referred to him as 'the greatest living historian'. He was a perfect example of the definition of an intellectual, someone who thinks ideas matter more than people. On the only occasion I met him he referred to human beings as 'unimportant as individuals, interesting only in large masses'. He was very tall, quite a womaniser, harsh, keen on money and indefatigable. He spent his late eighties writing an enormous, unfinished *History of the Communist International*.

Anthony Carson's real name was Peter Brook. He changed it at the request of the theatrical person of the same name: big of him, I thought. He belonged to a species of writer going back to Grub Street in the mid-eighteenth century, and now extinct: able and industrious but improvident and always needy, often unable to sign a cheque with safety, and in constant fear of debt collectors, duns, tax men, council officials, landladies and even the police. He wrote 'middles' of a personal nature, mainly about travel and foreign countries. They were often based on his experiences as a courier working for travel agencies, escorting groups of tourists round European, especially Mediterranean, resorts. This was his normal trade, in so far as he ever had one. It bored him – and he found the work, and the tourists, increasingly repellent. In the end, exasperated by a particularly tiresome contingent, he quit, not before hurling his courier's bag, containing all their tickets, hotel vouchers and passports, into the lake of Geneva.

Throughout my time at the *New Statesman* I employed him as much as I could. I loved subbing his little essays, each a jewel of its kind, containing sweetly turned descriptions of places, of the odd and eccentric people he met, of ancient customs now disappearing, and of ludicrous incidents in which he had been involved. There was much wit, choice jokes, neat epigrams and flashes of wisdom. They were not easy to write and sometimes I had to lock him in a room until he had finished. I learned never to pay him in advance, but always to fork out, in cash, on delivery. This was the procedure he liked and which brought the best results. My old editorial secretary, Edna, was very fond of him. She'd say: 'I know that look on your face, Carson. Surreptitious glances at the clock, eh? Waiting for opening time, aren't you? I've seen exactly the same expression on the face of my poor old father.'

Carson was a saint. He was often at the Colony Room, in its heyday under Muriel Belcher. There I would listen to his remembrances, buying him pints of the strong lager he relished. He was big and powerful but placid and pacific by nature. Once I arrived to find him being attacked by a furious oil painter. What Carson had done to anger him I do not know – he did not know himself – but the man was in a frenzy, kicking, punching, scratching and even attempting to bite. Carson put up no resistance, except occasionally brushing him off with a mighty arm. It was like a bear being baited by a pack of fierce dogs. In the end, I had to drag the man off myself. This was one of the rare occasions when Muriel was not at her post: otherwise the incident would never have taken place. Carson just shrugged his shoulders. 'The fellow has a short fuse,' he said: 'Can't help it. Some people are like that.' He laughed. 'I was involved in a much worse scrimmage in Bologna. Just off the Cathedral Square . . .'

Barbara Castle (1910–2002) was vivacious and pretty with lovely red hair. Her hair gave her a lot of trouble. It was the one thing she envied Margaret Thatcher. 'Her hair's so fine. But it's always tidy. How does she do it? Witchcraft!' Barbara thought about her appearance more than most women, 'You have to. People are only too ready to dismiss a woman MP as dowdy, especially if she's Labour.' She despised Shirley Williams: 'Always a mess. A disgrace to politics, Labour and her sex.' At one time, Barbara tried a wig. But it was snatched off her by an overhead wire when she was on an official ministerial inspection of a building site. She loved pretty, well-pressed, tidy dresses with neat buttons and bright colours. And well-made, high-quality shoes. High heels but not too high. But she always bought shoes that were too small for her, or too smart for her feet. Once, when she came to lunch with us at Iver, she asked Marigold if she could take off her shoes. 'Of course.' Both her feet were covered in small pieces of sticking plaster, hiding corns, blisters and bruises caused by her shoes.

Despite her interest in her appearance, Barbara hated feminism of any kind. She refused to take up women's issues. She flatly refused to have anything to do with education, the usual route by which women, among them Shirley Williams and Margaret Thatcher, got into the Cabinet. I first knew her in 1955 when I joined the *Statesman* staff at the same time as she became our political adviser. This meant she attended our Monday morning editorial conferences, and gave us the low-down on what was happening at Westminster. She was hard-working, articulate and effective – perceptive, too. She taught me a great deal and I learned to admire her. Harold Wilson admired her more than any other of his colleagues. He believed she had the ability and guts to be the first woman Prime Minister, and in an ideal world he would have liked her to succeed him in 1976. But Barbara's future had been blighted by her unsuccessful attempt in 1968 to reform the trades unions, the 'In Place of Strife' policy. He had backed her to the hilt on this but the rest of the Cabinet, led by Callaghan, had 'turned yellow', in Wilson's words, and the proposed legislation had to be dropped. Since Heath, who came in in 1970, likewise failed to crush the unions, they were all-powerful in 1976 and Callaghan was their candidate for the leadership. Not only did he get it, he immediately sacked Barbara and ended her political career. She said: 'Having told me I was finished, he then came closer and said, "I hope you don't mind if I do this", and kissed me on the cheek. I must say, being kissed by Jim Callaghan is worse than being raped by any other man.'

As Barbara had been destroyed by Labour and its paymaster unions, she might have been forgiven for taking a more detached view of it during its disastrous decade of the 1980s. But she remained loyal. Of course she took a peerage, as they all did if they got the chance, old Labour hacks enjoying being lords and ladies even more than the Tories. Considering the contemptuous things Barbara had once said about the House of Lords, her visible delight in her ermine and title was pitiful. Her continuing devotion to Labour was a mystery to me. I had been shocked by Gaitskell's phrase in his notorious speech, 'To save the party I love'. How, I asked, could anyone *love* a *party*? And Labour was peculiarly horrible in many ways. But it was all Barbara had. She had no children. She told me a bad bout of measles (or was it mumps?) had done for that. Her husband, Ted, was a nice old booby but nothing more. So when I left Labour, in disgust at the behaviour of the unions, Barbara never forgave me, and eventually broke off all contact. On her eightieth birthday I painted for her a beautiful card. I know she got it but she never acknowledged it.

Barbara once said to me (it must have been in 1956): 'Paul, you are a clever fellow, and mean well. But you must realise that people are more important than ideas.' How true that is! And it is the one maxim I have never forgotten. What Barbara never learned is that people are more important than parties, too. Not least the Labour Party. But it was her religion, the only one she had, and she went to her grave believing in it. Poor Barbara: what a bright spirit she was, and how she was wasted in the barren wilderness of politics.

Coco Chanel (1883–1971) was the third best exponent of *haute couture* in my time, coming after Balenciaga and Dior, though her range was limited. She did daytime and early evening clothes, never full evening dress. She did not follow the seams but developed certain lines and stuck to them. The frocks she made in the fifties were essentially the same as those she made in the thirties. She was sharp, mean, totally selfish and seemed to be devoid of moral sense. I looked at her carefully to see what men saw in her but could discern nothing. Before the war she had Bendor, Duke of Westminster, who was besotted at one time. During the war she went for high-powered Nazis stationed in Paris and lived openly with a top SS man at the Ritz. Then she had to flee to Switzerland for a bit but returned when it was safe to do so. She usually found young men to accommodate her. Some people would not speak to her but most did. She was the only head of a *maison de haute couture* who refused to attend Dior's funeral. My friend Annette used to say, 'She ought to have been married to Talleyrand.'

Chou En-lai (1898–1976) was – is – an enigmatic figure. I suspect we shall never know the truth about him. He was regarded by the Western media as the 'acceptable face' of the Mao regime. He was Mao's first man who travelled abroad, met and negotiated with Western leaders, talked to the media and made himself pleasant. Unlike Mao, a brutal peasant thug with no manners, and, despite his pretensions, with little education or cultural knowledge, Chou came of a Mandarin family. He displayed, on occasion, beautiful manners. I met him twice. He reminded me of an old-fashioned nonconformist clergyman, in his black clothes, discreet, seemingly humble manner, and clasped hands. He said: 'Violence rarely achieves anything useful or permanent.' 'Dogmatism is foolish.' 'To kill a man for his opinions is a crime.' 'There are many truths. But the Great Truth is composed of multiple voices.' He specialised in such anodyne blather and took many people in. I did not like him. He stank of humbug. We now know he was personally involved in a great deal of violence, author-ised countless arrests and torture of enemies, and was actually the creator of Mao's secret police. It is amazing Mao did not kill him, as he clearly wanted to do on occasions. Mao certainly denied him the proper medical treatment for his cancer, and hastened his death. His complicated relationship with Mao is described in detail in Jung Chang's and Jon Halliday's life of Mao. But doubtless the full truth will never be known. It still makes me shiver to think of him.

Winston Churchill (1874–1965) was the first politician I learned to caricature, drawing him with my finger in the condensation on the train window on my way to school, 1935, aged six – huge, bald dome-head, button nose, lips clasped round big cigar, sloping eyebrows over sharp, determined eyes. I did him because he was the easiest (Baldwin, Lloyd George, Roosevelt, whom I also learned to draw, were harder: Hitler, Musso and Stalin just a little more difficult than Churchill because of uniforms). Though out of office then, he was always in the news. As Arthur Bryant wrote of him, 'His head was always above the parapet.' I had to wait until I was seventeen before I met him, but the occasion was worth waiting for. It was the autumn of 1946 and I was just about to go up to Oxford. He was attending the Tory Party Conference at Blackpool – or, rather, since the leader did not deign to attend the confer-ence itself in those days, addressing the representatives on this Saturday morning, at what was called the party rally. My widowed mother was living in Lytham. Churchill did not like any of Blackpool's hotels and instead stayed at the small but luxurious Clifton Arms in Lytham. My mother knew the manager who said: 'If Paul will be there at 9.20 I will see he gets into the front hall for a good view of Mr Churchill.' So I did. He came out of the lift with his post-breakfast cigar in his mouth and wearing his huge, squarish bowler hat. (Beaverbrook was later to tell me that, before the First World War, Churchill, noticing the cartoonists liked his hat, told his hatter to make it even bigger.) He got out his box of outsize matches – they were a quarter-inch thick and three inches long – and then, noticing me, gave me one: 'Here, boy, keep this in memory of me'; which I did. Thus emboldened, I said: 'Mr Winston Churchill, sir, to what do you attribute your success in life?' Without an instant's hesitation, he replied: 'Conservation of effort. Never stand up when you can sit down. And never sit down when you can lie down.' Then he lit his cigar and went out to his limo, carefully raising his hat six inches vertically over his head, as was his fashion, to the crowd waiting outside.

There was never a time when I did not hear his name. I noticed early on that those who disliked him called him 'Churchill'. Those who saw the point of him called him 'Winston'. He was always famous, or notorious. He was a marked boy at Harrow for pushing Leo Amery (later a Cabinet colleague) into the swimming bath, thinking that such a small boy could not be important, whereas he was head of his house; and then by his handsome apology: 'My father, who is a very great man, is also small.' If he did not hit the headlines with his exploits, he made sure they became known by writing about them. Thus the public heard all about his Indian Frontier campaign with Sir Bindon Blood; his charge at Omdurman in 1899 with the 21st Lancers; his capture by the Boers and his dramatic escape. This last made him world-famous, and ensured his rapid entry into parliament. Not content, he quickly changed his party, and joined the Liberals. And, following the formation of Campbell-Bannerman's government in December 1905, he was given office, the same week issuing the two splendid volumes of *Lord Randolph Churchill*, his life of his father, to universal acclaim. He later summarised all his early adventures in a masterly memoir, *My Early Life* (my favourite book of his), in which, without appearing vain, he pushed himself centre stage in late Victorian and Edwardian England. That was always his way: writing contemporary history, he tended to turn it into auto-biography. Thus, when he wrote his account of the First World War, A. J. Balfour, sent an early copy, told his friends: 'Winston has written an enormous book about himself and called it *The World Crisis.*'

Violet Bonham Carter, many years later, told me about the Churchill of these years. In 1908 her father became Prime Minister and, she said, 'treated Winston almost as a son'. She loved him all her life and would happily have married him. But Clementine Hozier was his choice, and remained so always. I said to Lady Violet: 'Churchill was a man of great daring and enormous ener-gies. Such men usually have sexual adventures. Yet one never hears tales about him. Do you think he was always faithful?' She said: 'One can never say such things as a fact. But to the best of my knowledge, and from the very depths of my intuition, I am certain he was true to Clemmie.' As a senior member of the govern-ment – President of the Board of Trade, Home Secretary, First Lord of the Admiralty – Churchill worked closely with Lloyd George, the Chancellor of the Exchequer, to lay the foundations of the welfare state. Lady Violet said: 'This was really *his* Finest Hour. He had been born in Blenheim Palace and saw the workers as servants, or private soldiers. He had never become conscious of the poor until Lloyd George taught him the vernacular of radi-calism. But he took to the business with wonderful enthusiasm and force. He was never so completely absorbed in politics, so magically motivated, or so happy. His Liberal days were his best.' Well, she would say that, wouldn't she? But the view is confirmed by a saying of Churchill, not long before his death. My friend Bill Mallalieu, MP for Huddersfield, on account of a fall playing rugger was given a temporary right by the Sergeant-at-Arms to use the old House of Lords lift. Churchill in old age had permanent permission. He got into it one day and found Churchill there. The old man asked: 'Who are you?' 'Mallalieu, sir. Member for Huddersfield.' 'Ah. What party?' 'Labour, sir.' 'Well, I'm a Liberal. *Always have been.*'

The First World War exhilarated Churchill and he learned everything from it. But it almost broke him. Somehow he was made to carry the blame for the Dardanelles disaster, and resign. Lady Violet put it thus: 'He could not quite understand what had happened to him. I heard his resignation speech. It was a passionate appeal for understanding and forgiveness, and quite useless. It was like a woman saying to her departing paramour – "For God's sake, go on loving me!"' She added: 'And there was a blood price, for many people blamed him personally for a dead husband, brother or son, killed, as they saw it, in vain because of Winston's arrogance. It explains the hostility of many people to him right up to 1940.' He was saved at the time by Lloyd George, who brought him back to office as soon as he decently could, gave him high office (War Secretary) and made him a pillar of the Coalition, up to its sudden destruction in 1922. Then he followed 'LG' into the wilderness. His relationship with the wizard was curious. They were never equals. Bob Boothby, who was at this time very close to both, told me why: 'The fact is, LG was Winston's intellectual and emotional superior. He was a better politician and a better war leader. Winston knew it.

'In the mid-1920s, when Winston was Chancellor of the Exchequer, and I was his PPS, it seemed a good idea to bring them together again – there had been a chill. I spoke to Winston and he agreed, and I arranged for him to go to LG's room in the Commons late one afternoon. I waited outside. He was in a long time. It was dusk when he came out. He seemed subdued, almost crushed. I asked him: "How did it go?" "Very well. In no time we were back to our old relationship – *master and slave!*'"

How did Churchill became Chancellor in 1924? He was at odds with the Tories and had never thought much of their leader, Baldwin. But 'Stanley', as he liked to be called, had just won a thumping election victory and could do as he pleased. He was a passionate Harrovian. And Harrovians at Westminster tend to stick together; they are much less numerous than Etonians, and get many fewer glittering prizes. So they try to push and protect each other. It helps to explain the Profumo affair. In 1925 an ebullient Baldwin said: 'I want to pick a Cabinet of which Harrow can be proud.' That meant including Churchill, who was not expecting anything. He was astounded to be offered the Exchequer. 'Can you take it?' asked Baldwin. 'Can a duck swim?' Churchill replied. 'I still have the robes which my father wore when he held this magnificent office.' The parliament ran its full term and Churchill presented five budgets in a single parliament, the only Chancellor in modern times to do so. He was blamed for putting Britain back on the gold standard, but this was not a personal decision but the view of the entire financial establishment. I saw a memo J. M. Keynes wrote to Kingsley Martin, in 1940, I think, criticising a reference to this: 'It is unfair to go for Churchill about gold. He really had no choice, I now think.'

The 1930s were Churchill's nadir. He made a fool of himself over India, and an even bigger fool over the Abdication. He revered the House of Commons – none more so – and humbly deferred to it even at his moments of greatest power, but he was some-times curiously inept in judging its mood. His speech on this occa-sion, defending his 'Old Master' (Edward VIII), as he saw it, was shouted down, something which hardly ever happens in the House, and never happened to Churchill before or later. Harold Nicolson told me: 'It was the most horrible thing I ever heard – unspeakably unpleasant. I didn't think any man could have survived it.' Happily for Churchill, the growing belligerence of Hitler and our obsession with the need to resist him soon gave him more important matters to think about. My memories of his ascent to supreme office in May 1940 are vivid. Just after the invasion of France I recall my father, who had been through four years in the trenches and bitterly remembered the Dardanelles, saying to my mother: 'There's talk of making that man Churchill Prime Minster.' But soon his tune changed: 'It looks as if we'll have to send for Winston.' I heard all his broadcasts to the nation that famous summer and can remember passages in them by heart. I never had any doubt at the time that we would win the war, and have no doubt now that, without Churchill, things would have been quite different, and infinitely worse.

We did not know at the time the extent to which Churchill depended on his wife for support during the strains and horrors of the long war. The story was later told in *Clementine Churchill* (1979) by their youngest child, Mary Soames. She was (and is) the best, and the best loved, of their children. Randolph, the son, after a golden youth, was a grievous disappointment and often an acute embarrassment. Sarah, born in the fatal year 1914, married a stand-up comic called Vic Oliver, whom her father disliked on sight and grew to hate. Harold Macmillan told me that during the Cairo conference Churchill was one day particularly depressed, and needed cheering up. Mussolini had fallen, though not before he had executed Count Ciano, whom he had made Foreign Minister after he married Musso's daughter Edda. So Macmillan said: 'Look at Musso. What a hopeless mess he is in. Who would be in his shoes?' Churchill glowered. 'At least he had the satisfaction of murdering his son-in-law.'

I recall the election of 1945 very well. I was at Stonyhurst, and watched all the Jesuits go off to vote, some by car, some on bicycles, on polling day. Everyone assumed Churchill would win handsomely. But not the Jesuits. They were the only people I heard of to predict a Labour landslide, possibly based on reports from their parishes in big industrial towns. The only other exception was Aneurin Bevan, as he later told me: 'I believed the British people were mature enough to distinguish between a popular national leader and his party. No other people, I think, could have made this distinction so decisively. Mind you,' he added with his huge, overwhelming grin, 'I was influenced by the fact I could not stand the fellow. Or he me.' Churchill, in his own account of the debacle, had an intuition of defeat at the last moment. On the day the votes were due to be counted, 'I woke with a sharp stab of almost physical pain.' When the extent of the disaster became apparent, Mrs Churchill said: 'It may be a blessing in disguise.' He replied: 'It appears to be very effectively disguised.'

In fact, Mrs Churchill was right. Her husband used the sympathy his rejection by an ungrateful nation inspired among the Whitehall mandarins to drive an extraordinary bargain with the Cabinet Secretary. Under this Churchill acquired not merely physical possession but legal ownership of all the wartime papers which might broadly be called personal, and the right to publish them, subject only to a veto by the Prime Minister of the day. He had already acquired valuable experience by writing his account of the Great War. During the Second World War he used the lesson he thus acquired to word many of his key letters and cables for future use and publication. The bargain he struck in 1945 enabled him to make his account of the Second World War a documented one from start to finish, based on top-secret papers that were not to be made available to any possible competitor or rival historian for many decades, in some cases ever. His fortunate rejection by the voters gave him the opportunity to get down to the immense task straight away and to work at it with all the concentrated fury which his frustrations at losing power inspired in him. By the time he returned to office in 1951, the bulk of the work had been done, and the *magnum opus* was well on the way to publication, years ahead of the other participants – generals, admirals, air marshals, rival politicians and enemies. Hitler and Roosevelt were dead; Stalin believed, wrongly, that the official Soviet account would serve him. So Churchill was essentially alone in the field, able to write an account of the entire war which was both personal and also official, since based on state papers. Hence his version became, as it were, not only the first but to most people the authentic account of the Second World War. It was set in concrete, indeed carved in granite, before anyone else had a chance. It still remains, in all essentials, *the* account of the war.

Looking back on Churchill's long and amazingly varied life, it seems to me that his capture of 'the truth', or his truth, about the war he won was the cleverest of all his achievements. I say cleverest because we have to remember that he was daring, courageous, hyperactive and resolute – all qualities of the heart and body – but also highly intelligent. His judgement was erratic as well as fundamentally sound but on this issue (as also with his deference to the Commons) inspired. In writing his account he held all the trump cards but he never overplayed his hand. It is never obviously self-serving. At no point does it make the reader, even an opponent, want to fling it down in disgust. In presenting his case he exercised self-restraint and magnanimity. It is not as well written as his book on the First World War – he was much older and subject to many more self-imposed restraints. But in every other respect it is more effective, especially in recording history. Not even Julius Caesar was more successful in getting his version to stick.

Churchill's post-war government, which I witnessed at close

quarters, was a mere coda. He did not undo any of the more foolish acts of the Attlee government, as he should have done, and that task was left to Margaret Thatcher when she took over in 1979; by that time immense damage had been done to Britain and the economy. His reasons were threefold: he thought the electorate, however foolishly, had spoken in 1945 and Labour had a mandate; he had a certain sympathy with the spirit, if not the letter, of what Labour tried to do in levelling; but chiefly he wanted to concentrate on foreign affairs. He was overwhelmingly anxious not be portrayed as a warmonger. He once told a friend of mine: 'Never allow yourself to be photographed with a drink or a gun in your hand. I avoided a drink but I have been stuck with that beastly photo, showing me holding a tommy-gun. It has done me more harm than any other single thing.' This wartime photo, taken when automatic weapons, US-made, first became a general issue to British troops, was made devastating use of by both Labour and the Soviets. He was painfully sore about it, and even sued the *Mirror* over its 'Whose finger on the trigger' jibe, which accompanied the photo. He inherited the Korean War from Labour, and told a group of Tories in the Smoking Room, early in 1952: 'I am glad of it. The Old Man has been good to me. If I had been in charge when North Korea invaded, I would have had to do exactly the same as Mr Attlee. But, unlike him, I would have been called a warmonger. So I am grateful to the Old Man.' Sir Reginald Manningham-Buller, then Solicitor General, was puzzled and asked: 'What Old Man?' Churchill roared: 'ALMIGHTY GOD, Sir Redvers.' He always called Buller 'Sir Redvers', confusing him with the Boer War general. Churchill was always irritated by MPs with double-barrelled names, and tended to get them mixed up. That was why Buller got the law office, and Sir Harry Hylton-Foster was nominated by Churchill as Speaker.

In his last phase he was obsessed by summitry. He never lost sight of the importance of the American alliance. He strongly disapproved, privately, of Eden's Suez adventure, or, rather, the way it was conducted. He said: 'I would never have dared to go in. But having gone in, I would not have dared to come out.' When Khrushchev started to intervene, he said: 'Anthony must scuttle back as fast as he can under the American Umbrella.' It is always well to remember that he was half-American. He had American expansiveness, especially in personal expenditure. He liked to be what he called 'well-mounted'. His war memoirs brought him in an immense income but he was not above taking freebies from the likes of Aristotle Onassis or Beaverbrook or his Yankee publisher. They would never be allowed nowadays to an MP, let alone a Prime Minister. James Cameron, who had a dinner with the Old Man and Beaverbrook, at the latter's Riviera villa, *à trois*, gave me a vignette of the occasion. Churchill was silent, not to say comatose, for much of the dinner, though he ate heartily and his glass was never full for long. When leaving, Cameron shook Churchill's proffered hand and, in his nervousness, grasped it too firmly, so it hurt. Churchill came to life, eyes blazing, face flushed, and said loudly: 'God damn you.'

Alan Clark (1928–99) was a rich, noisy ruffian at Oxford, who was allowed to run a big car, because Hugh Trevor-Roper, Censor at Christ Church in charge of undergraduate discipline, valued Alan's invitations to his parents' home where he met smart people – so he gave permission for the car. Alan benefited from wealth and privilege all his life. But he was not generous and never reciprocated kindness: utterly selfish. An ex-girlfriend of his told me that applied to his love-making: 'A terrible lover.' He had a wonderful Old Etonian, Tory MP drawl, *Aaawwaaah*, etc., of which Frank Johnson gave a superb imitation. He and Nicholas Soames made a fine duo together of upper-class toffery. When his *Diaries* came out, and he revealed the secret of his 'coven' – how he had seduced the judge's wife and two of his three daughters – there was a tremendous media frenzy, and I wrote a funny piece about it called 'The Siege of Saltwood Castle'. I got a long letter from the judge, giving a circumstantial account of what a shit Clark was. I was particularly told not to invite him to our summer party that year, but I did so and he and his wife Jane came. All the well-behaved upper-middle-class ladies begged to be introduced to him. Jane kept her cool admirably throughout the fuss. She took a dim view of the social status of the coven, and came out with a notable maxim: 'Below-stairs women always go to the papers.'

Kenneth Clark (1903–83). He was the best lecturer I have heard by far. His books (I possess them all) are well written, and his TV series, *Civilisation*, was a triumph, but neither gives any idea of his magic when he was talking to a live audience, improvising, interjecting a new idea which had just occurred to him, thinking aloud (or appearing to). He had a golden voice. He radiated charm, with which he entranced even the chilliest women. He seduced the audience (of course, in the Oxford Taylorian, most of them were women). He was old-fashioned. He pronounced Rembrandt 'Rumbrunt', and Tintoretto without the final 'o'. His rendering of Parmigianino I have never been able to imitate.

He was kind. Whenever I wrote to him with a problem or request for advice, he always replied promptly. He was modest. 'I am nothing, compared with Gombrich. He is everything, I very little.' And: 'I am a gentleman amateur.' He never had to work. He inherited the money from Clark's Cotton Reels. His wife Jane was an heiress, too, also in textiles. He bought paintings and drawings very shrewdly, when they were still cheap, and thus became a multi-millionaire, instead of an ordinary one. He told me (1947):

'Go for Gothic. It will come back. Get to love the Albert Memorial and All Saints, Margaret Street, and Strawberry Hill.' He told me: 'Strictly between you and me, Matisse is a fraud. And Picasso is worse.'

He was a ladykiller and a practised adulterer of the top class. He broke his wife's heart and turned her from a beautiful woman into a raddled drunk. Once, when she went to Court, tipsy, she attempted to curtsey to the Queen but fell over and banged her head. The Queen said: 'Oh, that *was* a bump.' Stephen Spender told me of visiting their house, Saltwood Castle in Kent, in company with Stravinsky and his wife. At the composer's insistence, they stopped the car at almost every pub they passed, so that Stravinsky could have what he called a 'nogeen'. By the time they arrived, Stravinsky was tight and beginning to sing the oboe part of *The Firebird*. He warned Clark: 'Some drinking has been going on, I fear.' Clark replied: 'Nothing to what has been going on here, I assure you.' At that moment, there was a tremendous crash and the doors to the room were flung wide open, revealing a furious Jane. She said: 'Who the hell are these people? Whaaaat's going on – whaaaat, eh?' and fell down. Stravinsky said: 'That calls for a little drinkie' – and sang the oboe bit.

The success of Clark's *Civilisation* was interpreted at the time as a triumph of culture over barbarism and a sign that TV was a good thing. In the long term it was a cultural disaster, for the politicians were struck by the phenomenally high ratings, and began to ask: 'Why are the attendance figures for public museums so low by comparison?' This was the beginning of the political pressure on museums and art gallery directors to go for attendance records by 'blockbuster' exhibitions and scholar-ships – a process which has done infinite damage to art in Britain.

Clark told me: 'My life could have been better if I had been sent to Eton, instead of sent to that horrible school Winchester. The moment I arrived, I was told to report to a prefect's room, where I was told: "Sport an arse!" [bend over] and was given six very painful strokes of the cane. They said, "That will teach you to speak to a senior without permission." Still,' he added, 'maybe all that taught me to like a Caravaggio when he was very much out of fashion.'

Claud Cockburn (1904–81) was an inspired fantasist, masquerading as a reporter. He was much loved, but was not to be depended on for anything, least of all the truth of his endless anecdotes. He was tall, gangling, uncoordinated (often falling over; but this might be drink), unshaven, craggy, with a deep musical voice and a gorgeous laugh. He was the great-grandson of the famous Scotch judge and biographer Lord Cockburn; his father was a diplomat and he was actually born in Peking. He was at Berkhamsted with Graham Greene, under the headmaster-father, then at Keble, where his cousin Evelyn Waugh, also at an unfashionable college, got him into Harold Acton's smart set. Cockburn was essentially an anarchist who, for much of the twenties and thirties, imagined himself a Communist. This meant he wasted much of his life. The only subjects on which even he was boring were Marxism and Soviet Russia. He left *The Times* for the *Daily Worker*, then had the sense (in 1933) to start *The Week*, a political gossip sheet he wrote entirely himself. He created the fantasy of 'the Cliveden Set', and much else. It was read and noticed. He claimed that among the subscribers were the main London embassies, Charlie Chaplin, Gandhi, Ribbentrop, King Edward VIII and Mrs Roosevelt. But all this was mendacious propaganda, for which he had a gift.

Behind the façade of *The Week*, Cockburn was an active spreader of Stalinist lies and disinformation. He delighted in the work, though he was strictly controlled by his 'minder', Otto Katz, under the supervision of Willi Münzenberg, Stalin's most effective operator in Western Europe. I don't pretend to know about this darker side of Cockburn's life, which has been glossed over by his friends Anthony Powell, Malcolm Muggeridge and Graham Greene, and by younger admirers such as Richard Ingrams and Cockburn's sons, Alexander and Patrick. The truth, or some of it, emerged with the publication in 1995 of Stephen Koch's important book, *Double Lives: Stalin, Willi Münzenberg, and the Seduction of the Intellectuals*. Cockburn's memoirs, *In Time of Trouble* (1958), and *I, Claud* (1967), are full of lies, half-truths and jokes about matters which were deadly serious at the time: often life and (especially) death for those involved. It was well Cockburn did not accept Stalin's invitation to come to Moscow. Had he done so, he would have been killed or starved to death in the Gulag. Stalin had Münzenberg murdered and Katz put to death in the post-war Prague show trials.

As it was, Cockburn slithered out the Communist Party by a mysterious process of osmosis, the secret of which he carried to the grave. In the post-war period, almost forgotten, he lived in the home pastures of his Irish wife, Patricia, in County Cork, in a beautiful but ramshackle house, on a site associated with Sir Walter Ralegh. She bred and sold horses, which was often their only means of support. When Malcolm Muggeridge became editor of *Punch* he 'rediscovered' Cockburn who danced a fandango of reminiscent half-truths, and concocted anecdotes on its pages. He also wrote stuff for us at the *New Statesman*, though Kingsley Martin, while enjoying his company, said to me: 'Never believe a word Claud says, and never lend him money.' Kingsley once came out of his office laughing, and said to me: 'Cockburn has just been on the phone to me from Ireland for half an hour, gossiping. That call will have cost him all he is paid for the article we are using next week.' 'It won't have cost him a penny, Kingsley,' I said. 'Surely you know Claud always reverses the charges.' Kingsley exploded in fury, and immediately rushed to the cubbyhole where Mrs Smith, our telephonist, worked, ascertained that what I said was true, and told her never again to accept a reverse-charge call from Mr Cockburn – 'or indeed from anybody else except with express permission from me'.

My family and I spent a summer in a rented house not far from the Cockburns and had fun listening to his stories. Marigold would cook delicious meals for him – fresh-caught crabs, for instance, and he would exclaim with delight when the dish was put before him. But he never actually ate anything. I have seldom come across a man who lived on so little. But he survived to the early 1980s. He must have had a strong constitution. And metaphorically he had a strong stomach, too, showing no remorse or even recognition of the sinister life he had led in the 1930s, that 'low, dishonest decade'.

G. D. H. Cole (1889–1959), always known as Douglas. A small, grey, grim, dull man, who was important at the *New Statesman* when I first started to write for it in 1952. He had helped to create guild socialism, a form of trades unionism with pseudo-medieval trimmings, as opposed to the genuine article of which Ernie Bevin was the archetype. He hated Bevin, and Bevin hated him. Cole went back almost to the origins in the Labour Party. When he married Margaret in 1918 (she was a Postgate, an important left-wing dynasty) they formed one of those formidable partnerships then characteristic of progressive society, along with the Webbs and the Hammonds. An invitation to a meal with the Coles was unwelcome but not to be declined, and one had to be well briefed on current affairs before going. The food was

Fabian, cold and meatless. Kingsley Martin was very dependent on Cole. He did not trust R. H. S. Crossman to edit the paper when he was away, so Cole was brought up from Oxford to preside, and make the paper safe and dull. He wrote long articles in constipated prose on tedious subjects of 'social policy'. Kingsley would open the Monday morning conference with an announcement: 'We shall have a fine paper this week. Douglas has written a long piece on pensions – powerful stuff.' A perceptible groan would go round the room. Cole was on the paper's board for many years, often as chairman. As he was extremely mean, as well as abstemious, Kingsley believed he was very hard up. A taxi was sent to meet the Oxford train at Paddington on board meeting days, and the company secretary was under strict orders to be on hand when it arrived at the office, to make sure Cole did not pay for it – and to pay the return taxi in advance, after the board meeting was over. I never met anyone who warmed to Cole. Kingsley, to tell the truth, was afraid of him. We all laughed sardonically when, after his death in 1959, his estate was proved at over £50,000 net, an immense sum then. Kingsley was shocked. Cole's widow Margaret, a much fiercer creature, made herself custodian of his flame and made a tremendous fuss if the sacred name was mentioned in print in anything less than reverent terms.

John Coleman (1927–2001) was the film critic of the *New Statesman* in the 1950s, 1960s and 1970s. He was one of these bohemian writers who leave little mark on the records, and whose life it would be hard to reconstruct but who, nevertheless, form a rich element in our literature. I first met him in Paris when he supported himself, and resident mistress (often two), by writing pornography for Girodias's Olympia Press. This sounds disreputable but Coleman was not like that. Puritan, rather, a literary Roundhead, weighing words for their moral content, and writing sentences to convey salient truths about the human condition and to be read *sub specie aeternitatis*. He had been a pupil of F. R. Leavis at Cambridge but had risen above the sour sediment of that grim linguistic cook's grey confections. To the unrewarding and often routine task of writing notices of new movies he brought all his concentrated power of verbal dexterity and passion. He wrote sentences which leapt from the page with joy, created metaphors, which poked you in the eye, and threw into this crackling bonfire adverbs and adjectives which went off like rockets. There was nothing pretentious about all this; no self-conscious display of a style. It was genuine magic. There was a spark of genius in the man. I can only compare him to Hazlitt. And, like Hazlitt, he had many troubles: with drink, women, money and deadlines. I once said to him, 'If I survive you, I will pay a tribute to the way you write English.' He replied: 'No. You will forget me, very easily.' But I have not forgotten him.

Canon John Collins (1905–82) was an odd fellow, even for an Anglican clergyman. He became famous for running the Campaign for Nuclear Disarmament, which he did very well, for he was a fully paid up member of the Establishment who radiated moderation and kept the extremists impotent. As soon as he resigned, and Bertrand Russell took over with his 'Committee of 100', it lost all of its influence and disintegrated. What few knew or remembered was that Collins, as an RAF chaplain, had been at the heart of Bomber Command HQ near High Wycombe and had routinely blessed our thousand-bomber raids on German cities. He would not talk about this to me. I used to meet him at Kingsley Martin's flat in the Aldwych and later at J. B. Priestley's for weekends. He had a clever, fierce wife – Diana – and one of his sons became a ballet dancer. He hated going to church unless he conducted the service. At the Priestleys', one Sunday morning, I asked: 'Are you going to church, Canon?' 'Certainly not. I'm on holiday.' He was bitterly disappointed when, in 1967, Harold Wilson declined to make him Dean of St Paul's. He was a striking example of the total lack of spirituality one finds in prominent, sincere and hyper-active Anglican divines.

Norman Collins (1907–82) was important to me because he signed the first £1,000 cheque I ever received. (At ATV, when he was deputy chairman, every cheque for £1,000 or over had to have his or the chairman's signature.) The sum was immense at that time (1957). Collins came from poverty. His father was only a clerk and died young. He himself came up through the publicity desk at the OUP, the *News Chronicle*, Victor Gollancz's Left Book Club, and the BBC. He virtually created BBC TV then, frustrated by their stuck-in-the-mud bureaucracy, left to campaign for independent TV. He succeeded, helped to write the Television Act of 1954, then set up one of the new companies, ATV. But here again he was frustrated by being forced to amal-gamate the company with another which had access to City money. Thus he never became chairman, though he ran it till his death. If anyone shaped British TV 1947–2000, it was Collins. He told me: 'I have had a fiery lifetime of doing top-level work for three number two spots, under Gollancz, the BBC and at ATV. Why? Didn't go to a public school or Oxbridge. I've made a lot of money, though, and had a lot of women. Ha ha!' (He was a bit tight at the time but perfectly lucid.) He might have added that he also found time and energy to write sixteen novels, some of them big fellows. *London Belongs to Me* (1945) sold 884,000 copies in hardback and went into a movie and TV. He was not so much a rough diamond, more a flawed ruby, shining fiercely in the dark of the media world. Amazing to think he became a pillar of the Carlton Club. He was the most successful pressure group leader in modern British history and worth a full-scale biography.

Robert Colquhoun (1914–62) and **Robert MacBryde** (1913–66) were always together and were known as 'the Roberts'. They were both painters but their heyday was the forties. Then they worked, and sometimes shared studios or houses, with John Minton, Francis Bacon and Freud, and consorted with grander artists like Graham Sutherland and John Piper. The Roberts were the pride of the Glasgow School of Art intake of 1933–4, and painted well for a time. Then their drinking became deleterious – by the time I knew them in the mid-1960s they were notorious Soho drunks, at the Caves de France, the French House, the Colony, and a place round the corner called the Cosmopolitan (also other names). In the Caves they could be seen with their arms round each other's shoulders one minute, in loving friendship, and fighting the next. I discovered it was impossible to discuss painting seriously with them, and gave them a wide berth – not always an easy thing to do. For a time they were thick with Julian Maclaren-Ross. This ended in a bust-up when both turned on him, 'and I was obliged to draw my swordstick', as he put it. Dylan Thomas, another ephemeral friend, said: 'They are dirty drinkers, and cannot be relied on to buy their round.' Colquhoun dropped dead suddenly in Museum Street (1962) and MacBryde, drunk, was knocked down and squashed by a car four years later. They were, ideally, bit players in a novel. But Anthony Powell decided (he told me) to ignore them as 'too sordid and unattractive'. Also, he did not like their work. Nor did I. Nor did, to tell the sad truth, many people. All either of them said to me was expletory.

Sean Connery (b. 1930) was big in every way. A former milkman, he sometimes joked that he had been at the same school as Tony Blair, Fettes – 'at least, I delivered the milk'. He was a tall man, well-built, formidable. A fanatical Scottish nationalist. Very friendly, loved a good laugh. I used to see him at Carla Powell's. He was very sensitive to criticism in the gutter press. He asked my advice about suing. I said: 'Ignore it. Everyone knows you. Everyone has made up their minds about you. Their image of you is not going to be changed by something they read in a rubbishy Sunday newspaper.' I admire Sean as much as I have ever admired any man.

His wife, Micheline, was French but of Sicilian origin. She had been at a French high school and done their top-form course in philosophy. Once, at Carla's, waiting for Sean to arrive, I said: 'Let's see what you remember about philosophy. Did you do Kant's *Critique of Pure Reason?*' '*Bien sûr.*' 'Well, give me a synopsis of the argument.' She did so, brilliantly. (She is a very clever woman.) When Sean arrived, I said: 'Your wife is a good philosopher. She told me all about Kant.' 'About *what?*' 'About Kant.' Unfortunately, in Sean's pronunciation there is no real difference between 'Kant' and 'cunt'. 'No philosopher can be called Cunt,' he said. Micheline: 'No Sean, not *cunt*, *Kant*.' 'I heard you the first time.' Etc.

It was she who advised him to buy the foreign rights of the French stage play *Art*. She had, she told me, a premonition about it. So he did so. It earned him a fortune.

Cyril Connolly (1903–74) and **Barbara Skelton** (1916–96). In the 1950s the three most vivacious ladies in literary London were Edna O'Brien, Sonia Orwell and Barbara Skelton. Of these, Barbara was the most desirable, and certainly the most desired. She had a panther look, and was the original of Pamela Flitton in Anthony Powell's *A Dance to the Music of Time*. She loved fat men, liked them to lie on top of her and squash her. Her grandest lover was King Farouk of Egypt in the days of his glory. He used to beat her arse with the cord of his dressing gown. She married two of her fat lovers, Cyril Connolly and George Weidenfeld, and oscillated between them, causing poor George much distress. She left a devastating portrait of Connolly – idle, self-pitying, funny, recklessly improvident – in her clever memoir, *Tears Before Bedtime*. In the fifties and sixties, Connolly was by far the most talked-about and avidly read critic in town, even though he no longer ran *Horizon*. He and Raymond Mortimer were the big cheeses on the *Sunday Times* literary pages, Harold Nicolson and Philip Toynbee on the *Observer*. Everyone interested in books read all four every week (and V. S. Pritchett on the *New Statesman*). Nothing like that happens now. Of the big five Cyril was by far the most influential and enjoyable. I often watched him appear on the threshold of a literary party, surveying the scene, then turn on his heel in disgust. He was terrified of Evelyn Waugh, who loved and persecuted him, calling some of his more disreputable characters, like the mercenary general in *Black Mischief* and the slum children in *Put Out More Flags*, 'Connolly'. He is also caricatured as Everard Spruce in *Unconditional Surrender*. Towards the end, he despaired, moaning to me at the Beefsteak: 'Life is nasty, brutish and long, too long.' He always lived beyond his income, and died owing nearly £50,000, an enormous sum then. But a light went out of the literary world.

Maurice Cowling (1926–2005) spent most of his life as a Fellow, and tutor in history, of Peterhouse in Cambridge. But his name reverberated outside the university because of his success in training young men who afterwards became prominent, in public life and the media, to follow his conservative, not to say reactionary, principles. He had a very high, deep colour, and, though not very tall or big or even particularly burly, he was prominent because he looked like a human bomb about to go off. You waited for the bang. Sometimes it came. At other times there was a low seething or muttering or subdued growling, but with the ominous promise of detonations to come. He had a reputation for intense selfishness. Claudie, first wife of Peregrine Worsthorne, who was French, used to call him 'Number One.' Why so? *'Because dat is what 'ee is always tinking of.'*

Maurice was two years older than me, and went to school in Battersea; afterwards at Jesus, Cambridge. He served in the Queen's Regiment as a captain in India. His academic life was interspersed with journalistic spells, on *The Times* and *Express*, and as literary editor of the *Spectator*. He also twice stood for parliament, un-successfully. But from 1963 he was at Peterhouse for thirty years, with growing power in the college, and the University, until he wrecked it all by organising a foolish intrigue to make Hugh Trevor-Roper Master of the college. Why Maurice wanted Hugh as Master I never understood. He obviously did not know his man. Once Hugh was in the Master's Lodge he turned brutally on his backers, Maurice especially, and for the seven years of his mastership the college was torn in two. From being a rather cosy, old-fashioned, friendly place, it became hell on earth. Maurice never really got over this harrowing experience. He also wrecked the marriage of his and my friend, George Gale. Gale, like Worsthorne and Kingsley Amis, was part of the Peterhouse set, and Maurice was always in Gale's house in Wivenhoe, practically living there outside term time. They had rows, but Maurice had rows with everyone, me included. They involved a lot of shouting but were more noisy than anything deeper. He liked to shout and get even redder in the face than usual. Suddenly, something terrible happened. What exactly I never discovered. But George left home, eventually taking up with an Irishwoman, film critic of the *Mirror*, and going to live in Northumberland, where he came from. Wivenhoe was sold. And Pat Gale went to live near Swansea, where she came from. Maurice joined her there in 1993, when he retired from Peterhouse. George was very bitter, and refused to speak about the business. There was some question about the paternity of their last child. Pat was silent on the subject. When George died, Maurice said nothing and eventually died without ever telling what happened. It was very sad for people like myself and Perry Worsthorne, for the Wivenhoe circle, revolving around George and Pat, had been an important and delightful part of our lives – Perry even owned a house there for a time. Looking back on it all, I can see that Maurice, in his own way, was a destructive personality. John Raymond always called him anally retentive. He was an astonishingly constipated writer, and what he produced, after horrible efforts, was most difficult to read. He was as bad a writer as Leavis (whom he hated), but in a totally different way. He wrote a number of books, including a multi-volume *magnum opus* called *Religion and Public Doctrine in Modern England*. These books involved deep reading and were full of profound thoughts and *aperçus*, but barely readable – and remained largely unread, I think. Maurice lived on through his pupils, who regarded him as a superlative tutor. He had a terrible secret. He regarded the Christian religion as all-important to society in England. He saw it as the government's bounded duty to support it. He hated militant atheists or anyone or anything opposed to religious belief and practice. But he found it impossible to believe in God. 'Oh deary me!' as Pat Gale used to say.

Edward Crankshaw (1909–84) was one of the glittering collection of foreign specialists whom David Astor recruited to the *Observer* after the war, and who made it a great (though erratic and eccentric) newspaper. Unlike the others, however, Crankshaw was neither a drunk, nor a spy, nor a homosexual. Nor a hopeless neurotic. He was an exceptionally nice and cheerful man, marvellous to be with. His father was chief clerk in a London police court. He never went to university but insisted, at eighteen, on going to Germany, where he learned to speak the language almost perfectly and lived by translating. Then in the war he was sent to Moscow and learned Russian. He became Britain's leading Kremlinologist, though he claimed he wrote about the Soviet leadership 'as if I were reviewing a play'. I met him on a government trip to Yugoslavia in 1958. We became instant friends, for he could talk on music with authority, and art and literature with extraordinary insight. He told me all about his friend Artur Schnabel and how, as a boy, Schnabel met Brahms. The composer said: 'Well, boy, are you hungry?' 'Yes, sir.' 'Good. Make a good meal. When you have eaten well, you enjoy music more.' In Dubrovnik, Crankshaw and I had a lot of Bulgarian champagne, and afterwards tried to raise the drawbridge, which was then still in working order. We succeeded in moving it a bit more but were then arrested. Our Yug minder, the pressman at their London embassy, and a good Serbian egg, got us out. Crankshaw said: 'For the rest of our lives we'll be able to say, we raised the Dubrovnik drawbridge.'

Anthony Crosland (1918–77) I first met in November 1946 in the Oyster Bar at Whites, at the top of the Oxford High. He was tight and slumped over the bar. He had recently returned from a Good War, culminating in the liberation of Cannes, and was an ultra-fashionable Fellow of Trinity College. He was exceptionally good-looking, clever and assured. My companion, Hilary Sarson, was a dazzlingly pretty, north Oxford girl, exactly my age (just eighteen). When we went into the bar (forbidden to undergraduates like me, a rule occasionally enforced) she recognised

Tony and said: 'That's Tony Crosland, the most important don in the university, and I know him. Come with me and I'll introduce you.' She did that, adding: 'Paul is one of the cleverest freshmen and quite brilliant.' Crosland slowly focused on me and said: 'I'm a senior member of the University. Bugger off!'

Crosland later became (fairly) friendly, and he, Hilary and I, and his bosom friend Raymond Carr, Fellow of All Souls and historian of Spain, supreme exponent of the 'Academic Shout', used to drive around recklessly in the red MG Tony and Raymond shared, Hilary and I sitting on the dickey seats. Both of them were tight most of the time, and how we avoided trouble I cannot think. Tony at least looked healthy but Raymond had a ghastly pallor, and tottered uneasily on his legs. I would not have given him five years in those days. Yet he is still alive, and going to parties sixty years later, having spent many years as the dignified Warden of St Anthony's, a college which, in our day, did not exist. Tony, by contrast, has been dead a quarter of a century.

Tony married Hilary, and they came to see me on their honeymoon, passing through Paris, where I worked. But the marriage did not last. How could it? Hilary, though ravishing and sweet, knew nothing and read nothing 'except silly women's magazines', as she admitted. Tony was contemptuous of those who could not keep up with his razor-sharp and lightning-fast intellect. He behaved very badly, she very well. She allowed him to divorce her, so as not to hurt his political career (he had become an MP, first for Gloucester, then for Grimsby). He married again, a girl from Baltimore, Susan, who made him an excellent wife and wrote his biography after his early death. His career prospered up to a point: he became Education Minister, then Foreign Secretary. He wrote a well-received and, for a time, influential book, *The Future of Socialism*. But, somehow, he never captured the heart of the Labour

Party. He was too sure of himself, too arrogant, insufficiently interested in the lives and minds and aspirations of ordinary people. And he drank a lot. I recall him lying full length at a party, half-drunk, looking at the other guests as they passed him, eyebrows raised (he was then Secretary of State for Education). He suddenly focused on a tall, plain and (as it happened) nice and clever girl, focused in exactly the same way as he had on me in 1946, and said to her: 'Hello, Ugly Face!'

R. H. S. Crossman (1907–74) descended on me in Paris in 1953 shortly after I had become Paris correspondent of the *New Statesman*. He took me out to a sumptuous dinner on the proceeds of a large fee he had received from NATO for giving them a lecture on 'Black Propaganda'. This was a device he developed in the Second World War: the dissemination of lies and misinformation to confuse the enemy. Dick was good at this, partly because his own allegiance to accuracy was questionable. At his birth the Good Fairy had endowed him generously with qualities most people would envy – high intelligence, power of argument, brilliant articulation, etc. – but omitted others which even the most ordinary take for granted: the ability to distinguish between good and evil, and truth and falsehood.

Crossman was the son of a Chancery barrister and had a successful career at Winchester and New College, Oxford, where he got a double first, before taking a fellowship. Then he spent a year in Germany where he acquired a lifelong interest in German politics and a wife. At New College he lectured with immense success and acquired the reputation of being a first-class tutor, but he married his second wife, the divorced spouse of a colleague in the SCR, a solecism of the kind he was always committing. It is worth adding that this lady, subsequently divorced herself, came up to him many years later and claimed acquaintance. Dick said,

'Hello, hello! Remind me where we met – was it at a Fabian summer school?' 'No, Dick, I was married to you, remember?' 'Oh yes. Ha ha!' Dick himself told this story, with relish. He married a third time in 1982, the daughter of an Oxfordshire gentleman farmer; she brought him a small manor house and estate but he sometimes completely ignored her when they were together. Dick's concentration on what he was currently doing, saying and thinking was total and excluded any other focus of interest. This made people accuse him of bad manners, insensitivity and contempt for ordinary people. Attlee did not approve of him for this reason and because Dick had quarrelled with his parents (whom Attlee knew). So Dick, despite his brains and ability as a speaker, got no job in the 1945–51 government. Gaitskell, Attlee's successor, also regarded him as irresponsible. Everyone who employed Dick came to distrust him, I'm sorry to say. He was a superb writer, particularly of high-level journalism and intellectual book-reviewing. His *Plato Today* (1937) is a wonderful read, on a level with Keynes's *General Theory* and Ayer's *Language, Truth and Logic*, two other big, highbrow successes of the thirties. He worked hard at the *New Statesman*, where his articles and lead book reviews were a key part of the paper's huge success under Kingsley Martin. But Martin learned to distrust him, refused to put him in line for the succession, and left a memo giving reasons why Dick was never in any circumstances to be made editor of the paper. When Lord Campbell (Chairman of the Board) and I appointed Dick as my successor in 1970 we did not know of the existence of this memo. But Martin proved right: we had to sack Dick ignominiously after he had been in charge for 21 months.

Dick got on well with Harold Wilson, who had him in the Cabinet, 1964–70, part of the time as Leader of the House. But he left little permanent mark. The new committees he set up, on American lines, did not establish the importance he envis-

aged and his *Diaries of a Cabinet Minister*, though they generated a great deal of legal and media excitement, are of no permanent interest. He was too busy to write them up daily. Instead
he dictated them once a week. This is no good, as anyone who
has kept a diary knows. So they are much inferior in terms of
accuracy to Barbara Castle's, or Tony Benn's, especially the
latter, as Tony always carried a tape recorder and put down
conversations immediately after they had taken place. Barbara
tried to take notes for her diaries during Cabinet meetings but
Burke Trend, the Cabinet Secretary, objected and Harold Wilson
told her to stop it. 'Oh Harold!' she said, 'I'm only jotting down
things I have to remember, laundry lists and so on.' 'Don't give
me that, Barbara,' said Wilson, 'I know what you're up to.' (She
always called her diaries 'my old-age pension'.) It's odd to think
that in 1975 the Labour Attorney General, in a plea before the
Lord Chief Justice, sought an injunction to prevent Crossman's
diaries appearing in book form, even though they had already
been serialised in the *Sunday Times*. I think one reason
Crossman's *Diaries of a Cabinet Minister* aroused little but
ephemeral interest is that during the Wilson government of that
time nothing of interest occurred – just slow, inexorable
economic decline and futile attempts by Wilson & Co. to
arrest it.

Dick was a big, noisy, vigorous man, full of good humour,
meaning well, excellent company and of sparkling intelligence.
But something was missing, somehow, and its absence prevented
him from being a great man.

Martin D'Arcy (1888–1976). When I was a boy, the Catholic
Church in England had a formidable intellectual profile. It had
several heavyweights, and many more skirmishers, who were
capable of coming to its defence with essays, articles, reviews

and letters to the editor, on a continual basis, and from time to time producing books, sometimes big ones. Such were, among the laymen, Belloc and Chesterton, Christopher Dawson and Arnold Lunn, Evelyn Waugh and Graham Greene, Douglas Woodruff and Maisie Ward; among the priests there were Fr Martindale, Ronnie Knox, Fr Corbishley and, not least, Fr Martin D'Arcy. The Catholic periodicals open to them, the *Tablet*, the *Month*, the *Dublin Review*, etc., were of high quality, and the main Catholic publisher, Burns, Oates and Washburn, was also excellent. The Church could put up a good show, and those who attacked it, doctrinally or historically, such as C. G. Coulton, did so at their peril.

Martin d'Arcy was the son of a barrister. He was educated at my school, Stonyhurst, and returned there periodically to study or write, to teach and to absorb its profoundly Catholic, recusant atmosphere. He also liked traditional, recusant country houses, particularly with a priest's hole, into which he would try to fit his bony frame. He was a striking-looking man, piercing eyes, bushy brows, a firm chin and a scraggy neck, and a huge bush of hair which went a brilliant white. At school he was known as 'sheep's head'. The other Jesuits were in awe of him, he was so clever and powerfully argumentative, not afraid to write critically to the Jesuit General on the way the Society of Jesuits was run, or to remonstrate even with the Pope. His sermons were tremendous. But afterwards you could not remember what he said or what they were all about. He told me: 'That does not matter. A sermon should disperse a species of spiritual magic, which lifts up the soul, the *sursum corda*, and make one's theological nostrils twitch.' There was always something a bit cloudy about him. His best book, and his own favourite, *The Mind and Heart of Love*, about the two kinds of love, *eros* and *agape*, is a display of intellectual fireworks, which I read with difficulty. It required perseverance, and I now retain nothing of it. He showed me an immense parchment, ten or twelve feet long, from the early seventeenth century, which appeared to trace his family back to the coming of the Normans in 1066, and of which he was very proud. I said: 'Does this kind of thing matter?' 'It matters to me. And it mattered to the person who wrote the Book of Genesis.'

His basis of operations was Oxford, where he became Master of the Jesuit hall there, popularising its new name, Campion Hall, and completely rebuilding the fabric to a splendid design by Sir Edwin Lutyens. He received Evelyn Waugh into the Church, and got him to write his book about the martyr, *Edward Campion*, which won the Hawthornden Prize and whose royalties Waugh generously gave to the Hall. Waugh was very fond of him and based his sympathetic portrait of a Jesuit in *Vile Bodies*, Father Rothschild, on D'Arcy. (D'Arcy was not pleased. He said it harmed his reputation in the Church.)

By the time I got to Oxford in 1946, D'Arcy had just left Campion Hall to become Jesuit Provincial. This meant he operated from the vast, gloomy terracotta house in Farm Street (just off Mount Street in Mayfair), a place he found uncongenial. He liked to pop back to Oxford, particularly as he was now adorning it on a considerable scale with works of art (or *objets d'Arcy*, as they were known). His tastes were theatrical and his knowledge of painting and sculpture perhaps not as reliable as he thought. It was said that some of the things he bought were suspect, even downright fakes. Moreover, although he got rich Catholics (or others) to finance some of these purchases, at a pinch he used the funds of the English province. It was said he was 'financially profligate'. There were other counts against him. That he mixed too much with the Catholic gentry, and not enough with the working class in the big industrial towns where the Jesuits had schools and parishes. That he was too social in London and Oxford. That he did not tell Jesuit HQ in Rome what he was up to. There were plenty of mischievous and envious spirits in the English hierarchy, and even with the Jesuits, to carry damaging gossip to Rome. In 1950 he was suddenly sacked. True, it is an old Jesuit habit to pull down high-flying members of the Society if they become too prominent. D'Arcy had told me about this himself. He said to me, in 1946, I think: 'Of our vows of poverty, chastity and obedience, poverty you soon get used to – it doesn't matter and everything is provided anyway. Chastity ditto, you never think about it after a few years. But obedience – there's the rub. Instant obedience to the foolish orders of people above you whom you feel are your intellectual inferiors – you never get used to that. To obey willingly, without even an inner grumble: it's hard, my boy.' He took his demotion hard, and the last quarter-century of his life, after such a brilliant youth and middle age, was empty. He spent as much of it as he could in the United States, where he was loved. He hated the liturgical changes introduced by the Second Vatican Council, and what was happening to the Jesuit Order itself, marked by its absurd 'Option for the Poor' and followed by a catastrophic fall in vocations. As was said of Curzon by Winston Churchill: 'The morning was golden, the noontide bronze, the evening lead.' But he kept his faith. May he rest in peace.

John Davenport was a leading figure in that last generation of bohemian writers, a phenomenon started in the 1580s by Christopher Marlowe, which was finally ended by the 1960s cultural revolution. He was broad, squat, almost square, and immensely powerful. He had huge biceps, strong neck muscles like a bull's, and big fists. At one time he made his living as an all-in wrestler, at another as a fairground boxer. He had also been a superb schoolmaster, at Stowe, where he taught Peregrine Worsthorne and Colin Welch. Usually he lived by writing reviews, introductions to books and other literary odd jobs. He had a high, thin voice, ultra upper-class accent, and used antique slang. A favourite term of abuse was 'short-arsed'. He had a huge acquaintance. He held court every Saturday morning from 11.30 at the Commercial (now renamed the Chelsea Potter) in the King's Road. There he would write letters, spreading the addressed envelopes for all to see: 'The Rt Hon Anthony Eden', 'Edmund Wilson Esq.,' 'Graham Greene Esq.', 'The Duke of Devonshire KG', etc. He had high standards of behaviour, especially towards himself, enforcing them with his fists. John Raymond used to say, complacently, 'I have never had trouble with John. My view is, everyone gets the Davenport he deserves.' But shortly afterwards, Davenport detected in Raymond what he called 'an impertinence' and knocked him down, so that was the last we heard of the maxim.

Davenport was notorious for his exploits at the Savile Club, where he detected the Lord Chancellor, Lord Maugham, in an 'impertinence', and put him on the mantelpiece in the bar. Maugham, brother of Somerset, was a short man but by no means a lightweight, and Davenport's action in lifting him bodily to a height of six feet, or more, was notable. Maugham shouted: 'Put me down! Put me down!' but John just laughed: 'There you are, you ridiculous old booby, just like a clock. Tick-tock! Tick-tock!' The club stewards had to get him down in the end, not without difficulty. Davenport was expelled from the club.

Another exploit of Davenport's was to arouse the ire of the Irishmen who frequented the rather low-down pub next to the Royal Court Theatre in Sloane Square. His drinking companion on this occasion was Gerald Hanley, author of that fine novel *The Consul at Sunset*. It was St Patrick's Day, and somehow Davenport contrived to insult the Republican Irish (he had a particular dislike for De Valera). The Irish in large numbers attacked, and he and Hanley fought back-to-back to repulse them. It was fifteen minutes before the police arrived, and this was one of the great bar fights of the fifties. Davenport referred to it as 'a little difference of opinion with friend Paddy'.

As the sixties progressed, Davenport's drinking, missed deadlines, belligerence, debts and other problems gradually undermined his status as a literary figure and his self-confidence. He had no money, his family was fed up with him, and he took refuge in Cambridgeshire with his old mother, who had means. So ended the Davenport story, sadly, as do all bohemian lives. The New York journalist Norah Sayre, who adored him, was collecting material for a biography, but died before writing it. The great love of his life was Mary McCarthy, who reciprocated it; but the practicalities of living with Davenport defeated her.

Robin Day (1923–2000) was the best of all political interrogators on TV and his fame and success lasted an entire generation, almost exactly thirty years. Before that he was nothing. After his retirement, he was nothing. But in between he was one of the most famous men in the country and far more important, politically, than most Cabinet Ministers, let alone MPs. I first knew him at Oxford where he was a star of the Union, an opinionated, articulate, noisy and pushy fellow, obviously destined for a life of public notoriety and mischief. Later I used to have regular lunches with him, chiefly in Fleet Street, at the Cock or the Wig and Pen Club, to discuss his 'difficulties with girls'. He was always worried about his relations with women: pursuing them and not getting them, or getting them and not satisfying them, or keeping them, and not satisfying himself. These difficulties persisted all his life, and towards the end he often made himself a nuisance. He was a pawer, and he never seemed to be able to tell whether a woman wanted his pawing or not (invariably not). With women, he was quite without intuition.

In politics, however, and especially broadcasting politics, his intuition and instincts were phenomenal. He knew exactly what to do and always had the courage and firmness to do it properly. He had read for the Bar and had all the skills of a trained barrister of the best type – that is, one who puts truth and justice first, and who sticks closely by the rules of evidence, does not ask leading questions and treats the witness as a human being first and not as an item of judicial livestock. He learned from Richard Dimbleby, the first star in this field, and improved upon him. Day told me: 'When interviewing someone on TV, you must remember you occupy this privileged position as a servant of the public. You ask the questions ordinary, decent, civilised people would ask themselves, if they were you. The object is to elicit interesting and important information, not to secure a forensic victory. You can be persistent and even sharp but you must observe all the formal language of courtesy. You must not merely seem objective but be objective. Bias is the mortal sin of the TV interviewer. I cannot emphasise too strongly this need to clear your mind of personal opinions, party spirit and likes and dislikes.' He also taught me how to frame questions to get good, meaty replies, rather than 'yes' and 'no', or evasion. I learned a lot from him. He always stuck to his rules, which he saw as moral as well as professional duties. He told me: 'In the present state of our politics, the TV interview of a Minister or party leader in a key programme like *Panorama* is part of the unwritten constitution, and must be approached in an appropriately responsible manner. To abuse your power is wrong, disgusting. I hope I never do it. I hope I never have done it.' On the whole he emerged from a long career of interviewing top politicians with the greatest credit. For one thing, he always did his homework, thoroughly. There was never anything slipshod, tendentious, bullying, deceptive, mean or cruel about his questioning. Being interviewed by him could be an ordeal for a shifty politician on the spot. But all was fair. He would have made a good judge.

Day was for many years a fixture on TV, an essential part of its human furniture. I had the highest respect for him. I also warmed to his many frailties and weaknesses. He had very bad eyesight and was lost without his thick, big, heavy, horn-rimmed glasses. Indeed, he looked quite different without them – naked, unprotected. At Brighton, on the night of the IRA bomb, he was (of course) staying in the Grand Hotel, the Conference HQ, which was blown up. He was not hurt, but in the hasty evacuation his glasses got lost or left behind, and he wandered about the Front, and the beach below, like a lost man, barely able to see a step before him; he was bewildered, shaken, almost tearfully upset. I came to his rescue and sat with him, until succour came, and he was able to discard his pyjamas and dressing gown for proper clothes. This relief was due to Alistair McAlpine, the Party Treasurer, who phoned up Marcus Sieff, Chairman of Marks & Spencer, got him out of bed, and asked for help. Marcus, a good and famous man, got the local manager of M&S to open up the big store there, so that those who had lost, or were being forced to leave behind, their clothes, could go in and pick an outfit, free. I guided Day to the emporium and helped to get him dressed. Then we found him some temporary specs.

Once he retired he was a lost man. As Malcolm Muggeridge often said, TV exposure was a kind of oxygen to some performers, a kind of drug, deprived of which they became desolate and incapable of normal activity. He ceased to appear. Others took his place. He lived in a Westminster flat to be on the spot, but parliament was no longer his backyard and its members were cool to a man they had feared but had no more reason to butter up. He did not help matters, or himself, by constantly complaining 'I'm a forgotten man'. He became a ghostly figure some time before death came as a release.

André Deutsch (1917–2000) was a poor man's George Weidenfeld, being a Central European in origin, a publisher chiefly of 'progressive' works and a shrewd businessman, too shrewd for my taste. He was the only publisher to get the better of me, persuading me to do a useful little job for him and never paying me.

Princess Diana (1961–97) was well made: tall, slender, but with good, strong muscles, beautiful bones, fair, clear skin, heart, hands and feet – good balance, powerful, athletic, swift. She told me she was as thick as two planks and 'no good at reading'. But I got her to read a page from *Robinson Crusoe,* which she said was her favourite book, and she did – very well. A nice, tuneful voice. She and I could sing together 'As Time Goes By' (she knew the words better than I did) and 'Smoke Gets in Your Eyes'. She had good, clean, elegant handwriting, much better than usual for her generation, so I assume she had an old-fashioned governess at some stage. I have several letters from her. She knew nothing, really, of what I would call knowledge. She said: 'What I wanted to be before I got married was an air hostess. But I wasn't educated or intelligent enough. And they said: "You're only fit to look after children." So that's what I did.' She may not have had acute intelligence but she had more and stronger intuition than anyone I have ever met. She could see into people and respond instantly to what she saw. This was magic – a gift. It made her a kind of instinctive genius at public relations – not PR, but relating to the public. She really loved people, of every kind, and they loved her back. She radiated friendship and happiness. She told me: 'He [Charles] said to me: they're not cheering you, you know, because you're you. They're cheering you because you are married to me. Get that into your thick head.' She added, 'I thought at first he was right and tried to be humble. But I now know better. Anyway, I'm not married to him any more, and they still cheer me. So I must have something.' 'Do you think he was jealous?' 'Yes. It stuck out a mile. I felt like reversing what he said: "They're not cheering you, because you are you. They don't like you any more than I do. They're really cheering you because you're heir to the throne."' 'Did you say that?' 'Oh no! You mustn't take their royal pride away from them. It's all they've got. Without it they hardly exist.'

Almost the first time we met she asked: 'Who was the Prince Regent? Why do they talk about him – you know, Regent's Park? Was he important? What does it mean, Regent?' I explained. I said he was very selfish. He was always waking up in the night and asking the time. He did this by ringing the bell for the page on night duty, who went to look at the clock. Since the pages hated this habit, they rigged up his largest fob watch at the head of his bed, so he could see it. He always had candles burning so he could tell what time it was without disturbing the pages. But he still went on ringing the bell.

She was fascinated by this story. 'But that's exactly like you-know-who. Once, in his dressing room, he complained to me about shirts. His valet had put out three shirts to choose from, but he didn't fancy any of them. They looked perfectly OK to me. Anyway, he rang the bell. His valet came and he said: "Don't like those shirts." So the valet went across the room and picked out two or three more from the shelves. When the valet had gone I said, "Look – why did you ring for that man and make him come? All you had to do was to walk across the room and pick out the shirt you like for yourself. Why make him?" He said, very fierce, "He's paid to do it!"'

By way of teaching her history in a way she would like, I made a list of all the heirs apparent from the Norman kings onwards, or the heir presumptive – and how both had fared. I still have the list we used. We discovered that heirs apparent from birth had tended to make bad kings, because they had been spoilt from the cradle by flattering, obsequious courtiers. Outstanding examples had been Henry III (weak), Edward II (weak and murdered), Richard II, Henry VI, Edward VII and Edward VIII. The exceptions tended to be those whose childhood and youth had been troubled by civil war, exile, etc. Richard I was one; Edmund I another; Edward III, Henry V, Charles II. She said: 'Well, it looks as though poor William will have a troubled childhood and youth, so he ought to be OK according to your theory.' She said William (or 'Wills') was very nervous and worried. Not at ease. But with very good principles. 'He wants to grow up into a good person.' On the other hand, Harry doesn't care a damn. 'He's happy-go-lucky. I never worry about him.'

She said: 'Don't hate Charles. I ought to. But I don't. I just feel sorry for him. And for the people who have to deal with him.'

She often asked my advice. I said: 'No sex. No dealings with the media. Never give interviews. You think you can manipulate them. But you'll find, from bitter experience, they will get the better of you. So live an entirely private life. If you don't like it, hard cheese.'

She said: 'You give me good advice. I'll follow it.' But she never did. All wasted on her. She refused, in particular, to give up her relations with the media. Or to give up sex. And she was the worst picker of men I've ever met.

Once she told me: 'They wait for me at the bottom of Palace Gardens. They [photographers and reporters] are not allowed on the road itself. But they are just outside the entrance, night and day. So what I do is this: I phone for a taxi. It comes, and I spread newspapers on the floor, then I get in and lie down on the floor, on the newspapers, so as not to dirty my clothes. Then they shut the door and the cab drives off into Kensington High Street. All the press people see is an empty cab with the light off. Once I'm well past the mob, I can get up and sit down. Then I can go shopping or see my friends.'

When I heard this was how the Princess was forced to behave to escape the media, I thought: 'What are we coming to in this wretched country?'

Alec Douglas-Home (1903–95), 14th Earl of Home and later Lord Home of the Hirsel. He was far from stupid, as Harold Wilson tried to maintain. Indeed, shortly after he became Prime Minister, at the end of 1963, he got the better of Wilson, who had harped on the fact that he was 'the fourteenth earl', which he found very funny. Asked about this on TV by Robin Day, Home said: 'Well, I suppose he's the fourteenth Mr Wilson.' This got a big laugh, and 'the fourteenth Mr Wilson' stuck for a time. Home's estate was on the Scotch side of the eastern borders, and he lived in a big, rather desolate house called the Hirsel. He was bony, delicate-looking, and gave the impression that he needed a square meal. But a lot of the Homes were like that. They had thin, friable bones. Charlie Douglas-Home, his nephew, for a time editor of *The Times*, and husband of the beautiful Jessica, was always breaking his bones, not just riding but doing much less dangerous things. It proved the death of him. Home did not break his bones but he looked vulnerable. At Eton he was considered a heartbreak and big boys, and masters, felt protective towards him. So did the headmaster's daughter, and she contrived to marry him. In the Commons, Home was PPS to Neville Chamberlain at the time of Appeasement, and accompanied him to Munich. He told me: 'I would still defend the agreement Mr Chamberlain made. It was the least unpleasant of the various unenviable alternatives open to us, especially war. Relative to Nazi Germany, we were much stronger in September 1939 than we were a year earlier, especially in aircraft and radar stations. Without Munich and the year it gained us, we could not have won the Battle of Britain.' I asked him about the curious attraction Chamberlain seemed to have for some Tories – for instance, Chips Channon, as revealed in his diaries. 'Well, Chamberlain was a very likeable, even lovable figure. If you were on the same side and agreed with him. By comparison, Eden seemed to me flashy and Churchill wrong-headed and dogmatic. I saw Churchill make a fearful ass of himself over the Abdication, and couldn't take him seriously. Of course, one changed one's mind in 1940.'

Home made two mistakes when Macmillan, in effect, appointed him his successor. He should have insisted that Butler be tried out first, to see whether he could form a government. And he should have made a bigger effort to keep Macleod and Powell on board. His admission that he did economic sums by counting matches from a matchbox was also unwise, though it later seemed endearing. He also invited ridicule by telling the press that his favourite hobby was arranging flowers. When you think of it, it is a soothing thing to do, and when I visited the Hirsel, and noted how Spartan it was, the great redeeming feature was the magnificent flowers in all the rooms. To remain PM, Home renounced his peerage and fought a by-election for the safe Tory seat of West Perth and Kinross. I went up to cover the by-election for *This Week* with a large TV crew (that was in the days of all-powerful unions). The late autumn weather was perfect and I have never seen Scotland looking so delectable. We were based at the King George Hotel in Perth, where we had magnificent five-course breakfasts. When we first arrived, the Number Ten media experts had not taken over the campaign and local Tory officials were in charge. The boss was Major Drummond-Murray of Drummond Castle, who regarded journalists as upper servants, if that. At the first gathering he told us: 'I hope you fellows are going to behave yourselves and not cause needless trouble. This is an old-fashioned place and we are not used to the press intruding.' By the end of the campaign, of course, things were on a different footing. The final, televised press conference took place at the major's castle in the garden, and my ruffianly crew made heavy weather, dragging equipment across his parterres and borders, doing a lot of damage. Suddenly I saw the major approaching and thought: 'Oh God!' But he was by now a crushed and brainwashed creature: 'I do hope you people have got everything you need. If not, please give me a shout and I'll come running.' Home's wife, however, was made of sterner stuff and kept us under her beady eye. She ticked me off several times. Home himself staggered me by his naivety over economics and his readiness to agree to increased spending. It was a characteristic of his short government, and had a bad effect on his successor, Wilson. Indeed, the sixties were a terrible decade for economic profligacy – Macmillan's refusal to be 'frightened by the inflation scenario', as he put it, Home's ignorance and Wilson's weakness. But in some ways Home was not a bad Prime Minister and got steadily better as he proceeded. He was also a good campaigner, and if the election had lasted another week I think he could just have won it, or got a dead heat. As it was, Wilson had only a majority of four over all other parties.

When I went to the Hirsel I was not offered lunch, or a drink, or even a cup of tea, most unusual in Scotland. I got an impression of extreme parsimony. Perhaps this was accidental, but Tony Lambton, some kind of cousin of Alec, explained. He said that when Alec inherited, the old agent, or factor, for obscure reasons of his own told him that the estate was virtually bankrupt, and that without the severest economy huge tracts of land would have to be sold off. Alec believed him and did as he was told, and the headmaster's daughter, being brought up Dotheboys, was only too glad to impose austerity. Whether or not things improved, the Spartan regime was never changed, and only at the end of his life did Alec dimly realise that the estate was in very good financial shape, and probably always had been. In the meantime he had denied himself all the comforts. His flat in Westminster had so little spent on it, for so long, that the council almost condemned it as 'unfit for human occupation'. Or so Tony Lambton maintained. I like to think of the 14th Earl as the last gentleman eccentric to occupy Number Ten.

Tom Driberg (1905–76) was the most persistent and promiscuous homosexual ever to sit in the House of Commons. He had learned the vice at Lancing, supposedly a moral, High Church school, where he was a contemporary of Evelyn Waugh. The latter was fascinated by him, but always referred to him as 'sinister'. Driberg was shameless and fearless in pursuit of vice. He was a persistent 'cottager', accosting men in public lavatories, and asking them: 'May I suck your cock?' How he escaped gaol is a mystery. One reason was that, in the thirties, he wrote the highly successful William Hickey column in the *Daily Express*. Like Osbert Lancaster's cartoons, it gave the paper an air of sophistication which complemented its strident populism, so Mayfair people had it as a second paper to *The Times*. Hence Beaverbrook valued him, and several times got prosecutions of Driberg dropped. When, many years later, all Beaverbrook's papers became part of the Beaverbrook Library, near Fleet Street, A. J. P. Taylor, appointed its custodian, showed me a shelf of files, named 'Driberg', containing the incriminating material. Beaverbrook said to me: 'Aw, that Driberg. He is a bad man. He will go to Eternal Perdition! He is Devil's Meat!'

At the Colony Room, Driberg often invited me back to his 'place', in order, he said, 'to discuss Gnosticism'. 'Oh, is that what you call it, Tom? No thanks!' His fondness for fellatio made him no respecter of persons. When he was Chairman of the Labour Party, he and Jim Callaghan, the Prime Minister, had to attend a Labour occasion in the north, involving a long car journey. They stopped to have a pee behind a hedge. Driberg, ever alert, exclaimed in delight: 'Ooh, I say! What a beautiful cock you have, Prime Minister! May I have a closer look?' For once, Jim was at a loss.

Driberg had a horrible propensity to be rude to servants. When some of us did a Saturday stint on *Reynold's News* (myself as diplomatic correspondent, Anthony Howard as political correspondent, Driberg as columnist), its location, beyond King's Cross, meant there was not much choice of place to have lunch. There was one little Italian bistro which served passable pasta and veal cutlets. Driberg was so harshly and persistently rude to the waiters that everyone from *Reynold's News* was banned permanently. He also behaved disgracefully at a rather grand dinner Lady Pamela Berry gave during a Labour Party Conference at Brighton, in the top-floor restaurant of the Metropole Hotel. I complained to Pam, and she forced him to leave the table. I asked: 'Why do you have Driberg anyway?' She said: 'Oh, he gives a suitably low tone to balance the grandees.'

Driberg was capable of finding low homosexual life anywhere. When in Moscow, Guy Burgess complained he could not find partners. Driberg, though a mere visitor, soon fixed him up and told him exactly where to go to find more.

John Foster Dulles (1888–1959) was one of the best-briefed foreign ministers I've come across. You could never catch him out on a fact, a date or a law. His background was awesome. One of his grandfathers, John Foster, had been Secretary of State; so had his uncle, Robert Lansing. He was senior partner in the famous Wall Street law firm of Sullivan and Cromwell and in the First World War had been part of the special team set up by President Wilson, in Manhattan, to provide the expertise and documentation for the Versailles Treaty negotiations. As both Keynes and Nicolson testified, the Americans were always the best informed during the treaty-making. I had long sessions with Dulles at the American Embassy in Paris in 1954, and again in 1955, over Vietnam in both cases. He knew everything, and his lawyer's mind was razor-sharp. But everything had to be referred to Ike, who allowed him no real discretion. Dulles was related to the mother of my then American girlfriend, Euphemia, and was very kind and friendly to me. He said: 'In diplomacy, to go to the brink without going over it is the necessary art.' What struck me was that he held a glass of whisky and ice in his hand but never drank from it. He would put in his finger, and suck it instead. This is known as the Wall Street Finger Sip.

Anthony Eden (1897–1977) was the best-looking politician of his time, and the last to give his name to a hat (a type of homburg). He popularised the double-breasted suit among the elite. He came from the Yorkshire gentry – his father was the 7th Baronet, a man who had bouts of uncontrollable bad temper in which he smashed furniture, etc. Eden was the same. But much better-looking – 'like a beautiful, hysterical woman'. Two brothers were killed in the First World War, in which he served in the Green Jackets (KRRC), got a good MC and was brigade major at twenty, youngest in the army. He was devoted to the regiment. His son Nicholas and I were in the KRRC together and slept in adjoining beds at Bushfield Camp, the regiment's basic training centre outside Winchester, where the regiment had its depot. I had no idea

Nicholas was queer; later, he was the first prominent English victim of AIDS. Eden himself was not, I think, queer. He had two wives; the second became a good friend of mine after Eden's death. Eden was at Eton, then Christ Church; took a first in Persian and Arabic, and also spoke French well. He got the safe seat of Warwick and was in the Commons from 1923 until his retirement. A poor speaker, really – Churchill said: 'He used every cliché except "Kindly adjust your dress."' A poor writer, too, except in his book about his early life, *Another World, 1897–1917*, which he wrote right at the end of his life and published in 1976, the year before he died.

Eden did well until the late thirties, and resigned at the right time. But he allowed himself from then on to be overshadowed by Churchill, who overworked him in the war and caused the illness, aggravated by bad doctors and surgeons, which ruined his premiership. He was an unlucky politician, but it must be said that he had bad judgement. He handled the Suez Crisis, from first to last, with extraordinary ineptitude. My book on Suez, the first I wrote, done in ten days at the end of 1956 and published a week later, was too hard on Eden from a moral point of view but not hard enough on his incompetence in running a war. Churchill, with all his knowledge and instincts for war, never interfered in the details of operations. Eden did all the time, telling the RAF, for instance, to use smaller bombs on Egypt, to avoid civilian casualties. At the same time, the service chiefs were never given clear orders on the objective of the operations, the reason being that Eden did not know, or could not decide, what it was. Guy Mollet told me: '*Pas magnifique, et pas la guerre non plus*' (adapting General Bosquet's verdict on the Charge of the Light Brigade).

Clarissa Eden told me her husband, never a good sleeper, became a chronic insomniac during the Suez Crisis, which lasted from July to December, partly because of the time gap between

London and Washington (five to six hours), which meant he had to take phone calls from Ike and Dulles in the small hours. And, at the same time, his guts were causing him more and more pain and distress. After the decision to withdraw, caused primarily by US hostility, Eden was advised to rest, and was persuaded to go to Ian Fleming's house, Goldeneye, in Jamaica. This was totally unsuitable, a horribly uncomfortable house (see the gruesome descriptions in Annie Fleming's letters). So he came back worse than he went. At that point my father-in-law, Dr Thomas Hunt, Senior Consultant at St Mary's, was called in, as the country's leading gastro-enterologist. Why he wasn't consulted before, I don't know. After examining Eden, he was emphatic. 'If you carry on as Prime Minister, you will in my view be dead within weeks. If you resign now and sever yourself completely from the stresses of public life, you may live many years in reasonable health.' He was clear that politics, as well as bad surgery, was to blame. Eden, pressed by Clarissa, followed this advice scrupulously. He resigned immediately and refused even to advise the Queen about a successor. He did a deal with *The Times* on his memoirs, being paid £100,000. He was thus able to buy a fine manor house in Wiltshire, where he lived for twenty years. His memoirs (three volumes) are no good but better than Macmillan's. They leave all the big questions over Suez, such as collusion, unanswered. There is no good life of Eden, and it would require a genius to write one.

Dwight D. Eisenhower (1890–1969) I saw occasionally when I lived in Paris, at his office in SHAPE HQ. He had quite a temper. His uniforms were always beautifully pressed. He was not the man he seemed. He deliberately gave the impression of being laid back and lazy and always playing golf. In fact he was extremely hard-working, got up very early, and had important meetings and phone calls before breakfast. This was particularly marked during his presidency, 1953–61. His absurd press secretary, James Hagerty, gave out a daily schedule of Ike's activities, which omitted some of his most important doings. His logbooks and phone logs, published long after his death, tell a totally different story. Equally, he gave the impression that he handed over foreign policy to John Foster Dulles. Not so – Dulles had to report to him in detail every evening. Richard Nixon, his vice-president throughout, told me: 'Mr Eisenhower was the most devious person I ever came across.'

Ike was like Washington on religious matters, believing it essential to social coherence and order but having no interest in doctrine. He said: 'Every American ought to have a religion – and I don't care what it is.' He also coined the phrase, or popularised it, 'the military-industrial complex'. I thought him a very odd and complex man, and he deserves a really good biography which he has not yet received.

T. S. Eliot (1888–1965) I met only once, in 1953. He was standing just inside the entrance to the drawing room on the first floor at 50 Albemarle Street, headquarters of the publishing firm John Murray for over two hundred years. In that room Byron's letters from exile to John Murray II had been read to the London social literati, and in its grate the sole copy of Byron's memoirs had been burned, before witnesses. The then head of the firm, 'Jock' Murray, was famous for the strength and quality of the dry martinis he served at his parties. I loved to go to them for you never knew what might happen. Eliot loved them, too, though he worked for a rival firm, Faber & Faber. The only remark he addressed to me before we were interrupted was: 'There is nothing in this world quite so stimulating as a strong dry martini cocktail.'

I suspect he required a spur to write poetry, being shy, and alcohol provided it. His second wife told me, long after his death, that the poem of his which meant the most to her was 'The Journey of the Magi', written in 1927, when she was fourteen. She heard a recording of him reading it and it made a great impression. Later, after they were married, she asked him about writing it. He said: 'I wrote it one Sunday after matins. I had been thinking about it in church and when I got home I opened a half-bottle of Booth's Gin, poured myself a drink, and began to write. By lunchtime, the poem, and the half-bottle of gin, were both finished.'

Queen Elizabeth II (b. 1926) once rebuked me. It was at a party she gave at Buckingham Palace, part of a 'meet people' scheme introduced by Belinda Harley. The week before, I had written a fierce 'Page Eight' (chief feature article) for the *Daily Mail*, against a weak-minded decision by magistrates in the West Country, letting off a particularly obnoxious criminal type. I tore into the Chairman of the Bench, one of William Waldegrave's bossy elder sisters. But, as often happened, the *Daily Mail* put on top of the piece an unnecessary inflammatory headline. The family found it offensive. At the party, another of the sisters, Marmaduke Hussey's wife, Lady Susan Hussey, who was on duty as the Queen's lady-in-waiting, came up to me with a cross face and upbraided me: 'How dare you,' etc. The Queen was close, so she spoke in a fierce whisper. I replied, defending myself, also in a fierce whisper. This exchange continued until suddenly the Queen turned round and, eyeing us both with a comprehensive monarchical glance, said sharply: 'Stop bickering, you two!' Both of us fell into an abashed silence and the Queen moved on, complacently.

William Empson (1906–84) was an example of the importance of a title in launching a book and a reputation. His *Seven Types of Ambiguity* (1930), which made him, was originally an undergraduate essay. Both his mother and father were Yorkshire gentry.

He had a brilliant Cambridge career, was elected to an immediate fellowship at Magdalene, then had it taken away after a college servant found contraceptives in his jacket pocket. This drove him to the Far East, first Tokyo, then Peking, which became his life work until he returned to a chair at Sheffield, being now a universal genius. He was wild-looking, with a funny sprouting beard on his face, chin and neck. I found his conversation impressive but incomprehensible and afterwards could remember nothing of what he said. But I was told, by his Cambridge acolytes: 'That is the mark of genius.' At a big *New Statesman* party (he often wrote long difficult-to-read pieces for our books pages) to celebrate the fiftieth anniversary of the paper, in 1963, held at the Connaught Rooms, he got formidably drunk and interesting. His wife was even more drunk and went crashing through a glass door. Much blood was spilt, and the reason for the rumpus was yet another type of ambiguity.

David English (1931–98) transformed the *Daily Mail* from a sagging former market leader into the best popular newspaper in Britain, pushing aside the *Express*, *Mirror* and *Sun*. He and George Gale, who was fond of him, had been reporters together. English was clever, hard-working, absolutely ruthless and a shit. 'Yes, he's a shit,' said George. 'But he's our shit.' 'He's not my shit!' I said. He played a nasty trick on me. I told him a true story, at a party in the Savoy, about the wretched Andrew Neil, known as 'Brillopad' because of his peculiar hair. English used this in such a way as to identify not only Neil but me. Neil was dreadfully upset. To make it up, I had to invite him to my house, to a *tête-à-tête* lunch, and hear all about his mother, 'the only person of any importance in my life'. But not long after this act of treachery, English suddenly died – it was said, by his enemies on the *Mail*, as a result of persistent overuse of Viagra. But I don't believe this. He always looked to me as if he could pop off without warning, a frequent fate of successful newspaper types. His successor, Paul Dacre, has been even more successful, without being a shit at all.

Henry Fairlie (1924–90) was the most talked-about political journalist of his generation, and among his friends he is still talked about with a mixture of affection, admiration, amazement and disgust: 'How did he get away with it?' He was famous for popularising or inventing the term 'the Establishment' to describe Britain's ruling elite, and focusing on colourful members of it like Lady Violet Bonham Carter; for writing in the fifties a brilliant weekly column in the *Spectator*; and for his exploits in bamboozling editors, publishers and bank managers, seducing women and spending three or four times what he earned. He had a saying: 'I can get a hot-cooked supper anywhere in north London', and it is true. He specialised in pretty, lower-middle-class suburban housewives. But he had many other conquests. One was Pamela Berry, after she and Muggeridge parted. She wrote him passionate love letters, one of which I saw and read, since Henry left it behind a cushion on a sofa in George Gale's house in Wivenhoe – Pat Gale found it and read bits of it out loud. Another was Nigel Lawson's wife Vanessa, or 'Queen Nefertiti', as I called her. She told me: 'I met Henry and fell in love. I couldn't help myself. Then, one evening, he said to me: "Look, darling, this affair we are having is all wrong. It must end. We must do the right thing. You must get divorced from Nigel. I must get divorced from Lisette. Then we must marry." I looked at him, astonished, unable to believe my ears. A spasm of sharp happiness such as I have never known convulsed my whole being. "Henry," I said, *"are you serious?"* He said, *"I was never more serious in my life."* The expression on his face was of total gravity and earnestness. He looked saintly, so we arranged to go off the following evening, to Paris. So next day I packed a bag, wrote a farewell note to Nigel, and went to join Henry in the Rivoli Bar, downstairs at the Ritz, at 6.30. What I did not know, but what I soon was told by people who knew Henry much better than I did, was that Henry was obviously drunk at the time. He had the capacity to be totally pissed without betraying any of the signs to the smallest degree. And in his drunken bouts he had the opposite of total recall – total oblivion. So when he woke up the next morning he had no recollection of our conversation or what he had promised to do. Well, I packed my suitcase. I wrote a letter to Nigel. "You must have realised for some time that things were not going well between us. And I have now met a man whom I think can transform my life," etc., etc. Put it on the mantelpiece. Then with a beating heart took a taxi to the Ritz. Six-thirty precisely. No Henry in the Rivoli Bar. "Mr Fairlie, madam? Usually comes in a bit later." 6.45. No Henry. 7 p.m. No Henry. At last, at 7.30, I realised Henry was not coming but Nigel was – home! Could I get back in time to retrieve the letter? Well, I did, just. I was tearing it up into tiny pieces when I heard his key in the lock. I never told him.' (She later did leave Nigel and married Freddie Ayer; but died of cancer soon afterwards.)

Henry was involved in many escapades, involving drink, women, lies and – most serious, perhaps – neglected work and missed deadlines. In those days, if you were set an assignment for a paper like the *Daily Mail*, for which Henry worked for a time, you went to the cashier with a chitty from the editor, and he gave you a big wodge of notes (a 'goldbrick') in advance. Henry used to tuck it into his top jacket pocket, where he always kept his spending money, and head for – north London! And the suburban house-wives. He did this once when he was supposed to be travelling with me to the Paris Summit in the 1960s. Marigold came, too – and Lisette was supposed to be going with Henry, she never having seen Paris. Marigold saw her at the hairdresser's, very excited, poor girl. But Henry never got to Paris. He was spending the gold-brick. By this time his journalistic career in London was drawing to an uncertain close, and he had his eyes on America. But before he went there he became involved in an unfortunate libel action. It was on a live early evening programme called *Three After Six*, on which I also often appeared. He libelled a lady who had just produced a book on children which the programme was discussing. Henry said that, in view of the woman's amorous escapades, perhaps she was not the ideal person to publish such a high-minded book – or words to that effect. Henry then went to Washington to start writing for the *New Republic*. The woman sued. The TV programme company, unable to get hold of Henry, had no alternative but to settle, and in due course a sum was handed over. Later, the case came before a judge, for the company to apologise and make a statement admitting the libel was false, in open court. Henry was not there. The judge was irritated. He said: 'I now come to the co-defendant, one Henry Fairlie. He has failed to put in an appearance, though duly summoned to do so. He has failed to answer any letters, from the plaintiff and her solicitors, from his co-defendant and their solicitors, and from this court. I am told he is the United States of America. So be it. But let it be known to Mr Fairlie, that if he ever returns to England and comes within the jurisdiction of this court, it will be at his peril!' These ominous words were conveyed to Henry, and he took them to heart. He never returned. The woman dropped the action against him – obviously, there was no more in it for her – the case was forgotten by the TV company and everyone else, the judge, full of years, died. But Henry remained in America, and died there.

It was not his only brush with the law. Earlier, he had been declared bankrupt, and before – long before – he got his discharge, he broke the terms of his insolvency guarantee by writing a cheque. This came before a judge, who also showed intense irritation, and put Henry into Brixton Gaol for contempt of court. There he remained for a few days until he purged his contempt and told the judge he was sorry; Lisette accepting the situation philosophically: 'Well, at least I know where Henry is.'

Henry was a good-looking fellow, with a red-brown countryman's complexion. Billy Hughes said he 'looked like a homicidal ploughboy – we often get these types in court'. His charm was a miracle, for men as well as women delighted in his company. A few are still alive, and are delighted to have known the legend.

Geoffrey Fisher, Archbishop of Canterbury (1887–1972) was the last man to hold his post in the old style, without apology or the smallest doubt about his position or his fitness to occupy it. His predecessor, William Temple, had only lasted two years. Temple was big, stocky, red-faced, enigmatic, noisy, confident – also diffident and self-doubting – and hyperactive: obviously a bad insurance risk. The old Duchess of Kent said that when he made his obeisance to her, shaking her hand and bowing to the waist, 'it was like looking down on the back of a large bullock'. Fisher was a smooth operator who had been a highly successful and severe headmaster of Repton, turning it from a bit of a shambles into one of the best public schools. He succeeded none other than Temple. He was only twenty-seven and very fit, and needed to be, for he believed in beating badly behaved boys, and always did it personally, if possible. It is said that he once beat the entire school, taking a whole afternoon to do it. I have never been able to find out whether this was true, and if so how many boys he beat and how many strokes each received – or what their offence was, either. The future Archbishop Ramsey was a boy there at the time, so Fisher must have beaten him, too, the one occasion I know of when an Archbishop of Canterbury thrashed his successor. On the one occasion I met Fisher, at a party in Church House for an ecumenical occasion, I funked asking him about the beatings. He had quite a forbidding personality and was not the kind of person you could take liberties with. He conducted the Coronation with great authority and in the best prelatical style. I watched it in Paris on TV at a big party given by the American hostess Mrs Margaret Biddle at her house. She had three TV sets in a room full of little gilt chairs. In the middle of the front row sat the Duke and Duchess of Windsor. The Duke was absolutely riveted by it all, and afterwards expressed his delight. He used a curious expression about Fisher: 'That Archbishop of Canterbury, he's quite a goer, isn't he?' Later, Fisher was said to have played a role in persuading Princess Margaret not to marry Group Captain Townsend. He is supposed to have arrived with a pile of volumes of canon law, etc., each docketed, and she is supposed to have said: 'You may put away your books, Archbishop. I have already decided I shall not marry Group Captain Townsend.' But Princess Margaret, years later, told me there was no truth in the story. She said she went to Lambeth Palace and Fisher had no books. She said they talked mainly of other things, for an hour, as her mind had long been made up. She said: 'I never blamed Dr Fisher. I blamed the man Lascelles. He is the person who ruined my life.'

Fisher retired in 1961 and lived another eleven years as an assistant curate.

Constantine Fitzgibbon (1919–83) was by profession a novelist but was chiefly famous for the spectacular rows, indeed fights, with his wife Theodora. I met him through his friend Billy Hughes, who was their lawyer at the time. 'Con', as he was known, was of distinguished Irish descent from the Earls of Clare, but he was born in America, and spent part of his war in the American army on the staff of General Omar Bradley, Commanding 12th Army Group. In the 1940s, when I knew him, he was a prominent figure in literary London, his work culminating in his novel *When the Kissing Had to Stop* (1960), describing a Soviet takeover of Britain, which was serialised in the *Express* and had a spectacular, though brief, vogue. He wrote fourteen novels in all, and other books, including *The Life of Dylan Thomas*, Thomas having been his drinking companion. Con was married several times, but Theo was the wife I remember. She wrote cookery books, very well, and was in every way his equal, intellectually, socially, in invective and abuse and, when it came to the point, in fisticuffs. Con and Theo were a Punch and Judy turn in their cups. At a certain point in the evening he would 'go critical', a moment always signalled by a regular swinging movement of his right arm, a lowering of his voice and a sombre expression which turned his face into an iron mask. Theo would detect this, and prepare herself with another large swig of whisky. Then the fun would start. The marriage inevitably ended in divorce, and in due course Con took the pledge, wrote a passionate denunciation of alcohol, *Drink* (1979), and campaigned for abstinence. But he was never so interesting or popular, as when he and Theo were 'at it'.

Ali Forbes (1918–2005) was known to me as 'Old Name-dropper'. I never knew anyone who had this tiresome propensity to the same degree. It is true he knew some grand people. He was connected with the Kennedy family, on one side of the Atlantic, and with the Churchill family on the other. And he was sometimes to be seen in the Royal Box at Wimbledon or Covent Garden. But how he went on – and on, and on – in a rasping voice! He was also malicious and rude. His one heroic act was to resign from the *Sunday Dispatch*, at the time of Suez, because the paper supported Eden. He wrote a regular column for it, which he valued, so it was a genuine sacrifice, and he never got another job. Instead he wrote reviews for the *Spectator* – far too long, 'dropping names like confetti', and immense sentences, longer even than Bernard Levin's, but without his sense of syntactical artistry. He lived in Switzerland, mainly, on an exiguous income, and came to London for parties and to distribute malicious insults. All the same, when he died ('not before time', as was said), I missed him.

Gerald Ford (1913–2006) became American president simply because he could remember names. He and I were both Fellows at the American Enterprise Institute, a Washington think-tank, in 1980. He remembered my name, Marigold's name, and the names of my four children, though only told them once, when he asked. It was this extraordinary capacity, which he had to a degree I have never come across in anyone else, which led to him becoming House Minority Leader. Hence, when Nixon resigned, Spiro Agnew, the vice-president, having already been disgraced, Ford went to the White House. Ford was amiable but, apart from his name remembering, had no other qualification. His only other characteristic was a remarkable propensity for falling over. I saw him knock over a glass of water, trip over somebody's feet, back violently into a tea trolley and elbow a waiter, causing him to drop a tray of glasses, all in a single lunchtime.

E. M. Forster (1879–1970) lived to a great age. I saw him once, in Pall Mall, standing on the steps of the Reform Club. He wore an old mackintosh, stained, greasy and crumpled. The figure struck me as the epitome of the Man in the Dirty Raincoat. It began to rain as he hesitated on the top step. Then he turned up his collar so that only his big, sharp nose showed, moved gingerly down the steps, crossed the road and headed for Soho. Going cruising, was he? Cottaging? Better say: looking for copy.

His name cropped up once when I was staying with J. B. Priestley at Kissing Tree House. I said: 'I think Forster is rather overrated.' Priestley stiffened. 'I don't agree with you,' he said loudly. Oh dear! Had I foolishly disparaged a writer who, it would now be revealed, was one of Priestley's oldest and most valued friends? I need not have worried. Priestley continued: 'I don't agree with you. Forster is not *rather* overrated. He is *very greatly* overrated.'

General Francisco Franco (1892–1975) ruled Spain for longer than anyone else in her history, and during a period of the greatest possible difficulty. When I was serving in Gibraltar, 1950–51, the consensus in the Garrison Officers' Mess was that he had done well to keep Spain out of the war and remain in the saddle so long, 'the dago being a difficult brute to stay on top of', as one of the staff put it. On my brief meeting with him, he said: 'The trouble with Spain is that there is nothing between the landowners and the peasants, or the capitalists and the workers. I want to create a large middle class, as you have in England. Then we will have a tranquil state in which democracy can work. But that will take time.' In fact, by the time he died his work was done. A middle class had come into existence. His skill in handing over to a constitutional monarchy was successful. And Spain now has an economy roughly on the same level as the rest of Western Europe, for the first time in her history. All this was Franco's doing.

When I was writing *Modern Times*, I studied, with great care, and as much objectivity as I could, the Spanish Civil War. I came to the clear and unshakable conclusion that, morally, there was nothing to choose between the two sides. Cruelty in general, atrocities, murder of civilians, torture and massacre of prisoners – just about the same. They differed on one point. The CP in Catalonia murdered a lot of their internal enemies. Franco was never so foolish as to do that. Otherwise there was nothing to choose between them. Franco won the war primarily because he ran the economy better. Also Germany and Italy were more altruistic in helping than Stalin was in helping the Republic. All he wanted was their huge gold reserve – and he got the lot. It is true that, when he had won, Franco massacred the Communists who were left behind. But they would have done the same to his people if the Reds had won. And the fact that Franco destroyed the CP was precisely what ensured Spain's reunification and made her new prosperity possible.

Paul Preston's biography of Franco has many merits but leaves an unresolved contradiction. If Franco was as horrible as he states, and made all the mistakes he lists, and was so stupid and ignorant as he implies, how was it he was able to rule unopposed for so long, and so creatively, as Spain's subsequent history so clearly shows? He must be accounted, overall, as one of the most successful politicians of the century.

He was much smaller than you expected, like a movie actor. Strong bright eyes. Prissy mouth. Soft voice. Good manners for a soldier. He was extraordinarily eccentric. Fascinated by the cinema. He wrote a film script and then got the government film unit to shoot it with himself taking a role. He also regularly did Littlewoods Football Pools, and occasionally won modest sums. He wrote letters to the *Daily Telegraph* and signed them 'Thomas Babington Macaulay'. What did he most admire about the English, apart from having a large middle class?' 'Sense of humour.'

Dora Gaitskell (1901–89) was a plump little lady, of Russian-Jewish origin, whose maiden name was Creditor. In 1956 she came up to me at a party and said: 'Your name is Paul Johnson, isn't it? I heard you say something nasty about Hugh on the radio. Take that!' And, on tiptoe (she was under five feet), she swung her heavy handbag in a great arc and whopped me on the head. She was what the Yankees call feisty, and I much preferred her to her husband.

Hugh Gaitskell (1906–63). He was a typical Wykhamist. It is curious that when he and R. H. S. Crossman were contemporaries at the school, it was Dick, not Gaitskell, who became head boy. Gaitskell was hated by the Bevanites with a passion and intensity that now seems inexplicable. He made things worse by his own obnoxious habit of niggling. He was not content with a victory over his opponents in the Labour Party but had to rub their noses in it, and made them admit they had been wrong. His famous 'fight, fight and fight again' speech at the Party Conference was inflammable and made matters worse. His willingness to fight 'to save the party we love' struck me as evidence of a peculiar mentality. As with Barbara Castle, I did not see how anyone could love a party, particularly not Labour with its tunnel vision and endless rows. He was a divisive figure, and I do not think Labour could ever have won an election under his leadership. So his sudden and mysterious death (due to bad doctoring) was a merciful release. Within weeks of Wilson taking over, the party closed ranks.

Gaitskell made an ass of himself, under Attlee, by a ministerial statement saying people should not have more than six inches of water in their bath (to save fuel). People joked about his washing habits. The real trouble, however, was his taste in clothes. He had a liking for brown suits with strongly pronounced stripes. After meeting him, I saw for the first time what Curzon meant when he said, 'Gentlemen never wear brown'. He was a polished dancer in a *palais de dance* style, and not unattractive to women. Annie Fleming doted on him for a time.

General Charles de Gaulle (1890–1970) suffered from halitosis.

Malcolm Muggeridge believed the affliction was the key to his character – to forestall people retreating from his bad breath in revulsion, De Gaulle himself rejected them with hauteur. Diana Cooper told me that, in Algiers in 1943, she, as wife of Duff, the minister attached to the French, had to give a dinner at which he was guest of honour, and sat next to him. She had never really met him before, and was scared. In her nervousness, she began to tell him about the strange animals she had come across in Australia, where she and Duff had spent 1942. 'And then there were these wombats.' *'Les quoi?'* 'Wombats. WOMBATS.' *'Et puis?'* 'And the devils. The Tasmanian devils.' *Et puis?'* 'And the koala bears.' *'Et puis?'* She began to talk faster and faster, naming more and more strange species. Finally, she ran out of names. There was a silence. De Gaulle laid down his fork. *'Oui,'* he said. *'Il parait il y a des* kangaroos!'

She also told me that, in Paris in 1946, she gave a dinner for the De Gaulles and the Embassy. He had just resigned as Head of the Government. Madame de Gaulle was a severe figure in black, a pillar of the church in their home village, Colombey-les-Deux-Eglises, where they had a small chateau, and where he would accompany her to Sunday mass, carrying her large breviary. At the dinner, someone asked her, in English, what she was most looking forward to, now her husband was relieved of his onerous responsibilities. She replied, to the consternation of the table: 'A penis.' In the silence that followed, De Gaulle spoke; 'No, *ma chérie*, you 'ave mispronounced the word. You mean 'appiness.'

Nancy Mitford used to joke about Madame, and ask: 'Which of the two churches does she drag him to?' De Gaulle was a master of that characteristic French male gesture, the elaborate shrug. In 1956, a year or two before he came back to power, he held a press conference in the Hôtel Voltaire, near the Assemblée

Nationale. He gave his views on the progress towards European Unity, the Coal-Steel Pool, the Schuman Plan, etc., adding: '*A mon avis*, these economic arrangements are not decisive. The spirit of Europe does not lie in coal and steel and tariffs and money. *Non! Pour moi, l'Europe est l'Europe de Dante. Et de Goethe. Et de Chateaubriand.*'

I interrupted him. '*Et de Shakespeare, mon Général?*' He looked at me with intense hatred, then suddenly relaxed, gave one of his enormous shoulder shrugs, and said, as if in resignation: '*Oui! Shakespeare aussi.*'

After his return to power, on the backs of the Algerian *colons* and army officers, he abruptly reversed his position, and abandoned *Algérie française*. Jacques Soustelle, who had been Governor General there, and remained loyal to the *colons*, remonstrated with him. He put his views and added: 'All my friends agree with me.' De Gaulle told him, '*Alors, Soustelle! Changez vos amis!*' Years later, I asked Soustelle if the story was true. He said: 'Yes! 'Ee did say zat. 'Ee was a terrible man!'

El Glaoui, Pasha of Marrakesh (1879–1956) was a man of formidable power in Morocco in the 1950s. He was the man through whom the French ruled the country (which was not a colony but a protectorate) when they decided to dethrone the Sultan. When I was an officer in the British garrison in Gibraltar, I used to stay often in Marrakesh, in a palace in the old town. It was owned by some Romanian friends of mine. They knew the Pasha and took me to see him. He was a figure from the Middle Ages, tall, fierce, a tremendous cavalryman, and rider, who showed me how to use his curved sword, a sort of scimitar, which he carried when on horseback. He swished it up and down, from side to side, and round his head, saying '*On fait* ça! *et* ça! *et* ça!' He maintained his power by his mounted warriors, grouped in brigades of two hundred or so. They carried out what were called *ratissages* in villages known to be pro-Sultan, riding through them slashing with their swords, firing rifles and setting fire to one or two huts. His authority in Marrakesh, the capital of the desert, was absolute, and extended on both sides of the Atlas, well into the Sahara. His family had fought the family of the Sultan for hundreds of years, or so he told me. We had a feast which included a turkey roasted in an oven, with an outer shell of chestnut paste, very tender within. We ate with our fingers, and he picked out tasty bits to give me. We squatted or lay on cushions, very uncomfortable and inconvenient. His great friend among the French was Maréchal Juin, a tough old bird whom I also met, who told me: 'The Moroccans will not be ready for independence for a hundred years. El Glaoui is what they need.' But when Juin was replaced the power of the Pasha began to decline. After the Sultan was reinstated, he was put under house arrest, and died a broken man. Of course he was a violent old ruffian, without an idea in his head. But the Sultan was no better. Churchill said of El Glaoui: 'He gave us some idea of what Saladin must have been like.' Exactly. I was very glad to have met him – an old warrior from the past, unlucky enough to survive into the treacherous modern world.

Grace Wyndham Goldie (1900–86). When I knew her she was (from 1954) Head of TV Talks at the BBC. She started the *Tonight* programme and picked Donald Baverstock to run it. She was a clever woman but spent too much time in the hospitality room. In 1962 she was promoted Head of Current Affairs, and started to frequent the hospitality room when prominent politicians were doing a programme. This led to rows. In 1965, during a BBC party, I discovered her in a broom cupboard locked in a passionate embrace with George Brown, then Secretary of State for Economic Affairs.

Victor Gollancz (1893–1967) was long past his meridian by the time I met him in 1955, and had acquired an unenviable reputation for being impossible to work with. I remembered his denouncing *Lolita* to me as a 'disgusting book, a work of pornography of the most vicious kind', without saying he had tried to buy it, and failed. He was furious with Attlee for not offering him a peerage, with Canon Collins and J. B. Priestley for not giving him the leading role in CND, and with David Astor and Arthur Koestler for crowding him out of the anti-capital-punishment campaign. He more than once asked me: 'Why does Kingsley Martin hate me so?' I said: 'He doesn't, though he might have good reason to. Why do you never advertise in the *New Statesman*? You have an advert every week in the *Observer*, though it doesn't agree with your views.' 'Well, I've no need to advertise in the *NS* as they give me free plugs anyway.' I thought he was an utterly self-centred man, mean, and an example of the lack of moral qualities in left-wing thinkers. He was also personally unpleasant. He was a hypochondriac, and always terrified of contracting VD. He would constantly take out his penis to inspect it to discover whether it showed signs of VD or indeed whether it was still there at all. In his office he would perform this ritual several times a day, near a frosted window he believed to be entirely opaque. The girls in the building on the opposite side of the well pointed out that this was not so. They sent him a round robin saying: 'We've seen enough of your cock now, Mr G. Can we see something else?' He was furious and sent a pompous complaint to their boss. Pomposity was his chief characteristic in old age, and he strutted to eternity.

Arnold Goodman (1913–95) had a universal reputation for worldly wisdom, fine judgement and everything to do with the law, politics, business and human nature. But I always found him a booby and a muddler. He was the senior partner in Goodman, Derrick, Solicitors and Commissioners for Oaths. He did constant work for Howard Samuel who made a fortune in property in the years immediately after the Second World War. That is how he got into political circles, for Samuel used his money to bankroll *Tribune*, which was Nye Bevan's organ. He introduced Goodman to Bevan, and to Michael Foot, the editor. And he started to work for both these two, and they in turn passed him on to Harold Wilson, who made Goodman a life peer and got him to do fixing jobs, e.g. in Rhodesia. I first met him when I wrote *The Suez War* for MacGibbon & Kee, the publishing firm Samuel had just bought, at the end of 1956. Goodman read it for libel. He did not find any libel but he claimed that much of the inside information it contained, which I had got from various sources, was a breach of the Official Secrets Act. I do not now believe Goodman ever understood the Act, or had even read it properly, and today I would have brushed his objections aside – but then I was much less experienced and confident, and anyway Samuel believed in Goodman's omniscience and his warning: 'You would go to gaol too, Howard, not just Paul.' So some of the best bits in the book were taken out, though nothing like as much as Goodman wanted. He was an enormously fat man with a huge head and countless double chins. At our final conference before publication (everything was done in a rush, for the book was written in a week and published ten days later), he suddenly shifted his ground, getting more and more angry: 'This whole book is a breach of the Official Secrets Act from start to finish, and I must solemnly advise you, Howard, that not one jot or tittle of it can be published with safety.' And all his chins wobbled with indignation. I told him he was a goon, and a coward, and exceeding his brief. He backed down, eventually, and we put out the book as it stood. There was never the slightest trouble with the authorities and I believe it could have been published in its original version quite safely. After this experience, whenever I heard Goodman praised as a wizard, I would say: 'Balls!'

However, he usually meant well, was kind-hearted and I dare say often helped people who were in a mess. He reassured them anyway. And he didn't charge people he thought were hard up. He did his important fixing at breakfast in his Portland Place flat. How he got so enormous I don't know. I never saw him eat anything. But perhaps he ate secretly.

Goodman was fat all over. Once, when he and I had been at the Commons, we were given lifts in Dick Crossman's ministerial car (he was at the time Lord President of the Council). Dick got in next to the driver, I took one seat at the back. The other was occupied by Dick's papers, a big red dispatch box and a pair of suede shoes, for he had been to the Palace to see the Queen, who objected to suede shoes, so Dick had had to change into black leather ones. Without giving anyone a chance to dispose of the pile, Goodman backed into the car, as he always did, and sat on top of the lot, enveloping them under his vast arse. He did not even notice. So it was the princess and the pea story – in reverse. Dick, unobservant as ever, was quite unaware of Goodman's amazing feat. But the driver and I exchanged winks.

Goodman was unmarried – what woman in her senses would want him? – but as his fame and importance mounted, various widows were proposed for him by busybodies – Clarissa Eden, for instance, and Annie Fleming. I don't suppose either of these two fastidious ladies would have seriously considered him for one second. But they were happy to be taken to the opera, and parties, by him. Harold Wilson, as PM, made use of Goodman for all kinds of top-secret purposes. But nothing much came of his activities. As Jim Callaghan said, 'It is all piss and wind', and when he became PM, Goodman was 'put on the back burner'. He was supposed to be in receipt of fascinating confidences and to know the inner workings of many dark political deals. But when his eagerly awaited memoirs, *Tell Them I'm On My Way*, were published, it was found to contain s.f.a. of interest, as I expected. His final years were of sad declension, and growing shortage of money. In pursuit of fame he had neglected his practice. He was also inclined to take on too many roles, and this led him into unresolved conflicts of interest. Indeed, in one such case he was the object of serious litigation on behalf of the Portman family, still pending at his death, so he left this world a worried man. His life was yet another adverse comment on the evils of worldliness, though it should be said that vanity, not greed, was his weakness.

Katharine Graham (1917–2001), who owned the *Washington Post*, inherited from her husband, Phil Graham, was a great power in US politics, solely because of her control of that key paper. She had terrific courage. It enabled her to win a strike battle with the fierce print unions, by using helicopters to lift copies of the paper from the roof of the *Post* building, to the impotent fury of the union pickets. But she was in many ways ignorant, stupid and tiresome. Pam Berry regarded her as her best friend in Washington (she was a notable hostess there). Though Pam agreed with many of my criticisms, she would never allow me to attack 'Kay' in print. 'If you go for her in public,' she said, 'it will be the end of our friendship.' So I submitted. What did it matter? Nobody now cares tuppence for old Mrs Graham, and today few have ever heard of her.

Graham Greene (1904–91) and I had various dealings when I was an editor – he sent me short stories and the occasional article. I have quite a collection of brief letters from him, usually on business. I found him creepy. The trouble with Greene was that he went to a school (Berkhamsted) where his father was headmaster. This set up in him an unresolvable conflict of allegiance – should he be loyal to his friends or to his father? – and this led, in practice, to a deep-rooted instinct to betray. Hence, though employed in the Secret Service during the war, he sympathised with the Cambridge traitors and consorted with them when in Moscow. And, though he joined the Catholic Church in the thirties, he betrayed it again and again, consorting with, and praising, its enemies, especially in Latin America. I had rows with him about this. He also, during his affair with Catherine, the American wife of Lord Walston, made a point of embracing her secretly in Italian churches, once (according to his account) copulating with her in the darkness behind the high altar. His understanding of Catholic theology was defective and makes nonsense of the plots of two of his novels. Unlike Evelyn Waugh, a good theologian, he never understood what the Catholic Church was about. At heart he was a twisted Calvinist. There was a strong streak of irrationality in his view of the world. This made him a good contriver of original plots, and his journalistic training on *The Times* made him a sharp observer. As a descriptive writer he was as good as any writer of fiction in the twentieth century. He once told me: 'Write a long paragraph about a place – a town, a street, a room, an office – then take out all the adjectives, and most adverbs. Then leave it. Then come back to it and put in fresh adjectives and adverbs. Try it, see if it works for you.' He had a slow production rate. He regarded five hundred words a day as very good. Waugh told me he could manage two to three thousand when 'flush', as he put it. Greene's anti-Americanism, part of his itch to betray, made no sense, and was as stomach-churning as (later) Pinter's. But Greene was the handsomest member of his ugly family.

Sir Hugh Carleton Greene (1910–87). He was a huge man, six foot six, and big in proportion. He could down a magnum of champagne without noticing. Before the war he had been an ace foreign reporter for the *Telegraph*, then joined the BBC. He was the first inside man to be made Director General of the BBC, in January 1960. The date is relevant for Greene did more to make the sixties a significant decade for change and folly than any other individual. Under him, the BBC led left-wing programme fashion, with programmes like *That Was the Week That Was*, as well as near-the-knuckle shows like *Till Death Us Do Part*. Harold Wilson grew to hate him, and in 1967 made Charles Hill the Chairman, hoping to provoke Greene's resignation. But Greene stayed on another two years. When he finally resigned in March 1969 he asked me round for a drink. We chatted in his office, and he poured out his hatred of Wilson. When I left he took me downstairs into the famous lobby of Broadcasting House, with its engraved Latin motto, beginning 'This Temple of the Arts'. He had a glass of champagne in one hand, and with the other held a magnum by the neck. He said: 'I have worked for the BBC, on and off, since October 1940. I have always wanted to say to hell with the BBC, and drink champagne in this beastly hall under that silly motto. After nearly thirty years, that's exactly what I'm doing.' And he drained his glass, refilling it from the magnum. And how the commissionaire and the ladies behind the desk stared!

Geoffrey Grigson (1905–85) was notorious for being the most savage reviewer of the century, particularly of poetry. When John Raymond was assistant literary editor of the *New Statesman* and wanted me to do a harsh review of a bad new book, he would call down to me: 'Fix bayonets – I want you to do a Grigson.' There were rival explanations for his harshness to writers. One was that he loved literature, poetry above all, so much that he could not tolerate anything below the best. He wrote poetry himself – some said first-class poetry – and in the thirties he edited *New Verse*, one of the best poetry reviews. But another version was that he was horribly unhappy. He was a late child of clerical parents, who had already had six sons, and they packed him off to boarding school at five. He described his sufferings in a memoir, *The Crest on the Silver*. To make matters much worse, three of his brothers were killed in the First World War, and the other three in the Second World War, leaving him alone. (He had marriages but they usually did not last.) This case of family slaughter must be unique. When I was an editor I was intrigued by his literary cruelty and had him into my office to see what sort of a fellow he was. To my surprise he turned out to be tall, handsome and well preserved (he was then in his sixties) and absolutely charming. But poets, as a rule, regarded him with dread. After he was dead and safely buried, I mentioned his name to Stephen Spender and a look of undisguised terror swept over his features: 'Oh God! That man!'

J. B. S. Haldane (1892–1964) was the rudest man I ever met. He was naturally bad-tempered but it was believed his anger was 'clinical' and arose from injuries, physical or psychological, received in the Great War when he conducted experiments on new weapons at great danger to himself. So people were more tolerant than his behaviour warranted. He had had a row with the *New Statesman*, and as a result it was agreed a member of the staff would call on him periodically, at his flat south of the Strand, to deliver things. This disagreeable chore was performed by my colleague Norman MacKenzie. But shortly after I joined the staff, he revolted, and said he would put up with Haldane's rudeness no more. So I was sent instead. Haldane answered the door. He did not invite me in, but berated me from the doorstep. After a bit his wife appeared, too, and joined in the abuse. What they said made little sense, so I was not personally rattled. But I objected to the recurrent use of the term 'lickspittle', so eventually I said: 'Professor Haldane, if you were not an old man, I would punch you on the nose', and left.

Gilbert Harding (1907–60) illustrates the terrifying power of television to elevate individuals into blinding celebrity, then return them (at death or even before) to the primeval darkness from which they emerged. He told me he was born in a workhouse and educated in an orphanage. This was half true. His parents both worked and lived in a workhouse in Hereford. His school was the Royal Orphanage, Wolverhampton. This was an excellent academy and got him to Queens' College, Cambridge, though he only managed a third there. 'I was idle,' he said to me, 'and self-indulgent. I should have been a don. I have the temperament of a scholar. I love clever young men. I would like to help them. As it is, I have wasted my life, and now, at the end of it, I am paid a fortune to display my worst fault – bad temper.' He was in turn a schoolmaster at the kind of schools described by Waugh in *Decline and Fall* (he was by temperament a homosexual, though never, I think, a practising one), a professor in a dim university in Nova Scotia, a policeman, a newspaper correspondent in Cyprus and a law student. During the war he worked for the BBC, like so many other educated drifters.

In 1947 he got his chance, as quizmaster of the BBC radio show *Round Britain Quiz*. The quizmaster was a new profession invented by the BBC in the forties, which required a combination of the schoolmaster, the authority figure and the entertainer. Harding had all these characteristics but in addition possessed an eccentric vein of sarcasm, springing not so much from a love of knowledge as a contempt for the ignorant. This gave him distinction in his new role. He flourished in *The Brains Trust* and *Any Questions?*, and, when TV arrived, he became the star of *What's My Line?*, another quiz show, perhaps the most successful of all. At times in the fifties he was, after the Queen and Churchill, the best-known face in England. He looked like a schoolmaster of the worst type: fat and overindulgent, red-faced, hirsute, with a bristling moustache of strong, spiky hairs, hair growing wildly over his eyes and out of his ears, and on the backs of his hands, a strong but hoarse, asthmatic voice, a longing to punish, humiliate, put down and inspire fear – and a rare capacity to do these things. Like many schoolmasters, he enjoyed making his jokes before a captive and sycophantic class, which was exactly what TV provided in those days. The BBC put professional laughers in studio audiences. His bad temper was absolutely genuine. When not exercising it on the airwaves, he liked to sit just inside the main bar at the Savile Club (half of whose members worked at the BBC) and comment on people entering, to himself or, occasionally, to people like me who relished his awfulness. 'Oh, it's you, is it? Looking for a friend? What makes you think you *have* a friend? Here, or anywhere else?' Or: 'Ah, if it isn't old name-dropper. Nobody here, old chap, worth you sucking up to – might as well go back to wifey.' Or: 'That man carries the stale breath of Broadcasting House around with him and the sly whiff of its chronic intrigues. Had a good day of malice aforethought, eh?' Some entrants, seeing Harding, would beat a hasty retreat. Others would try ingratiation, not as a rule with any success.

Harding was the English equivalent of Alexander Woollcott, or, rather, the noisy, overbearing eccentric portrayed in *The Man Who Came to Dinner*. But he had a soft heart. A bleeding heart, as they used to say. He was always on the side of the underdog – except when kicking him for personal reasons. He hated colonialism, capital punishment, flogging and caning in schools. He was humble in the presence of Nye Bevan, but I have seen and heard him going for Herbert Morrison. He loved his mother passionately. His autobiography was dedicated to her: 'To Mother, who deserves so much more, and so much better.' This love emerged painfully and dramatically when he appeared on John Freeman's *Face to Face* programme on TV. One of Freeman's stock questions was: 'Have you ever seen anyone die?' When he put this to Harding, there was a long pause, then tears, bitter, prolonged tears. Harding had seen his mother die, and it had shattered him. Freeman had not known this, otherwise he would not have put the question. There was a national outcry and Freeman was much abused, in print and by mail. Harding said the episode 'did me much good'. 'Got out of me something which had been twisting and torturing my soul.'

I always thought of him as a sick man: sick in spirit, knowing he ought to be doing something better but guiltily enjoying the good things in life his telly fame brought him. Sick in body, too, throughout his life, with periodic crises. He gave up smoking, but drank more as a consequence. After leaving Broadcasting House in November 1960, following a *Round Britain Quiz* performance – 'the gilded treadmill' he called it – he suddenly dropped dead in Portland Place. They gave him a slap-up requiem mass in the Cathedral at which the Cardinal preached and the great and the good-for-nothing (as he liked to put it) attended. The tremendous plainchant *Dies Irae*, which was still allowed in those days, was a glorious-gruesome experience, and I noticed some grim faces in the fashionable pews. After it was all over, he was no more. Where had he gone? Into the airwaves?

Sir Arthur Harris (1892–1984), Head of Bomber Command during the war. He always acted strictly under orders, but was made the moral scapegoat of the ruthless destruction of German cities. Everyone behaved badly to him, even Churchill. He took it stoically, but was bitter. He used to drive around at high speed in a huge Packard, the kind of car Chicago gangsters used. Once he was stopped by a young policeman. 'Sir, you were well over the speed limit. If you go on like that you will end by killing somebody.' 'Young man, I kill thousands every night.' I owe this story to Canon John Collins, who was the chaplain of Bomber Command HQ.

Denis Healey (b. 1917). For many years he was the roughest fighter in the Labour Party, and made countless enemies. His favourite term of abuse was: 'You are out of your little Chinese mind.' Once, during a Party Conference at Brighton, I found him by himself, walking on the front. 'Denis, why are you alone?' He said: 'Because I have no friends.' Before the war he was a Communist, then became an army major, a pillar of Labour orthodoxy, and got a fine seat in Leeds, then overwhelmingly right-wing Labour. He was an unpleasing man, with a livid face, hirsute with fierce, bushy eyebrows. He had some skill at the piano, and could knock out well-known tunes, which made him briefly popular at party social gatherings. He was the best-read politician I ever met, from German philosophy to detective stories, and could remember everything he read. Once, when he was Secretary of State for Defence, he asked me to lunch at Admiralty House where he was living. I found him alone in the fine drawing room, a trolley with coffee and sandwiches on it. The room was full of sound and he was stretched out full length on a sofa, a volume in his hand. He said: 'I am reading Heidegger, and listening to Honegger.'

Ted Heath (1916–2005) in a way introduced, or symbolised, a new era in British politics. Just before the war, at Balliol, where he was an organ scholar, he was interviewed by the careers don and asked what he wanted to do in life. He replied: 'I intend to be a professional politician.' The don was put out. He had never heard the phrase used before. It sounded ominous and unBritish. Well, it was, wasn't it? But by the time Heath retired, all members of the House of Commons, Tories as well as Labour, were professional politicians.

Heath had the worst manners of any politician I have ever met. He was particularly uncivil, often rude, to women, but was really rude to everyone. He never wrote thank-you letters to hostesses. He hardly ever said thank you verbally. If the person sitting next to him at dinner was of no interest or use to him, he ignored them. Margaret Thatcher gave me a characteristic vignette of him. When Keith Joseph funked standing against Heath for the Tory leadership after Alec Home resigned it in 1975, and she was persuaded to stand instead, she thought it courteous to go to Heath's room in the House and tell him personally. So she did so. When she entered his room and told him, he was writing at his desk. (It would never have occurred to him to stand when a lady entered the room.) He did not look up, but continued writing, and said: 'You'll lose, you know.' That was his only comment. So she left the room, closing the door quietly.

I never got the impression Heath was musical. To play the organ you don't need to have a sense of tone or touch – the registration does it all, and that is purely an intellectual exercise. He had no ear, as far as I could tell. Of course he was *interested* in music, and got pleasure from it. He seemed to love conducting. A professional musician who had played under him told me: 'He kept up with us reasonably well. Always a quarter-beat behind.' The nicest thing I know about Ted Heath is what he said to my wife Marigold at dinner once: 'The thing I would really like to have done in my life was to write a successful musical comedy. You know – one whose tunes are whistled by errand boys.'

Heath was at his best as Chief Whip, a job for which he was fitted. He was invaluable to Macmillan in 1957 – he was the first man Macmillan talked to after the Queen had asked him to form a government. They dined *à deux* at the Turf Club. He would never have become party leader, and so PM, if Reggie Maudling had not been so idle. On the other hand, Maudling was dishonest, so perhaps it was just as well.

Derick Heathcoat-Amory (1899–1981). This strong, self-confident, jovial man, changed history by what he didn't do. He came from the most ramifying, county-political family in the West Country. They had a textile business and an estate, and went to Eton and Christ Church, Oxford. He never married and was a senior scout-master but there was never any scandal. Before the war he served in local government, then as a half-colonel in the army and was wounded at Arnhem. He had no sense of fear at all and was quite reckless about what he said. In 1945 he took over the seat at Tiverton held by a cousin killed in the war, soon rose, and was a minister from 1951. I loved talking to him, or rather hearing him discuss his colleagues. One 'always has his hand in the till'. Another a 'bloody coward'. A third 'a rapist, if he dared'. In 1958 all the Treasury ministers, led by Peter Thorneycroft, resigned in a body, hoping to break Macmillan. He dismissed it as 'a little local difficulty', but it would have been more serious if Amory had not been there to take over Thorneycroft's job. It was only seven weeks before the budget, but Amory was cool and confident, and in no time the incident was forgotten. Supermac was very grateful to him, and there is no doubt at all that Amory could have succeeded him as PM. But he left Westminster in 1960. He told me politics disgusted him, 'a sewer'. But I think it was to do with his homo-sexuality. He felt that, as a senior minister, he could not, in the country's interest, take risks with his sex life. Otherwise he would have succeeded Macmillan with the support of the entire party in 1963, and beaten Labour soundly the following year. Thus the Harold Wilson era in politics would never have occurred. I liked 'Derry'. Who didn't?

Cardinal John Heenan (1905–75). When he was Archbishop of Liverpool, he finally cancelled the project to build the vast cath-edral designed by Sir Edwin Lutyens, his masterpiece. It would have been the greatest work of the twentieth century. The crypt, in all its complex magnificence, had already been built, but work stopped with the war, and was not resumed. Heenan not only cancelled it but had built instead a miserable tent-like thing whose only merit was cheapness and which the Protestants immediately christened 'Paddy's Wigwam'. I told Heenan, a pink-cheeked fellow, very pleased with himself: 'You are a man of little faith. Catholics are poor but they are generous, and the Catholics of Lancashire would have been glad to meet the bill. You have done a very wicked thing.' He took this well, and said: 'You may be right. If so, I will be punished in the next world.' Me: 'And in this, by your feelings of guilt.' Later, when he was Cardinal of Westminster, Heenan said to me: 'You were right about the cath-edral, as I now see.' I apologised for my harsh words, but I still feel angry at this missed opportunity to create something wonderful for God.

Ernest Hemingway (1899–1961) was one of the very few writers who invented a new kind of prose. I met him twice. The first time was in Paris, in 1955, when I was sitting at La Coupole with my deli-cious girlfriend, Jackie. He arrived with his *cuadrilla* (a bullfighting term he liked, meaning entourage or team), and sat at a nearby table. He liked the look of Jackie and asked us to join him. So we moved the tables together. He ordered seven dry martinis, and lined them up. 'Seven strong soldiers on parade for their last campaign,' he said, then drank them all, each at a loud gulp. Afterwards he said: 'Now for the end of the world.'

I saw him again at Havana Airport in 1960. Castro had just nationalised the oil companies, revealing for the first time that he was an out-and-out Communist dictator. There was a panic, and people were leaving the country as quickly as they could. Airlines were overbooked and passengers were being bunked off the planes to New York. This happened to me and to Hemingway, who was very angry. Then the Chief of Police happened to pass by, and they greeted each other with a huge hug. Hemingway was invited to have a drink, and he said to me: 'Come along and we'll sort it out. It will be fun.' But I preferred to get on a plane, and eventually I and another Yank found one going to New York, which let us on board. We made sure our luggage travelled with us by dragging it ourselves on to the aircraft. All this required a lot of bribes. We took off, with passengers standing in the aisles, the only time I've seen this on a scheduled flight. All this time Hemingway was drinking with the cops. Later, I heard, he went back to his *finca*, twelve miles from Havana.

Hemingway said he learned to write good English partly by studying the excellent style sheet of the *Kansas City Star* and partly by learning journalistic cable-ese. I have the famous style sheet near my desk, and from time to time look it over. I have composed three style sheets myself and occasionally think of Hemingway when I'm searching for a word.

David Hockney (b. 1937) struck me as the most hard-working painter I had come across. When I was with him on Lake Como he was at work as soon as it was light and carried on until the light went, using a multitude of sketchbooks to capture fleeting effects which struck him, as well as formal canvases. When not painting or drawing he was discussing art, for he had innumerable visual interests and theories. He was never content with what he had done but was always pushing into new areas and dimensions – of scale, subject matter, medium, colour. He was a typical Yorkshireman: dogmatic, argumentative and assertive, with a hard carapace concealing a soft centre of geniality and generosity. He always travelled with three people who ran his professional affairs and helped to make his life easy so that he could concentrate on his work. When not talking about art he liked to rage against the anti-smoking campaign which he took as a personal invasion of his life and freedom, and to dwell on how much better things had been half a century before. This last led him to rediscover North-East Yorkshire, where, he claimed, life had stood still since the 1950s. His sister had a house there and he set up a studio in it, doing huge canvases and watercolours of the country round Bridlington. He did a drawing of me which took him exactly one hour and ten minutes. It was sold at his next show for $125,000. I reproduced it in my *Art: A New History*, though it made me look like an embittered old man of 150.

Quintin Hogg, Lord Hailsham (1907–2001) was unlucky not to become Prime Minister, which he might have done in 1963. But enough people thought him overexcitable, a hothead, a crybaby, a silly billy and a bigot, to damn him, although he was none of those things. His overexcitability was calculated. I have seen him quite deliberately work himself into a rage in a TV hospitality room just before, and also just after, a broadcast. He was by temperament and heredity a barrister and did this courtroom-rage act as part of a brief. Thus he planned to seize the chairman's bell at a Party Conference, and shout out (misquoting Donne) to the socialist enemy: 'Seek not to inquire for whom the bell tolls. It tolls for thee.' Equally he planned his 'intemperate' attack on Profumo on TV, in which he used the term 'extra-marital intercourse', putting the stress in 'marital' on the 'i'. He loved putting on funny hats, always with a purpose. The only time I saw him do an eye-catching thing unintentionally was at the notorious Tory Party Conference of 1963, when his second wife had just had a new baby. This was in Blackpool in the conference hotel. He came down the big staircase to find a host of journalists waiting for him at the bottom. He had been feeding the baby and in each hand he had an open tin of Heinz baby food. The first question was provocative and before giving an angry reply he raised both arms to their fullest extent, forgetting he was carrying the tins. So their contents shot all over the journalists standing near him. I shall never forget the enormous figure of Derek Marks of the *Express* wiping carrot purée out of his eye, parallel to the equally large Michael King of the *Mirror* rubbing condensed milk off his natty suit. 'Ha! Ha! Ha!' roared all those who had not been hit. 'He! He! He!' smirked Quintin, belatedly handing the now empty tins to an aide.

His life was punctuated by dramas which would have been funny if not so serious. In the war he fought in the Middle East, returning to find his wife had been having an affair with a very Free Frenchman. His return was unexpected and unannounced, and he found the telltale *képi* deposited on a console table in the hall of his flat. Jeremy Thorpe used to do a marvellous imitation of the scene that followed. His second wife was killed in a riding accident in Sydney – I have been shown the spot. But that was not at all funny. Margaret Thatcher adored him, and not only gave his career a new life by restoring him to the woolsack but kept him there year after year. He said to me: 'Am I not too old to be in the Cabinet? Should I not retire?' I said: 'If you were an ordinary Cabinet Minister, the answer would be "yes". But a Lord Chancellor should be old. Indeed, very old. Think of Lord Eldon. Or Lord Halsbury. Stay on, dear Quintin, stay on!' He said: 'By God, you are right! Age is the true tenant of the Woolsack. Lord Eldon! What a thought!'

Philip Hope-Wallace (1911–79) was a dear friend and mentor. His death, sudden and unexpected (he went to a health farm, slipped, broke his hip and died in a nearby hospital) was a grievous blow to me and I miss him more than I do any other friend. I gave the address at his memorial service, and wrote his entry in the *DNB*. After Charterhouse, he went to Balliol, having already learned to speak French and German well on the spot. He began work in the slump selling vacuum cleaners (as did Julian Maclaren-Ross) then started to write about music for *The Times*. Most of his life was spent writing about theatre and opera for the *Guardian* and for the BBC, on the famous *Critics* programme. He lived a bachelor existence with his two elder sisters. He fought an endless battle with *Guardian* subs and copy-takers. His complaints were met with: 'That's what we call a self-correcting error, Mr Hope-Wallace.' Much of his copy was dictated straight, without notes, from a call box. He told me of dictating a concert review with a final paragraph on Elgar's overture 'In the South', adding finally 'The end'. This came out 'a magnificent rendering of Elgar's overture "In Southend"'.

But he loved all the business and agonies of daily reporting. He arrived early every evening at El Vino with a mass of newspapers and magazines clutched to his bosom. Some of the best talk in London could be heard at his table there. His noble head, his mellifluous voice, his thesaurus of anecdotes and shafts of wit, sharp but never cruel, which he played on the personalities of the day, attracted a gifted circle of writers, editors, lawyers and public men, over which he presided with grace, generosity and a quiet but unmistakable moral authority. 'One always behaves better when Philip is listening,' said one clever young man. 'One doesn't say cruel things, one boasts less, one is more civilised and serious.' But the jokes were endless, too. To his young admirers, who were legion, he epitomised the best characteristics of the pre-war generation: breadth of culture, fine breeding, flawless manners and delightful urbanity.

I have a poignant memory of Philip, after a long, happy Sunday lunch at my home in Iver, sitting in the garden sunshine and watching the children and their friends playing under a hose. 'Pure, innocent bliss,' he said. I valued his praise more than that of anyone else, and his (rare) rebukes went home. I never inquired into his private life. He never mentioned his homosexuality – a man of his breeding never did in those days. He was lonely, and that made friendships of supreme importance to him, so he abided by Dr Johnson's wise adage: 'A man should keep his friendships in constant repair.' In return, his friends who are still alive keep his memory fresh in their hearts.

Frankie Howerd (1917–92) was sitting opposite me at a dinner given by Bob Maxwell. I had never met him before but always admired him. I had only to look for five seconds at his long, lugubrious face to start laughing. In its lines and contours, its hills and valleys and eruptions, was written all the tragic-comic hopelessness of mankind's search for illusory joy. 'What are you laughing at?' 'Your face, Mr Howerd. It is the most valuable face on earth.' 'What do you mean?' 'Well, you have good lines and tricks but it's your face which is the basis of your genius for making us laugh. The ability to make large numbers of people laugh in the midst of their misery on earth is the greatest of all gifts.

Tycoons and generals and politicians may have the power to rule
and crush and stamp on us. But only great comics, like you, Mr
Howerd, can raise us up above the human condition, and show
the way to the stars. You are God's most useful gift to our species,
and I salute you!' Suddenly I noticed great tears were welling into
his eyes, and coursing down his old, tired mug. 'That's the nicest
thing anyone's ever said to me,' he muttered.

Cardinal Basil Hume (1923–99) created, as Cardinal-Archbishop
of Westminster, a reputation for sanctity he did not deserve. He
got on well with Anglicans, Nonconformists, atheists and
heathens, but old-fashioned Catholics disturbed him. He was
always thinking of the media.

He panicked when accusations were made against one of his
priests. Our parish priest, of St Mary and the Angels, Father
Michael Hollings, was attacked in the *News of the World* about
an incident with a young man said to have occurred twenty years
before. There was no truth in this, as the police eventually established, clearing Father Hollings of all suspicion. But immediately the newspaper story appeared, Hume suspended Hollings,
without even seeing him or getting his side of the story. The
poor man, who had had a gallant career in the Guards during
the war, and had been seriously considered for high office in
the Church – including Hume's own job – spent months of
agony, while the police inquiry trudged on. Eventually, after his
clearance, Hume had the nerve to come down to reinstate him,
in full pontificals, and say mass. In the porch, I told him he had
behaved badly and had been disloyal to one of his priests in his
hour of trouble. His chaplain tried to interrupt. So I said, 'Hold
your tongue, sir!', and continued with my rebuke. Soon after,
Father Hollings died, broken by it all. He was an unusual priest,
much disapproved of by some, loved by others. I once visited

him in his tiny, overcrowded study. Over the desk was a notice: 'Please God, bless this mess.'

Hubert Humphrey (1911–78) was the jolliest politician I ever met, always smiling, joking, joshing and expanding. He said to me, in 1965, 'I am a happy man because I am doing what God made me for, playing a part in leading this great nation to new heights of prosperity and good-fellowship.' 'Do you really believe that, Mr Vice-President?' 'With all my heart and soul.' He made a famous speech in 1968 at the beginning of the election campaign, saying: 'Here we are, the way politics ought to be in America, the politics of joy.' But poor old Humphrey was doomed to disappointment, for LBJ's dog-in-the-manger selfishness made it impossible for Humph to win the election. After that – nothing.

Marmaduke Hussey (1923–2006) was called 'Dukey' by his friends and 'Duke' by those who didn't know him. He was always cited as the classic example of an overpromoted man. When he died, various obituaries made this point venomously, especially one in the *Guardian*. It is true he was not particularly good at anything. He had no talent for newspaper management, but was made head of Times Newspapers. He knew little about broadcasting, and cared even less, but was made Chairman of the BBC. He had nothing to say on public issues, but was made a life peer. He was severely wounded at Anzio, losing a leg as a result, and was very brave about it. So people felt sorry for him. His wife worked for the Queen, and I suppose that helped. He was good-natured, innocent-minded, decent and always assumed other people were as nice as he was. This was why he mishandled the strike at *The Times* of 1978/9 so completely – he thought the unionmen and *The Times* journalists were good chaps. 'Dukey!'

I would say, 'You have to bear in mind that most people are shits.' 'Oh, I don't know about that.' 'And journalists are shits in spades, Dukey!' 'Do you really think so?' When he was offered the Chairmanship of the BBC, I told him not to accept unless he was provided with a car and driver, because of his leg. 'What a splendid idea! Do you think it will work?' Later: 'It did, old boy. Thanks very much.' When he was running *The Times*, he took me to lunch at Brooks's. When he was at the BBC, he took me to Claridge's. He said: 'People think this place is a bit dull. But the food's not half bad if you stick to simple things. And it's convenient. And, damn it all, it's so cheap.' After his death, I thought: he did quite well for himself. Shows a gentleman can still prosper in a shit's world.

Leonard Hutton (1916–90), the great Yorkshire batsman, was my favourite cricketer when I was a boy. I once saw him play, at Old Trafford, Manchester, not long before he made his record-breaking 364 against Australia, at the Oval in 1938. I would have given anything for his autograph. Time passed, and in 1947 I again saw him play, at The Parks in Oxford. He played a leg glide, the most beautiful stroke I have ever seen on the cricket field. I finally met him in the sixties, at a Foyles luncheon. I no longer collected autographs, but I said to him: 'Sir Leonard, there was a time when to possess your autograph would have sent me into seventh heaven. So may I have it now?' He said: 'I very much admire your writing, Mr Johnson, and *your* autograph would be very welcome. Let us swap.' So we did. We then talked, and he told me: 'The first match I played for the Yorkshire first eleven, I was seventeen. I had made quite a name for myself outside it. But when I went into the Players Dressing Room, there was a silence. The Senior Professional said to me: 'Art thou 'Utton? Right, ah thowt so. This 'ere is thy locker. Put thy togs in there. And doan't speak until th'art spoken to.'

Leslie Illingworth (1902–79) was for a time (in the fifties) Britain's highest-paid cartoonist. He invested his money buying flats all over London. When Henry Fairlie, through his improvidence, was homeless, Leslie let him live in one, rent-free. He was mild, kind and generous, and not surprisingly his cartoons lacked bite.

Sidney Jacobson (1908–88), number two at the *Mirror* in its days of power under Hugh Cudlipp, and one of the life peers, from that Augean stable, was raised to eminence by the harassed Harold Wilson. His parents ran an unsuccessful ostrich farm in South Africa. His father was drowned at sea and he was brought up by Lewis Silkin, who held legal office in the Labour government. He was a fine rider, and a successful steeplechase jockey in India, though he told me he had 'bad falls', and it is amazing he survived at all for he was very tall. He had a good war, won the MC and was promoted half-colonel, commanding an infantry battalion. Jacobson thrived under Cudlipp but was no good on his own. When the TUC gave up subsidising the *Daily Herald* and it was transmuted into the *Sun* under Jacobson's editorship, it made such appalling financial losses that Cudlipp practically gave it to Rupert Murdoch. He made it a roaring success and in due-course it ousted the *Mirror* from its number-one spot which it had held for a generation. Jacobsen brooded on this disaster, and the steady economical and moral decline of the *Mirror*. I found him gloomy and depressing company. He came back once, after a party, to my flat in Lennox Gardens, and I have an image of him trying to put out his cigar in what he thought was an ashtray but was actually a bracelet of Marigold's she had put on a side table. We still have the table with the burn marks on it, a reminder of the hard-drinking men who made and unmade the *Mirror*.

Pope John XXIII (1881–1963) was full of jokes. I first met him when he was papal nuncio in Paris, and a favourite at dinner parties for *le tout Paris*. He said: 'When a lady comes into dinner *trop décolletée*, you would think that all the other guests would look at her. *Mais non! Ils regardent le Nonce!*' He also told me: 'My great weakness is to go down to the kitchen, and sit and gossip. It gives me more pleasure than anything else. *Et après tout!* It is fairly innocent, and I learn a lot there. Surely no one was ever sent to Hell for gossiping in the kitchen? But perhaps it's different for an archbishop.' All this, however, was before he became Pope, and turned the Church upside down with his Second Vatican Council.

Pope John Paul I (1912–78) was Patriarch of Venice, and seemed a bright, chirpy fellow who wrote little holy books for children. Harmless he was, and I suppose he was chosen at the Conclave as a papal innocent, after the muddled papacy of the indecisive Paul VI. I was present in St Peter's Square when he appeared on the balcony, after having been elected Pope. He already appeared to have a hunted look. He lasted barely a month. He was all alone and lonely in the Vatican. He seems to have had no family and nobody close to him. The rumours about him being murdered are obviously absurd. There was, however, something especially pathetic about his death. No one realised how ill he was. No one attended to him. There were no friends or associates near him. He died alone and neglected in the cavernous vastness of that ugly old palace, his dead body being discovered the next morning by a servant. It is curious how a man, in theory one of the great potentates of the earth, can be left to his own devices and die a lonely stranger in the midst of such magnificence. In the long history of the papacy there is no stranger tale. Poor pontiff – poor, lonely Vicar of Christ!

Pope John Paul II (1920–2005) was unknown to most journalists when the Conclave met to elect a successor to the sad figure of John Paul I. As usual I reported the Conclave for the *Sunday Telegraph*. The Vatican press office had issued useful biographies of all the cardinals attending. Insiders knew that Cardinal Wojtyla of Cracow was a serious contender but did not expect him to be chosen so quickly. Then the white smoke came out and shortly afterwards the *camerlengo* (chamberlain) appeared on the balcony of St Peter's to announce that the Pope had been chosen – the first non-Italian pope in modern times. There was pandemonium in St Peter's Square, which was packed. I had to struggle through it and then, literally, run all the way to the Stampa Estera on the other side of the Tiber, in central Rome. There I found the *Telegraph* stringer. Told him: 'Just get me a line to the office copy-taker, and leave the rest to me.' He was panicky, but he could do that, and did. I then dictated a two-thousand-word story for the front page, without a single note, but using, of course, the biography. It is the only time in my entire journalistic career I had to do this. However, it made all editions and we beat the competition hollow. The *Sunday Times* special correspondent was so confident no pope would be elected that afternoon that he went off to Castel Gandolfo, and filed no story at all. The *Observer* special correspondent was tight. So we had it all to ourselves.

The way in which John Paul set about rescuing the runaway Church from its unchecked descent into careless liberation and pointless change has been described in my book *John Paul II and the Catholic Restoration*. His was a noble work. It has continued under his successor, Benedict XVI, whom he might have chosen himself. John Paul was a great man, an outstanding Pope in the tradition of Gregory the Great, Hildebrand, Innocent III and Pius X, and a saint, who will, I hope, shortly be declared so. He radiated spiritual power and authority. In his primacy you really felt you were with the Vicar of Christ. When I presented him with a copy of my *History of Christianity* in its Polish translation, and he blessed me and the book, Marigold burst into tears. 'Why is your wife crying?' he asked. 'Because she is overwhelmed by Your Holiness.' 'Oh, I am just an old pope, giving a blessing,' he said. 'Nothing to be afraid of.' But I think he struck most people who actually met him, or got close to him, as someone special whom they would not meet again in a long lifetime. A man chosen by God to express the spirit of goodness which lies in every man and woman, and to preach a doctrine of dedication to divine service, in a horribly cruel and materialistic world. I thank God he was raised to the papacy, and for giving me the privilege of meeting him.

His final struggle for life, and his ennobling death, and the magnificent funeral service which followed in St Peter's Square, were episodes in spiritual experience we can never forget.

Hewlett Johnson (1874–1966), the notorious 'Red Dean' of Canterbury, was a figure at Soviet Embassy receptions in the 1950s, which is where I met him. He said to me, after we had an argument, 'Cultivate serenity.' Good advice. He was tall and his legs looked well in gaiters. He had long white hair, carefully washed and brushed. He had a pectoral cross of solid gold, a weighty bauble, given him by the Soviet government (who also gave him the valuable Stalin Peace Prize). His chief characteristic was vanity. He was reputed to be very rich. His father, a

Lancashire mill-owner, left him a fortune. His first wife was rich, too, and he got all the money when she died. His book *The Socialist Sixth of the World* (1939) was boosted by the Soviet machine all over the world. He boasted it had sold more copies than any other book except the Bible. This may not have been true, but the royalties were prodigious. He was trained as an engineer and took a B.Sc., originally intending to go into the family firm. Then he took a degree in theology at Wadham College, Oxford, and went into the Church. Ramsay MacDonald was blamed – unfairly – for creating the Red Dean. He made Johnson Dean of Manchester in 1924 on the advice of the then bishop, and promoted him Dean of Canterbury in 1931 on the advice of Archbishop Lang, and his successor William Temple. Johnson was then a believer in C. H. Douglas's Social Credit theory, and his hero was Henry Ford. It was only after reaching Canterbury that he was enthused with the Soviet Union by a Marxist Extra Mural Tutor called A. T. D'Eye. His first visit to Russia was in 1932 and thereafter he went often; later to China, going there last when he was ninety. The Russians could not, or would not, distinguish between the Dean and the Archbishop of Canterbury, and Johnson made no effort to enlighten them. He loved being treated in Moscow as an archbishop and head of the English Church. This infuriated Dr Fisher, who in 1947 put out a public statement: 'The Dean's office and jurisdiction in this country does not extend beyond the confines of the Cathedral body of which he is head. Outside those limits he speaks and acts only for himself. The Archbishop of Canterbury has neither responsibility for what the Dean may say or do, nor the power to control it.' Johnson invariably took Stalin's side, praised Soviet achievements and flatly denied its horrors and acts of wickedness. He needed to believe and once dabbled in psychical research. His Communism was a form of table-tapping. He was High Church and an extreme Ritualist, like many left-wing figures of these times, such as the Rev. Conrad Noel and Tom Driberg. But Tom did not like him. He told me: 'He is a fraud and should have a red-hot poker up his skinny arse.' The canons eventually persuaded him to resign. But by then (1963) he was already eighty-nine, so he had a good run for his red money. There are icons of him by Soviet artists, and a bronze by Epstein (never seen). But photos say it all. Kingsley Martin liked and envied him. He said: 'Well, it shows there must be something to be said for Christianity. He believes it all about Jesus, just as he believes it all about Stalin. What's the difference?'

Lyndon B. Johnson (1908–73) was, in my view, a bad man with some good qualities. He had been a teacher in Texas, his home state, and his feeling for the (white) poor and his desire to give them a better life, and knowledge, was absolutely genuine. It was instinctive, too. He also had an acquired desire to raise the blacks but this was more an intellectual conviction than an intuitive emotion. But whatever he thought in his heart, his conduct and manner were conditioned by the corrupting effects of many years of power-seeking and exercise, by the deals he had done, almost every day of his successful life in Congress. He was the most powerful and experienced senator ever to occupy the White House. Remember: he did so by the accident of Kennedy's assassination. I doubt if he could ever have got the nomination, and won, on his own personality and record. People knew too well that he was morally damaged. Some thought he should have gone to gaol over one scandal. Jack Kennedy, and still more brother Robert, had a low opinion of LBJ as a person. One of them, I don't know which, said: 'I doubt if he has a soul. But if he has he's already lost it.'

LBJ was an exceptionally big man, with a huge head. He was

not pleasant to get close to. And he liked to move close to you. He knew that, in most cases, he could thus inspire fear. All his professional life he had flourished – especially as majority leader of the Senate, and as the big cheese in Texas – by generating fear or, among the few fearless, the respect which the fear-inspirer usually receives. He exulted in this power. He liked to humiliate those who feared him or were under his power. He would say: 'He's the kind of guy who can come and see me when I'm on the can.' Or: 'I expect him to kiss my ass in the window of Macy's, and tell me I smell of roses.' He was rich in vulgar sayings: 'I'd rather have him inside the tent pissing out than outside pissing in.' The first time I went to see him I was accompanied by Michael Berry, proprietor and Editor-in-Chief of the Telegraph Media Group, Hugh Cudlipp, who ran the *Mirror*, and the editor of *The Economist*, Alastair Burnet. We saw LBJ in the small sanctum he had off the Oval Office. He had four TV sets built into the wall, so if necessary he could watch the four main channels simultaneously. They were always switched on but he turned down the sound in our honour. He was not particularly polite, and when Hugh Cudlipp asked him about reports of torturing prisoners in Vietnam, he turned up the heat. It was an unpleasant and, I thought, profitless encounter for everyone. Just before, we had had a long and acrimonious exchange with LBJ's Secretary of State. This was partly my fault as I had provoked him. I had not had a drink, as I was at the far end of the table. But he was at the drinks end, and had been amply served. He came in with us, oiled, and tried to add to what LBJ was saying in defence of his conduct of the war in Vietnam, until the president brutally shut him up. On the second occasion, in the same room, I was alone, and the president was war-weary. But he still, instinctively, tried to inspire fear, moving his rocking chair (or whatever it was, on runners) nearer and nearer to me, so that his huge face loomed close. He had truly enormous ears, so that it was like being approached by a wild African elephant. He seemed to be able to make his ears flap, too. He smelt of power, or something distasteful, and his pockets were full of bits of paper – cardiograms, for instance, to prove his heart was sound, and other bits of medical stuff. I asked him why he did not leave the Vietnam War more to the military. 'Because I don't trust them.' But this was the whole trouble. A democratic leader ought to lay down the objectives of policy and give clear orders accordingly. But then leave the actual execution to the generals. This was what Churchill – however reluctantly at times – did in the Second World War, and which Eden conspicuously failed to do at Suez. I tried to explain this to LBJ but he was not in a mood to listen. He controlled the war politically and in detail, and in the hope of forcing the Viets to a political solution, and so he lost it. He could not understand anything outside the political sphere, which had been his entire life.

His Great Society programme reflected the generous side of his nature. But, in addition to the war, it was too much for the American economy of the sixties. Almost for the first time in the country's history, America came up against the physical limits of its enormous potential. LBJ had to face the prospect of reining in, and that he could not do. He was broken by the time he pulled out of the race for re-election. By that time he had wrecked whatever chances Hubert Humphrey ever had of winning, leaving the road open to Richard Nixon. There is a good biography waiting to be written about LBJ, with all his enormities, and virtues, and physical awfulness. How Ladybird Johnson, a grand woman, could bear him, I have never understood. But a good biographer would explain.

Elwyn Jones (1909–89). He was a run-of-the-mill political lawyer who, for want of much competition, held various law offices under Labour and eventually became Lord Chancellor. He did nothing of significance, but resurrected the Lord Chancellor's Right of Rebuke. This was an ancient practice under which, if someone did something contrary to the national interest and the good governance of the realm, the Lord Chancellor would summon the offender to his office, and solemnly rebuke him. The miscreant was supposed to be on his knees while being thus admonished. While Jones sat on the Woolsack I wrote a series of articles in the *Sunday Telegraph* on the ills of the nation. This included a savage attack on the Law Centres which provided free help to litigious busybodies and nuisances. Jones was put under pressure by Labour lawyers to punish me in some way. He decided all he could do was rebuke me. So I was summoned to see him, being told a failure to attend would be 'at your peril'. I went, and he explained the grievance against me. I was not made to kneel down. His demeanour was solemn, but not particularly severe. I made my defence. He said: 'That is inadequate. I have no alternative but to rebuke you. Accordingly, I do rebuke you.' I seem to remember he wagged his finger. I said: 'Is that all?' He said: 'I should think it quite enough. You will remember this all your life.' Well, in a sense, I have.

Nicky Kaldor (1908–86) was probably the ugliest man of his time. He had other disagreeable characteristics. Norah Sayre, who married his best friend, and was dismayed when Kaldor came on honeymoon with them, told me: 'Nicky could fart in seven different ways, each worse than the last.' He was born and educated in Budapest but came to London in 1927 and thereafter was an ornament of English academic life, at the LSE and then at King's, Cambridge. He was a follower of Keynes but a socialist of the most punitive kind, believing in heavy personal taxation. He was responsible for the introduction of capital gains tax in its pecu-liarly destructive and inefficient form in Britain. He advised foreign governments, too – India, Ceylon, Ghana, Turkey, Iran, Venezuela; after his advice was taken, and it usually was, riots swiftly followed. 'Nicky's meddling is always the prolegomenon to trouble,' said his friend/rival/enemy Dr Thomas Balogh. In the 1964–70 Wilson government, Balogh advised Number Ten, Kaldor Number Eleven. This was a part of Wilson's disastrous 'creative tension' strategy. Both were given peerages. Both became rich but Balogh boasted: 'I am richer than Nicky Kaldor.' Both, but particularly Kaldor, grossly underestimated the evil consequences of inflation, and Kaldor played a major role in stoking the inflationary furnaces in the sixties and seventies. I found him tiresome, arrogant, charmless and volubly dogmatic and, whenever we met, put him down, no easy matter. By comparison, Balogh, also an unpleasant man in some ways, was an angel.

Kenneth Kaunda (b. 1924), of Northern Rhodesia, I came across at Salisbury Airport, where he was in difficulties with the author-ities. I managed to extricate him and we flew to Lusaka together. He was a man of the greatest possible charm, courtesy and moral integrity. His father had been the first black missionary in the area. Later, he ran the country as honestly as he could, so long as he could, but I shall not forget what he said to me: 'Why should Africans run their affairs any better than the White Settlers, if they are without God? The settlers are materialists and that is why they have failed. But if Africans try to rule without God, or against God, they will fail even more disastrously.'

Christine Keeler (b. 1942). At the time when she was the down-fall of Jack Profumo she was ravishingly beautiful, and for some time after. Once, in Muriel's bar, which had only one loo, used promiscuously by men and women, I found it locked when I tried the door, and a female voice within said prissily: 'It's occupied.' So I waited. Soon, Francis Bacon, drunk and bursting to pee, arrived. I said: 'There's a woman inside.' And he shouted: 'Come out of there, you bitch!' Then he began to kick the door. Nothing happened, so more kicking and shouting followed. Eventually, the bolt was drawn back, the door opened and a beautiful woman emerged, nose in the air. It was Keeler. She did not look at us, but strode back to the bar. All she said was: 'Men!' A lifetime of experience went with that one contemptuous word. Intrigued, I got into conversation with her in the bar by apologising for Bacon's behaviour. But she proved of no interest whatsoever. Mandy Rice-Davies, whom I also met, was by contrast a real fizzler. She proved a huge success as a night-club hostess in Tel Aviv. She also coined the memorable saying *à propos* of Lord Astor's denying that he had even met her: 'Well, he would, wouldn't he?'

Nikita Khrushchev (1894–1971) was the ebullient, ruthless, blood-stained and accident-prone Soviet leader between the end of the Stalin era and the long, comatose reign of Brezhnev. He was always doing things – often unwise, sometimes interesting. On 27 November 1957 the *New Statesman* published an 'Open Letter' from Bertrand Russell to Presidents Eisenhower and Khrushchev, on the subject of nuclear weapons. People in the West were just beginning to get neurotically worried about the subject. So Russell's piece was timely. He was not yet then the fanatical extremist of his final phase, when he founded the 'Committee of 100' and went to gaol for obstructing the pavement. But he was heading that way. His open letter was in places obscure and confused, and I had a lot of trouble straightening it out and clarifying it, and then clearing the changes with him. He was always difficult to deal with, especially on the phone. However, it appeared, and attracted some attention. Then, in mid-December, when the letters to the editor were brought to me on Monday morning for me to give them a preliminary sorting out before handing the best on to Kingsley Martin, I was surprised to find a long typewritten screed in Russian. So far as I could see, it was signed Khrushchev, in Cyrillic script. There was an accompanying translation from the Soviet Embassy which confirmed its Kremlin provenance. On close reading it seemed to be rather well done, the *NS* style of cool realism. In fact, a smart piece of propaganda, taking Russell seriously and putting the Americans on the spot. I wonder who had written it – Burgess or Maclean? Or the Third Man then being talked about? Or Gromyko, the Kremlin's all-purpose foreign export? (Later evidence suggested Philby, as yet unmasked and writing for the *Observer*.) Kingsley was too hysterically excited by the event to handle it rationally, and Russell arrived in the office, gibbering and spitting with self-importance. My instinct was to treat it as a perfectly ordinary event and use no special layout or typography, and that's what we did. It appeared on 21 December 1957. After all, Stalin had given us (and H. G. Wells) an exclusive interview in 1934 and we had published pieces by Lenin and Trotsky. My concern was to get a prompt reply from Eisenhower to round off the exchange. Despite my efforts, this proved impossible. He could not, or would not, do it. Eventually I got John Foster Dulles, Ike's Secretary of State, to do it. He produced a much shorter and rather effective piece, and we ran it on 8 February 1958. The affair aroused huge interest, did the paper's prestige a lot of good and helped to start CND, though that really arose from an earlier article written by J. B. Priestley, which we had published on 2 November.

My next vignette of Khrushchev occurred during his visit to London with his colleague Bulganin. After the Stalin autocracy Russia was supposed to be run by a collective of equals. But Khrushchev appeared to be more equal than the others and certainly more equal than Bulganin. He always did the talking and appeared to take the decisions. Eden, then Prime Minister, showed them around Oxford. He later told me that, during the drive there, as they passed through the industrial wilderness of Slough and the Great West Road (the A4 – this was before the M4 was built), Khrushchev astonished him by observing, admiringly: 'England is a very cultivated country.' 'I suppose,' said Eden, 'he meant "built up" or "heavily invested in".' He added: 'He had nothing to say about the Oxford colleges. I gathered he thought they were old-fashioned, should be pulled down, and replaced by modern buildings.'

The two visitors held a huge conference for the media in the Central Hall, Westminster, which I attended. It was arranged by the Soviet ambassador, who took all the questions, which had to be in writing, and decided which were to be answered. But Khrushchev immediately took over and reduced the arrangements to chaos. He snatched some of the written questions from the basket in which they were placed, tried to read them and constantly shouted orders to the ambassador. He answered some questions but, when it was Bulganin's turn, interrupted him and took over. There was a long, aggressive question from Randolph Churchill, then writing for the *Evening Standard*, which Khrushchev replied to with an angry rant. Then Isaac Deutscher, Trotsky's friend and biographer, stood up and asked a question, or made some remarks, in Russian. Khrushchev jumped to his feet, red in the face with rage, and angrily shook his fist at Deutscher. I had never actually seen anyone shake his fist before (or since) and it was a wonderfully comic moment. He and Deutscher stood shouting abuse at each other, until Bulganin and the ambassador calmed Mr K down. Deutscher then left, waving his arms, and held an impromptu press conference of his own on the steps outside.

I had a third glimpse of Mr K in action in 1960, at the Summit Conference in Paris. This was turned into high drama by the success of Russia in shooting down by rocket the high-flying U-2 spy plane, and capturing its pilot, who had parachuted to safety. Eisenhower, who was nearing the end of his second term, had nothing much to say, but Mr K had plenty. His speech in public on the subject of this blatant intrusion by the US of Soviet air space was a highly theatrical performance, though as Mr K was incapable of following the script, it got out of hand, and some very earthy expressions were used by him. When interrupted, he banged the podium with both fists, and when the interruptions continued he took off one of his shoes, and used the heel as a hammer, banging away like a mad auctioneer. (He later repeated this performance at the UN headquarters in New York.) It made me and others laugh, but later we thought: is this man fit to be head of a great power which possesses H-bombs and means to deliver them on Western targets? On reflection, his abandoned display of rage and temper was frightening, recalling Hitler at his worst.

Having seen Mr K behaving like this, his reckless attempt to instal missiles in Cuba came as no surprise to me. But I thought that, if Kennedy, now the president, kept his head, stood firm and stopped the missiles from arriving, Khrushchev would have to climb down. I was in charge of the *New Statesman* that week, as John Freeman, the editor, was on holiday in France. Kennedy's 'Quarantine' solution seemed to me right, and I decided to back him (I phoned Freeman in Paris first and got his agreement). Apart from the *Daily Express*, we were the only English paper to do so. But it proved to be right and Khrushchev had to back down and take his missiles home. It proved to be his last major error of judgement, for, soon after, his colleagues got together and sacked him, for 'adventurism' and various other crimes, including 'uncouth manners'.

Well: he was uncouth – no doubt about it. He had crude manners and looked plebeian. His clothes were dreadful. He had a huge hat, which he wore perched on top of his head, and ill-fitting suits. His trousers were too wide, and too short – half-mast. After his fall, when he led a retired existence on the outskirts of Moscow, he seemed a pathetic as well as a comic figure. I supposed he was lucky to be alive.

Cecil King (1901–87) was an enormous man, six foot seven, and broad. He said to me: 'I am told I have a resemblance to a Roman emperor of the Antonine period.' He also thought he looked like Bonaparte, and collected Napoleana. These included a chain from Fontainebleau, a pair of gold-bullion epaulettes, and a *tricorne*. He behaved in a much grander fashion than Northcliffe, his uncle, who had founded the Associated Newspapers empire, although he never owned any of it by inheritance. He was never a rich man. He accumulated no capital and was entirely dependent on salary, expenses and stock options for his grand way of life. But he shared Northcliffe's delusions. He claimed he could make himself invisible. I once saw him walking up Fleet Street, just opposite the glass palace of the *Express*, obviously in this belief. He always looked up as he walked, and with his height could not see passers-by. As he could not see people he assumed they could not see him. He had other superstitions and was generally creepy. Once, at a party at the residence of the US ambassador in Regent's Park, I was talking to Dora Gaitskell and suddenly felt a chill. I said to her: 'Do you feel cold?' 'Yes, I do. Very. Do you?' 'Yes, look!' There was King standing quite close to us, in the corner, and hemmed in by furniture. He looked at the ceiling.

He had not been there a minute before, and we could not explain how he had got there without leaping over the armchairs. We clutched each other in fear, then moved off. When we looked again he had gone. It is the only time in my life I have had a psychic experience.

King wrote an autobiography which Weidenfeld published. It was sent straight to the printers without being vetted by lawyers. I received a proof copy. Then I got a panic call from the publishers saying they were recalling all copies. I said, untruthfully, that I had mislaid mine. When an expurgated copy was eventually published, I compared it with my own proof to see what had been cut. There were a score or more of grievous libels, chiefly about members of his own family, or business associates, all still living. King was extraordinarily reckless in what he said, or wrote.

This marked his campaign against Harold Wilson as Prime Minister, culminating in a front-page article in the *Mirror*, which King wrote himself, saying Wilson must go. As Roy Thomson said shrewdly to me at the time, 'Cecil is behaving as if he owned the equity.' But of course he didn't. He also tried to involve Mountbatten in a kind of putsch. Mountbatten was a silly man, but not that silly. Also he had to advise Solly Zuckerman, who was present at the crucial meeting, and told him that what King was proposing was treason, and later described the scene. Meanwhile, Hugh Cudlipp, also alarmed, was plotting the coup which ousted King as chairman. I ran into Cudlipp at a party Jim Callaghan, then Chancellor, gave at 11 Downing Street, and said: 'You must get rid of King. He is turning the *Mirror* into a proprietorial paper, which it never has been. He will ruin it unless you stop him.' I repeated Roy Thomson's remark. Hugh looked alarmed. Perhaps he thought I had got wind of his plot. He speeded it up, and King was duly ousted.

But though Cudlipp carried out his putsch with great bravery and skill (as he later set out in detail) he proved no good as

Cecil King's successor. Once he took over the chairmanship, the huge edifice – at that time the largest publishing company in the world – which King had built up with wizardry, bluff and chutzpah – began to shake. Cudlipp was the greatest journalist of his day. But no good at running an empire. It soon changed hands and eventually landed up in the greedy clutches of Maxwell.

Jeane Kirkpatrick (1926–2006) wrote a fine article in *Commentary* about 'double standards'. Mr Reagan read it, and as a result made Jeane US ambassador to the UN, a job she loved and did very well. She was an AEI scholar in Washington at the time I was there. She was a very noisy woman. I always got in early and could tell when she arrived because, when she slammed her door, everything in my office shook violently. I'd say: 'That's Jeane, ending the Cold War with a bang.'

Henry Kissinger (b. 1923) was a good man to meet at a party or to run into by chance. He always told you something you didn't know, and which was worth knowing. He held strongly to the view that power in men acted as an aphrodisiac on women. It didn't matter how ugly you were or how fat you were; if you had enough power the women were yours. Once, at dinner in London, at a time when the notorious Alan Clark diaries were revealing the number of his conquests, and causing scandal, Kissinger asked me: 'What does this guy Clark have? Sure, he had some kind of job under Thatcher. But he *wasn't even in the Cabinet.*'

Rev. Father Ronald Knox (1888–1957) was a sad little man with a wry smile. I liked him though I did not think his *Punch*-type jokes very funny. His father was Anglican bishop of Manchester.

Ronnie was a brilliant scholar at Eton and Balliol before taking Anglican orders. Then, during the Great War, he 'poped'. The Catholic hierarchy, even more stupid and philistine than it is now, made little use of his talents, though he was given the cushy job of chaplain at Oxford University, where he wrote his best book, *Let Dons Delight*. He used to return to Oxford periodically when I was up to preach a sermon at the chaplaincy, never quite as witty as he hoped. He was a small, ugly fellow with a big, slobbering underlip and a huge nose, always pipe-infested. He had a saying: 'This room has a suspicious smell of not having been smoked in.' He loved party games of every kind, crosswords, which he made more difficult for himself by reading only the across clues, Scrabble, gossip and 'old Catholic' country houses. He was a sort of permanent house guest or chaplain first with the Actons in Shropshire, then the Asquiths at Mells. He wrote a serious book, *Enthusiasm*, about those dangerous people who think they have a direct line to the Holy Ghost. He wasted ten years of his life making a new translation of the scriptures which nobody read and which has never been used. Evelyn Waugh was devoted to him but found him, as he aged, a burden and a bore, and writing his life a penance. The best thing he did was to compile an accurate map of Trollope's Barsetshire by close study of the novels. I find the contemplation of his life depressing – it depressed him, increasingly – and wonder what God was up to. He told me: 'The only escape-route is mysticism', and that is why, at the end, he translated the autobiography of St Thérèse of Lisieux. Evelyn Waugh admitted to me: 'He was born a jester, he strove to be a saint, and so ended up a melancholic.'

Arthur Koestler (1905–83) led a life of sound and fury which in the end signified little. He knew a great deal about science as well as politics and his experience in the workings of Communism, especially Stalinism, in Russia, Central Europe and Spain, was unrivalled. His *Darkness at Noon* (1940) I read in my last year at school on the advice of the Jesuits. They were right because it cured me of any possible tendency to embrace the far left. But it is misleading in one important respect. It implies that Stalin relied on psycho-political forces to get old Bolsheviks to confess imaginary crimes at the Moscow trials. We now know they were broken down by old-fashioned torture and brutality. There was no difference between the OGPU and the Gestapo in this and in most other ways. Koestler had no respect for truth. He lied about politics and history and his own career with as much freedom as he lied to pretty women in order to get them into bed. There is a brilliant and scorching description of Koestler's seduction technique in Simone de Beauvoir's novel, *Les Mandarins*. Years later Marigold was the object of a similar attempted seduction by Koestler when he lived in Knightsbridge – hilarious (and pathetic). He described to me his imprisonment in a Franco gaol in 1937 (see his *Spanish Testament*) when every morning he expected to be taken out and shot. He said it made him an opponent of capital punishment, and later he played a key part in the campaign to abolish it in Britain under the aegis of David Astor's *Observer*. He was born to believe and since he could not believe in God he believed first in Communism and then in the paranormal, rather like Aldous Huxley (whose mind his resembled in various ways). This obsessed him in the last twenty years of his life, and he wrote books about it. Indeed, having become rich through his writings, he left half a million pounds to endow a chair in parapsychology. His cruelty to the women who fell for him was well known even in his lifetime. He boasted of having cuckolded Dick Crossman, Bertrand Russell, Jean-Paul Sartre and others.

His final act of wickedness to women was to persuade his naive last wife to commit suicide with him in 1983. He had Parkinson's and terminal leukaemia but there was nothing wrong with her. What remained of his reputation for probity was destroyed by a well-researched biography written by David Cesarani: *Arthur Koestler: The Homeless Mind* (1998). The author told me he had begun by admiring Koestler but the evidence of his lack of moral sense was overwhelming. He is a powerful lesson to all who believe in intellectuals. As Pat Gale used to say, surveying all the very clever men she knew: 'Oh dear!'

A new life by Michael Scammell makes a determined attempt to restore Koestler's reputation. But both books should be read.

Tony Lambton (1922–2006) amazed me by being caught out with a call girl and obliged to give up his political career. I thought he was a man of the world. He wrote his cheques with his own name, and had his official car parked just round the corner from her flat. He took no precautions at all. Of course he had been spoilt for many years and had inherited far too much money. He had five daughters as well as a son. I once saw the five all together, sitting in a row, on a bench in Julian Barrow's studio in Tite Street. Quite a sight. They should have been painted together by Sargent, who had the same studio. Tony looked sinister because his eyesight obliged him to wear tinted glasses, and he affected a snarlish look at times. The left were delighted to have him as a cartoon upper-class ogre to hate. But actually he was an amiable innocent; quite harmless, except to members of his own family, who found him a trial and an embarrassment. But, then, most Lambtons were that. He told me: 'I have had a delightful life and cannot grumble if I came a cropper from time to time.'

Osbert Lancaster (1908–86). An ugly man with a pockmarked face, as if from smallpox, and hirsute, sprouting foliage all over his face, ears, etc., and bristling military moustache. He looked ferocious and perhaps was. Philip Hope-Wallace, who was his fag at Charterhouse, said he was beaten unmercifully by Osbert. He became the best society cartoonist since Beerbohm, his 'Pocket Cartoons' in the *Daily Express*, in the days when it was England's best popular newspaper, giving it a distinction no other rag at this time possessed. Although he was thought of as a wit and a sophisticated man of letters, I never heard him say anything of the smallest interest. He was a poor man's Bowra. But I remember him at the Beefsteak, ordering an orange gin (like a pink but with orange-coloured and flavoured angostura) and getting it. Some of his jokes still make me laugh. E.g.: Man in 1956 [Suez year] waiting in long bus queue in Chelsea: 'I suppose they're sending the Number Nine round by the Cape.' And Lady Littlehampton, spooning peas into her mouth on a knife: 'What I say is, if it's me, it's U.' But who would understand them now? It's odd that the short and ugly Osbert should have married the tall, svelte and (in her day) handsome Anne Scott-James, fashion writer on the *Express*, where they met. But the marriage seemed to work, even though Osbert got Max Hastings as a stepson.

Cosmo Gordon Lang, Archbishop of Canterbury (1864–1945), I knew only through the stories A. L. Rowse used to tell. They were both Fellows of All Souls together for many years. Rowse thought Lang much nicer, and a much better man, than he was painted – not least in his official portrait by Orpen. Before starting, Orpen said: 'I see seven archbishops.' But the one he chose, said Lang, was threefold, 'proud, prelatical and pompous'. Bishop Herbert Hensley Henson of Durham, another Fellow of All Souls, asked 'To which of those adjectives does Your Grace particularly object?' Rowse added, who was Henson to talk? He called his autobiography *Retrospect of an Unimportant Life*. If that were so, why did he require three volumes and eight hundred pages to describe it?

Lang was a snob. He once held a luncheon entirely for dowager duchesses. After it, his chaplain, Alan Don, said: 'They didn't seem any different from anybody else.' Lang replied testily: 'That just shows, Alan, how mistaken you can be.' Lang revered the Royal Family. He thought Edward VIII would make a disastrous King and hailed his replacement, George VI, whom he respected and liked, with secret delight. The Abdication papers were signed on 10 December 1936. Three days later Lang broadcast to the nation, saying the ex-King 'sought his happiness in a manner inconsistent with the Christian principles of marriage, and within a social circle whose standards and ways of life are alien to all the best instincts and traditions of his people'. This was thought to be kicking a man when he was down. Lines for which Osbert Sitwell took credit, but which were actually sent to Lang at Lambeth Palace through the post, anonymously (his chaplain contrived to keep the letter from him) expressed the mood of many:

> *My Lord Archbishop, what a scold you are!*
> *And when your man is down, how bold you are!*
> *Of Christian charity how scant you are!*
> *And, auld Lang swine, how full of cant you are!*

In fact, Lang twice warned Edward, both as Prince and as King, that he was heading for disaster. After he went, he wrote in his diary, 'I cannot bear to think of the kind of life into which he has passed.' It was his belief that, to a man used to a busy life, one of idleness must be agony. But, feeling this, why did he resign in 1942? He bitterly regretted it, living in Kew in loneliness and irritable inactivity until 1945.

Philip Larkin (1922–85) was in my view overpraised and over-rewarded for his rather meagre output of poems. But then he lived in an age when genuine poets were rare. He was a librarian all his life and a conscientious one. He illustrates the fact that the English always in the end warm to somebody who goes on doing the same thing for a very long time. He never did anything else except issue books and write poems and when he died he was given a service in Westminster Abbey attended by thousands.

He was a most unhappy and usually lonely man. He said to me on one of his rare visits to London: 'I have never had enough sex. It's the most important non-event of my life. I have never come within a million miles of having enough sex of any kind. I can tell you about every fuck I've had, and almost every fumble. It isn't right!'

Sir Alan Lascelles (1887–1981), unlike most courtiers, came from the upper aristocracy and was not in awe of the House of Windsor. He served the Prince of Wales in the 1920s but was appalled by his shocking, self-centred, bad behaviour, and when he resigned in disgust told him exactly why. He returned to royal service in 1935 working for George V, Edward VIII (glad to see the back of him) and George VI, then did ten more years under Elizabeth II. His diaries, though spasmodic, are well worth reading. He was not exactly mean but hated spending money, especially on himself, and above all on clothes. In 1925 he had a stroke of good fortune: his elderly Victorian uncle died, leaving him, among other bequests, all his shirts and under-clothes. These included a large quantity of what Lascelles called 'drawers', pants of the pre-elastic vintage, which you kept up by putting your braces through cotton fastenings. He wore these until the early fifties, when the fastenings wore out, and he reluctantly got new, modern trunks from Marks & Spencer. As the old ones had been bought in the 1860s and 1870s, they had lasted eighty years. He did not order a new suit between 1932 and the end of the war, when he was horrified to discover what tailors now charged. He then discovered Montague Burton, 'The Tailor of Taste', who did him a three-piece suit for £5. This lasted him the rest of his life. He was not the only member of his class with abstemious habits. His master, George VI, was similar, and during the war they joyfully competed with each other to obey government exhortations to 'save supplies' (and so money) by 'making do'. The King had leather patches put on the frayed elbows of his jackets. Both reused envelopes by gumming on labels – Lascelles continued to do this to the end of his life. He boasted he had not bought a tie since the 1920s. Holes in his socks were neatly darned, I think by himself. Princess Margaret hated him. He was the ringleader in the Court circle which made her marriage to Peter Townsend impossible. What Lascelles had against Townsend was that he was a flashy dresser whose clothes were 'a bit too fashionable for a serving officer – a bad sign'. After his retirement, Lascelles's last gesture to austerity was to grow a beard, thereby saving on razor blades.

F. R. Leavis (1895–1978) was so Cambridge-oriented, and un-urbane, that Oxford did not acknowledge his existence when I was up in the late forties. C. S. Lewis could hardly bring himself to mention his name, and I suspect that Professor Tolkien had never heard of him. Not that Cambridge seemed to like him much either. He was marginalised in dim colleges like Emmanuel and

Downing. It was more than thirty years before he was even given a readership. He never got a chair, though right at the end of his life he was a visiting professor in Wales and at Bristol. Of course he was fierce and made a point of being a rebel. In fact he was not working-class: his father, and the father of his wife Queenie – even fiercer than he was – were both shopkeepers. He attracted fanatical supporters and followers. They were taught to say, if asked what books they liked, 'works of literature do not exist to be liked; they exist to be e-val-uated'. Kingsley Amis did a good imitation of Leavis lecturing, even better than his Lord David Cecil, Leavis's polar opposite. Actually, on the one occasion Leavis and Cecil met, they got on very well together, talking chiefly about flowers. John Raymond compiled a list of Leavis's *obiter dicta*, including: 'Rupert Brooke shared Keats's vulgarity but with a public-school accent'; 'T. S. Eliot's work was founded on self-contempt, well-grounded'; 'The Sitwells belong to the history of publicity rather than poetry'; 'Raymond Mortimer would go down as the worst living critic, were it not that Desmond McCarthy is still alive – oh, and Harold Nicolson, too'; 'Dickens's *Pickwick Papers* is without the smallest possible merit'; 'a knowledge of Latin, and still more of Greek, is a positive impediment to the appreciation of English literature'. The most intriguing thing about Leavis was his intermittent, edgy, at times, surprisingly close friendship with Ludwig Wittgenstein, marked by long walks, mutual incomprehension and rows. Wittgenstein said to him, characteristically: 'Leavis, give up literary criticism.' Leavis wrote very bad English, clumsy, verbose and inelegant. It struck me as odd that the one practising writer he chose to savage personally, C. P. Snow, wrote English even worse than his own. I learned to give Leavisites a wide berth, as mean-spirited, spiteful and relentlessly malicious.

Jennie Lee (1904–88) was a fierce, bitter Scotchwoman from

Fife, a miner's daughter. She got herself a good education and was always a hard worker but her political hates poisoned her, and made her a disastrous mentor to others, especially Aneurin Bevan, whom she married in 1934. He told her: 'Why don't you get you into a nunnery and be done with it? Lock yourself up in a separate cell away from the world and its wickedness?' He also called her 'My Salvation Army Lassie', which showed there was some affection there. I could not abide her – her appearance, the way she did her hair, her looks, eyes, voice or sentiments on anything. She was solidified vinegar made flesh. The advice she gave Bevan was always wrong and did him infinite harm. She could not, anyway did not, give him children, which he passionately desired. She made his home life prickly and political instead of being restful and comfy. She had no sense of humour. She was in parliament for North Lanark 1929–31, and again in 1945 for the safe seat of Cannock, which she contrived to lose in 1970. Then she became a peer, as all those fierce Labour women did, no matter how comprehensively they had denounced the House of Lords in the past. Indeed, she revelled in the Lords and all its plush and servility and loved being called 'My Lady' and 'Your Ladyship' – woe betide anyone who forgot. Harold Wilson made her Britain's first Arts Minister, a ridiculous appointment, and she was foremost in founding that hopeless venture, the Open University. Her end was awful. After Bevan's death, and Wilson's retirement, she gradually came down in the world. She lived at a grand address, 67 Chester Row in Belgravia, but in the basement. Housebound, her only visitor, in the end, was Lord Goodman, and he eventually became so fat that he could not get down the stairs. So no one came except social workers. After her death a well-meaning but naive woman was asked to write her official *Life*, and inadvertently, without realising it, spilled the bitter beans.

Lee Kuan Yew (b. 1923) was by far the ablest politician/statesman I ever met. He went to Raffles College in Singapore, then Fitzwilliam, Cambridge – a lawyer. When I first met him in 1955, he had just created the People's Action Party and become a member of the Legislative Assembly. He was then known as Harry Lee in the old colonial style of giving 'natives' a familiar Christian name. He struck me right away as a monument of practical common sense, shrewdness about the present and an intuitive grasp of the future. I never knew him be wrong about an important issue of geopolitics. Not a trace of the emotional and personal distortions created, as a rule, by colonisation, so marked in Nehru, for example. Pro-West for exactly the right reasons. A very clever wife, also a Cambridge graduate. He became first Prime Minister of the new State of Singapore in 1959, and when I saw him there he was very much in charge. Sukarno was then dictator of Indonesia and wrecking it, destabilising the region and threatening his neighbours. Lee gave me dinner at his flat and took me out on to the balcony. 'See that island?' 'Yes.' 'That's Indonesia. They are as near to us as that.' 'My God!' Next day I saw the leader of the Communists, who made no bones about taking over Singapore by force. I had a TV film crew with me. We went with Lee to the Cameron Highlands in Malaya, in the hills not far from Kuala Lumpur, a beautiful hot-weather resort. Lee played golf with Tunku Abdul Rahman, a sensible, moderate man. I got the crew to film carefully their driving strokes, and gave them the results, so they could study their faults and eliminate them. Both were childishly pleased. Afterwards I told Harry about the Communists and their plans. He said: 'I know.' Me: 'If I were you I would lock them up in Changi Gaol!' 'Do you think so?' 'Absolutely.' This was one of the rare occasions when a political leader has taken my advice. It proved to be good advice, too. Once he took the Communist extremists out of the political equation, Lee never looked back.

Singapore prospered mightily. Though it had no raw materials whatever, only a tiny amount of land on which to grow food (though every square inch was, and is, farmed very efficiently), its GNP went up from less than US $100 a year to Western levels. It is now higher than the UK's. Lee was regularly re-elected until 1990, when he took a back seat, but still has decisive influence. Singapore is the best-governed state in the world: virtually no crime, no drugs, no pop music row, very high health standards, no corruption, no nonsense of any kind. All due to one man (and woman). Good jokes, too. Had he any faults? I dare say, but I don't know of any.

Bernard Levin (1928–2004). He came from the LSE where he had studied under Harold Laski, and had been a Marxist. But by the time I knew him, in the late 1950s, he had moved sharply to the right. His passion for music, especially opera, was such that he arranged to go to Covent Garden or a concert every single night. He liked very tall, thin girls: Vanessa Redgrave, then Arianna Stassinopoulos. He told me: 'I want a girl to be head and shoulders higher than me.' 'Why?' 'Then I know I am getting breeding, quality and value for money.' If he was taking out a girl, a messenger would arrive at her flat an hour before she was due to leave, bearing a corsage of orchids, or the like. This flustered most women. He never married. He had one of the worst phobias I have ever come across, a terror of spiders. His arachnophobia was such that he could not remain in a room where he knew a spider to be. He told me: 'I have killed over a thousand spiders.' He was also a chronic insomniac. He claimed he had not slept for over twenty years. This may be because he drank quantities of black coffee which he made himself, as strong as possible. He became senile at a comparatively early age, so that, halfway through an article, he forgot what he was writing about. Everything about him was in some way extreme. Derek Marks, editor of the *Express*, and a poker player, said: 'Bernard is always raising the ante.'

C. S. Lewis (1898–1963). He was the English tutor at Magdalen when I was up. He never taught me but he seemed to like me and we occasionally did Addison's Walk together (exactly a mile). He said: 'Has it occurred to you that English literature would have taken a quite different turning if Wordsworth and Coleridge had come here instead of going to Cambridge?' I read his *Preface to Paradise Lost* when I was fourteen: the first grown-up book I read voluntarily. It was an eye-opener and when I told him so he was delighted. He was a superb lecturer. He filled Magdalen's hall to overflowing, the girls on the dais sitting at his feet. It was said he got them so excited your best chance of seducing them was on the evening of the day he lectured.

Selwyn Lloyd (1904–78) was the son of a Methodist dentist practising in the Wirral, the wealthy suburban district across the Mersey from Liverpool. But he went to Fettes, Edinburgh, and Magdalene, Cambridge, and never had a trace of a Liverpool accent, so far as I could see. Indeed, he affected upper-class ways, and when Foreign Secretary took to the FO his two high-bred salukis. He got selected for the Wirral, a safe Tory seat, in 1939, had a good war, beginning in the RHA then going on to staff work, ending a brigadier. He held the Wirral seat 1945–76, when he went to the Lords. He never did anything, said anything, wrote anything or even thought anything of the slightest importance, though involved in great events. He was Eden's poodle at the Foreign Office, being involved in 'collusion' with Israel, something he never spoke about. Then he was Macmillan's poodle at the Exchequer, being sacked without warning in 1962 in 'The Night of the Long Knives'. Home brought him back as Leader of the Commons. But he left the front bench in 1966 to make money in the City for his old age. In 1971 he became Speaker, until 1976, and was moderately successful. He was very shy and inarticulate, bruised by a most unsuccessful personal life – deserted by a woman he once loved – and had few friends. I could make nothing of him and could get nothing out of him, even though I once tried hard to get him tight. He wrote two books, *Mr Speaker, Sir* and *Suez 1956*, neither of them of the smallest interest. Amazing, I often think, that such colourless and inert nonentities can get to the top, collect honours and awards. Of course, he always worked hard, having nothing else to do. The only person I knew who thought warmly of him was Jonathan Aitken, who was, I think, on his staff at one time.

But he did serve one purpose. When Tom Stoppard takes photographs and wants to make people smile, he says in a solemn, loud voice: 'The Right Honourable Selwyn Lloyd MP'. I have used this device myself, often. It always works, raising not only a smile but a real laugh.

David Lloyd George (1863–1945) I saw once at Beaumaris, when he was very old. He had come there with his daughter, Megan, who was Liberal MP for Anglesey. He still represented the Carnarvon Burghs in the Commons. He had a mass of white hair, a white moustache and a red-brown healthy face. He moved quickly and seemed full of energy, asking endless questions. He asked my name, what school I went to, what was my favourite subject and what I thought of the war. He told me I had a fine head. He was interested in heads and thought phrenology the key to character. C. P. Snow told me many years later that, in 1937, he was by himself on the Riviera one Christmas, staying in the same hotel as LG, who was there with a large family party. He invited Snow to join them for dinner. Afterwards, Snow asked him: 'What led you to ask me to dinner?' LG: 'I thought you had an interesting head.'

Merlyn Rees, who was Home Secretary in one of Harold Wilson's governments, and MP for Leeds at one time, gave me an account of an election meeting in, I think, Menai Bridge, where he was introduced to an old fellow who had known Lloyd George well. He asked, politely: 'What was the most striking thing about Lloyd George?' The old man said nothing for a time, then suddenly said in a very loud voice: 'Lloyd George had a prick as big as a donkey's.' Much embarrassed, Merlyn said nervously, 'Well, yes. He was a man of many parts.' The old man said: 'Yes, he was. But that was the part of him they were interested in down here.'

Frank Longford (1905–2001) came from a military Anglo-Irish family, the Pakenhams. The Duke of Wellington, the Iron Duke, married Kitty Pakenham, and her brother Ned was killed at the Battle of New Orleans. Frank's father was killed in the First World War. Frank could not adjust to army life in the Second World War and had to be invalided out – he felt this to be a disgrace. By temperament he was a don, and was a successful one at Christ Church: the 1930s and 1940s. He loved young people as soon as they were old enough to talk to him, and he was as kind to his friends' children as his own. He took a great interest in mine, and in their friends. He used to phone me regularly to talk over the news, right up to the end of his life. He was born a Protestant and Tory. He switched to Labour and was converted to Catholicism – hard to say which was more of a shock to his family and friends. But once he changed he was fanatically loyal to Labour and to Rome. He failed to get into the Commons so in 1945 Attlee made him a peer as Lord Pakenham, so he could serve in the government. (As his elder brother Edward was childless, Frank was due to get an Earldom and a seat in the Lords anyway when his brother died.) So Frank was an active member of the Lords for nearly sixty years and going there, daily, was an essential part of his life. His marriage to Elizabeth lasted almost seventy years. His was a very stable existence, revolving round London and Dublin. He never travelled abroad if he could help it. He made over Pakenham Hall, and the entailed estates, to his eldest son Thomas, to avoid two sets of death duties in one generation, so was never wealthy. But aunts, etc., were always leaving him things, such as his house, Bernhurst, in Hurst Green, East Sussex. When I first knew them, he and Elizabeth lived in a house in Chelsea Manor Street. Marigold shared the basement flat with their daughter Antonia, then with her cousin Henrietta Phipps, daughter of Frank's elder sister, Pansy. He regarded Pansy with some awe. Once at my house, Frank had been saying that he was not really British but Irish. Pansy exploded: 'Frank, you are a disgrace. You have sat in the Cabinet and you have had the signal honour of becoming a Knight of the Garter – how can you say you are not British?' He took this rebuke with sheepish humility. Frank was sent by Attlee to Germany, and he was so anxious to make it up with them and exercise the spirit of Christian forgiveness that, on arrival at Cologne Airport, he sprang out of the plane before they had properly wheeled up the gangplank, and injured himself. That was characteristic. He loved making humble gestures. When first presented to Pope Pius XII he tried to kiss his big toe, in the traditional manner, and had to be prevented. As a minister, he and his family lived for a time in Admiralty House, which his children (he had eight) loved and remembered later with great affection. Frank cared about education more than any other subject and when serving (as Leader of the Lords and Lord Privy Seal) in the 1964 Wilson government, he eventually resigned when Labour reneged on its promise to raise the school leaving age from fifteen to sixteen.

After education came the treatment of crime. Frank was a prison visitor for half a century and took it very seriously. He befriended a great many people. Of course there were one or two sensational cases he took up, including Myra Hindley, but most of the prisoners Frank helped were very obscure. Hindley no doubt deceived him, and so did others, but Frank expected that and did not take it to heart. His motto was 'Hate the sin and love the sinner'. He wrote a number of books, the most important of which was his original study of the Irish peace treaty of 1921–2. He hero-worshipped that old rogue De Valera, and went to see him regularly. Frank was not a good writer and took little trouble – just wanted to get his thoughts into print. He wrote several autobiographies, publishing diaries, etc., and also little volumes with titles like *Humility*. He campaigned against pornography, and enlisted Marigold's help in compiling the report of the committee he set up to investigate it (which included, oddly enough, Kingsley Amis and Elizabeth Jane Howard). He was once proceeding down Harley Street with a large suitcase full of pornographic material, when the cord holding the disreputable bag together snapped, and its contents fell all over the pavement. A lady phoned the police, saying: 'A scruffy old man is selling dirty books outside my house.' A policeman duly came up to Frank who was trying to stuff the magazines back into his case. ''Ullo, 'ullo, sir, who are you and what might you be doing?' 'My name is Lord Longford and this is my homework.' 'Is that so, sir, and would you please step this way to the station with your wares and we will sort it all out.' Frank was never unduly embarrassed by this sort of mishap. He did not mind being laughed at. Indeed, he laughed at himself. Dining at his favourite restaurant he inadvertently took away the wrong overcoat. How he got into it was a mystery for the sleeves were too small. But he never noticed such things, and went off to the Lords. In fact it belonged to a judge (a tiny judge) and in its pockets were his notes of a murder trial, of which he was in the middle of summing up. The judge was frantic, but Frank was greatly amused when told what he had done, and loved telling the tale. He loved food and ate whatever was put in front of him, never noticing what was on his plate. He might have got fat, but his hyperactivity kept his weight down. His family often ran to fat. His brother Edward was reputed to be the fattest man in the Republic: his chair at Pakenham Hall (renamed by Thomas, Frank's son, Tullinally, its original Irish name) had a huge recession in it, and his double bed was one enormous cavity into which you endlessly slid during the night if you were unlucky enough to be allocated it. The house was vast, had a magnificent library (the first room in the house, as often happens in Ireland), an organ in its huge hall and countless bedrooms, some with collapsed ceilings. But there was rarely any hot water. It was all very Irish – Anglo-Irish, really.

Some of Frank's children and grandchildren married into other philoprogenitive families (e.g. the eldest daughter married into the Lovat Frasers) and by the time Frank and Elizabeth died in their nineties they had many scores of children, grandchildren and great-grandchildren. When writing and revising Frank's obituary for *The Times* and the *DNB* I tried to make an accurate calculation, but failed, as more babies were being born to grandchildren all the time. Elizabeth, the most beautiful Oxford undergraduate of her generation, was middle-class Birmingham – related to the Chamberlains. Unlike Frank, she was a very skilful writer, as were some of her children. Her books on the Jameson Raid and on Queen Victoria and on Wellington were well received, and made a lot of money, part of which went on building a swimming pool at Bernhurst. (Both she and Frank swam daily until they were over ninety.) She was a woman of exceptional intelligence, charm and sound sense, interested in everything. I count my friendship with the Longfords one of the most fortunate things in my entire life.

Lydia Lopokova (1892–1981). Russian ballerina and by marriage (to J. M. Keynes) a member of the Bloomsbury Set, who laughed at her. I had coffee with her and Leonard Woolf in 1956, when she was in her sixties. She had long ceased to dance but still moved with extraordinary grace. Her origins were humble, her father being a theatre usher and her mother the daughter of a municipal clerk in Riga. She was only five feet and she lifted up her face to speak to you in an endearing way. Her head seemed to be round, like a pink rubber ball, with big, dazzling eyes, very expressive. In the Diaghilev company she understudied, then replaced Karsavina, partnering Nijinsky in *The Firebird*. Massine created roles for her. After a divorce she married Keynes in 1925. He had her as an amusing trophy. As he was an aggressive and acquisitive homosexual, the marriage was never consummated. There is (for once) a good Picasso drawing of her, done in 1919, which gets her funny nose right, tip bent down. She moved her hands in a magical way. Her English was extraordinary. She told me Nijinsky was 'a flash in the pane'. 'Of glass?' 'Of course.' Diaghilev was a 'monument'. Everyone called her Loppy, but to T. S. Eliot, who adored her, she was 'Loopy Loppy'. Woolf told me that when she was away from Keynes she wrote him a weird little letter, every day. Were these letters kept? If so, they should be published, testimony to a strange, intense love. She and I got on. She said to me: 'I would soon get the hanging of you.'

Mary McCarthy (1912–89) left me with mixed feelings. She was clever – no doubt about it – but wrong-headed. Her novel *The*

Group, about her friends and contemporaries at Vassar, then an all-women college, is a *tour de force*. Her political judgements were nearly always wrong. She gave me a lot of trouble when I was editing the *New Statesman*. She made the mistake of getting mixed up with the CP and the Trots in the thirties, then compounded her error by marrying Edmund Wilson, who used to beat her up, though she often hit him back, with saucepans, rolling pins, etc. She wasted a lot of her talent and energies in ephemeral journalism for the *New York Review of Books*, spending more time on it than the results merited. So she did not produce the great book of which she was capable. On the other hand, she did take to task the awful Lillian Hellman. She wrote: 'Every word Hellman writes is a lie, including the "ands" and the "buts".' This was true, of course, but Hellman sued, and the thing would have gone to court had not the old witch suddenly expired. Otherwise McCarthy would have been ruined. She was a woman of great parts, but no wisdom. I had a row with her in Paris in 1968 and found her pig-headed, ill-informed, voluble but stupid, and oh so tremendously unattractive. She had an ugly mouth and drew attention to it when she talked, which was most of the time. I asked John Davenport, her quondam lover, what she was like. 'I suppose you mean, in your dreary lower-middle-class way, in bed? Well, the answer is, a bit on the lazy side, if you know what I mean. No, you don't, do you? What I mean is, not very active in attending to my pleasures. Like all Vassar girls. It's the way they were taught. Look after Number One.' Stephen Spender, with a giggle, said: 'She stretched her talent as far as it would go.' 'How far was that, Stephen?' 'Oh, as far as Pamela Hansford Johnson or Olivia Manning.'

Julian Maclaren-Ross (1912–64) was immortalised by Anthony Powell as X. Trapnell in *A Dance to the Music of Time*. Like

Anthony Carson, he wrote his stories from his experiences, and when he had mined them to exhaustion he dried up as a writer. He could not invent. He could, however, embroider. His master-piece is the story 'A Bit of a Smash in Madras', which actually happened to him in, I think, Cairo. But he successfully transferred it to India, though he had never been there. He had a gold-topped cane and a swordstick and a hat with a wide brim. His favourite drinking place was the French House, and the Caves de France also saw a lot of him. The only time I saw him draw his sword-stick was when MacBryde and Colquhoun were planning a joint attack on him for not paying his round. Like most bohemians, Ross became a bore, always asking for loans and telling long stories you knew were untrue. Tony Powell makes him more interesting than he actually was. The imitation of Boris Karloff was an inven-tion of Tony's, but Ross could certainly do impressions of Groucho Marx, Clark Gable and, surprisingly, Shirley Temple singing 'Animal Crackers in My Soup'.

Iain Macleod (1913–70) was one of the brilliant 1950 election intake which transformed the Tory Party. He was an Islander-Highlander, a Celt, a kind of poet. He won his reputation by standing up to Nye Bevan in debate and out-Celticising him in a superb speech. He was plain, with a wide mouth, a huge brow and little hair, brushed across the dome in pathetic strands. He could make good jokes, tell stories well, engage in witticism. But the remark by Lord 'Bobbety' Salisbury stuck: 'Too clever by half.' His health was wretched. He was more or less always in pain, and took pills and lots of whisky to deaden it. He died pretty soon after Heath made him Chancellor of the Exchequer after the Tory victory in the 1970 election – much to the loss of the party and the nation.

Macleod had a spell as editor of the *Spectator*. That is when

I knew him best. He could not stomach the way in which Macmillan, stricken with prostate trouble and obliged to resign, manoeuvred to get Alec Home to succeed him. Macleod refused to join Home's government. So Ian Gilmour, who then owned the *Spectator*, offered him the editorship, bundling out the current editor, who first learned he was sacked in the papers. Macleod began his reign by giving the inside story of Home's appointment as PM by what he called 'The Magic Circle'. It caused a sensation, put the *Spectator* on all the front pages and gave a huge boost to the sales. John Freeman, then our editor, took it calmly, but I decided we had to do something to restore our prestige as market leader. So for our next issue I wrote an article insisting it was all the Queen's fault as she did not need to take Macmillan's recommendation about his successor, and should have taken advice outside the 'The Magic Circle'. This was inflammable stuff, and quite true, too. It caused just as big a sensation as Macleod's article the previous week and put the *New Statesman* on the front pages, so our sales got a boost. Macleod was furious and accused me of 'sharp practice'. But amity was restored by a lunch John gave for him. A photo exists of just the three of us, rosy with good food and wine.

Harold Macmillan (1894–1986) had a long, apparently successful, but deeply unsatisfactory life. He told me he always felt there was something round the corner he was missing. His wife, Lady Dorothy, daughter of the 9th Duke of Devonshire, was clumsily – not discreetly – unfaithful to him, over a long period, with, of all people, Bob Boothby. Her daughter Sarah was Boothby's, not Macmillan's, or so Lady Dorothy insisted. When I was up at Oxford I got to know Sarah in 1947. She had only just discovered about her paternity, and was confused. She said: 'It has made me even more afraid of my father than I was already.' Sarah was not an undergraduate ('not clever enough') but was doing a secretarial course at Miss Sprule's Typing Academy, a great Oxford institution in those days. Debutantes who had failed to find a husband in their 'season' went to Miss Sprule's to learn typing-shorthand, so that they could get some kind of job (at Conservative Central Office, the National Trust or a private bank in the City). I knew four girls there: Sarah, my particular friend, not a beauty but with very pretty legs, and a sweet nature; Caroline, the biggest and richest, who got everybody she liked invitations to London dances, a blonde and amorous, but somehow unattractive; June, also blonde, was the prettiest but had thick ankles. Finally, there was Angela, who had been 'bunked' from Benenden for being found with her 'uncle' in 'inappropriate circumstances', as the authorities put it. Angela wailed: 'I'm always the one who gets caught. Lots of girls take their knickers off, but I'm the one who's discovered with a bare arse.' 'Well, if you use expressions like that, what do you expect?' huffed Caroline.

I got leave to go to a dance with Sarah and spend the night in London. Tom Boase, the Magdalen president, giving me permission, said: 'I advise you not to sleep with girls, Paul. It's not nearly as nice as you think it's going to be.' (What the hell did he know about it? I had already slept with more girls than he had.) Sarah said: 'My parents are away. You can stay at my house.' But that was not as easy as she thought. Her parents then had a house in Chester Square. That was all right, and Sarah had a front door key. But after the dance, when we went there, we discovered that all the bedrooms, except her own and her mother's, were locked. There were no servants around. She didn't know where the keys were. It was not done for a good girl like her to have a man in her room. 'So you'll have to sleep in Mummy's bed.' So I did, climbing between the tousled sheets and falling instantly and soundly asleep. I was woken by a man's voice: 'Who the hell are you?' Looking up, I saw the old walrus moustache of Harold Macmillan. He was not exactly gruntled to return unexpectedly and find a mop of bright red curly hair on his wife's pillow. However, he took it in good part. It was Sarah who had the jitters.

My next contact with Macmillan was in 1955 when I had to write a profile of him for the *New Statesman*. I got an introduction to Bob Boothby, who received me at his cosy little flat at the bottom corner of Eaton Square. He told me all about Macmillan's early career and his being sent to Canada as ADC to the Duke of Devonshire, Governor General. He said: 'It's a natural mistake, but a mistake nevertheless, for the ADC to marry the General's or the Governor's daughter.' This was his only reference to Lady Dorothy. But he did mention the Cavendish gene, which led to so much drinking in the family. Dorothy didn't have it but she passed it on to three of her children, including poor Sarah, who became an alcoholic and died of drink, and her brother Maurice, otherwise a nice, dull man, whose drinking was a source of much sorrow to his father. Andrew Devonshire also had the gene, and it blighted his life, though he continued to live into his eighties. Anyway, Boothby explained about the gene, and much else. He seemed to me a wonderful man of the world, and I hugely enjoyed his company, then and later. Macmillan liked the profile, called 'Keeper of their Conscience'. It was unsigned, but Sarah told him I had written it, and it stood me in good stead in our future relationship.

Macmillan was fundamentally shaped by the First World War, serving in the trenches with the Grenadier Guards. Several of his closest friends were killed, and another, Harry Crookshank, lost his balls. (Diana Cooper, a wartime VAD, was introduced to Crookshank in 1919 and said: 'I feel I know you already, as I carried your poor old balls, in an enamel tray, across an orchard in Normandy!') Macmillan used to say, 'All the best of us were killed. We are the unsatisfactory survivors.' But I don't think he believed this. He was a tremendous actor – and actor-manager, as Boothby said. He was also a world-class bore on the subject of 'the Trenches'.

Macmillan had a northern industrial constituency in the thirties, Stockton, and this made him a liberal in some ways. Or, rather, a Whig.

For political purposes, he adopted Cavendish emotions, and saw himself as one of the Whig elite, a Foxite, hating the self-ishness of Carlton Club Tories. He once told me a long story (all Macmillan's stories tended to be long) about the lengths his father-in-law would go to avoid stepping into the Carlton to keep out of the rain, preferring to get wet and go on to Brooks's. So during the appeasement period, Macmillan was a Churchillian, and got his reward when he was made Minister – Resident at Allied HQ Algiers in 1943, looking after North Africa and Italy, and dealing with all the generals, British and American, the French, Gaullist and Vichy, the Greeks and the Italians. It was the best stroke of luck of his entire career. He met everyone, had to deal with all kinds of problems. He learned lessons of this kind much more thoroughly than Eden ever did, and thus prepared himself for becoming Prime Minister. He also learned the absolute centrality of Anglo-American relations and (as he put it to me) 'how to keep your temper when dealing with the Yanks'.

Naturally Macmillan lost his seat in 1945 but by now was regarded as indispensable, so Churchill and Central Office quickly arranged a safe seat in the south for him. He had another stroke of luck in 1951, for Churchill made him Minister of Housing at a time when it had been decided to make house-building on an unprecedented scale a major item in Conservative policy. So Macmillan was able to proclaim a target of 300,000 houses a year in the sure knowledge that it could be reached. He thus became a 'successful' minister, with automatic promotion, first to Defence, then to the Exchequer. He had got on well with Churchill. But his relations with Eden, PM from 1954, were always edgy. Officers from 'the Brigade' were always suspicious of 'Green Jackets', but the feeling went deeper. In the thirties he was jealous of Eden, a glamour figure both politically and socially, whereas he was a fusty, moth-eaten, prematurely old fogey known to be a cuckold. He used to say that Butler, not Eden, should have succeeded Churchill. Equally, Eden was planning to get rid of Macmillan, retire him, in 1956, when all was changed by the Suez Crisis.

Eden later claimed, privately, that 'Macmilan got me into the Suez mess'. What he meant by this, as Robert Blake told me (he was privy to a lot of Tory secrets) was that on 25 September 1956 Macmillan, in Washington, had a secret talk with President Eisenhower in which Ike told him he would support British military action against Nasser, the Egyptian dictator, to get the Suez Canal back. The British ambassador, Sir Roger Makins, was present, took notes, and got a completely different impression. Macmillan cabled back his version of Ike's attitude, and that was the one Eden wanted to hear. Presumably he took no notice of Makins's dispatch. But the truth, of course, is that Ike was often ambiguous, not to say two-faced. Anyway, Eden went ahead, and compounded his error in using force without explicit American backing by using it in conspiracy with the French and the Israelis. All this was calculated to arouse Ike's ire, and did. Whether Macmillan gave Eden his explicit backing is not clear. He denied to me, many years later, that he had ever approved of what was called our 'collusion' with the Israelis. He said he was not a party to it, and certainly was not present at the secret meeting between Eden and Guy Mollet, the French premier, when the collusion plan was hatched with the Israelis. The only other Cabinet Minister there, at Villecombray airbase, was Selwyn Lloyd, a cipher. Macmillan told me: 'I prefer not to talk about Suez. Too painful.' I thought: 'Oh yeah? It did you a power of good.' And so it did. Macmillan, as Chancellor, completely underestimated the damage the Anglo-French invasion would do to sterling once active US opposition became known. It was calamitous, so Macmillan abruptly switched sides, and told Eden: 'The game's up – pull back!' Eden saw this as cowardice, then treachery, and eventually came to believe Macmillan had been Machiavellian throughout. But I doubt that. As he was fond of saying, and the Suez disaster confirmed it: 'What is the strongest force in politics? Is it policies? No. Is it personalities? No. It is events, dear boy, events.' I didn't agree with this rather Tolstoyian view, though the Suez story does tend to confirm it. After all, if Eden had known how quickly and completely the Egyptian forces would collapse before the Israeli attack, he would never have needed to intervene at all. And of course, he did not foresee, nor did anyone else, his own physical deterioration. Events did settle the matter, and in due course made Macmillan Prime Minister.

I laughed when Macmillan celebrated his new appointment by settling the new Cabinet with Ted Heath, his Chief Whip, over dinner at the Turf Club. This shocked some people as frivolous, but it seemed to me to show a bit of style – sadly needed in those grim days. So did Macmillan's appointment of John Wyndham as an unpaid private secretary – he being a cheerful, debonair, very rich man with a huge and beautiful house, Petworth, in Sussex. Macmillan also let it be known that, far from being overburdened by the pressure of dire events, he was reading Trollope's novels. And old Dorothy for once turned up trumps by transforming Number Ten, a rather forbidding place under Eden, with 'the Suez Canal flowing through the drawing room', as Clarissa Eden put it, into a rather cosy country-house-in-London place, with grandchildren scrambling all over the place, and golf clubs, shooting sticks and gun cases in the hall.

The skill and aplomb with which Macmillan extricated Britain from the Suez mess, got back on to good terms with Ike and the Americans, and healed the divisions in his own party, were striking. He seemed to be able to take anything in his stride as, for instance, when his entire Treasury team resigned early in 1958 because the PM would not take inflation seriously enough. About to leave for a tour of the Commonwealth, Macmillan dismissed it as 'a little local difficulty' – and that is how he made it seem for a time. Again, in 1958, when the bottom fell out of Britain's remaining positions of strength in the Middle East, and all our friends there were murdered, Macmillan and Ike acted together, the Americans 'stabilising' Lebanon with troops, while we went into Jordan. It seemed all right at the time, but it left the enemies of the West in power in Iraq, which mattered much more than either, and that too stored up trouble for the future. Macmillan resembled Baldwin somewhat, preferring an easy-going present to taking steps to deal with a threatening future. It looked good at the time. Macmillan, turning an attack by the cartoonist Vicky upside down, became Supermac – the chap who could pull off miracles effortlessly. He developed a turn with phrases. In South Africa he lectured the whites on 'the Winds of Change'. He told the British people, 'You've never had it so good.' He looked very masterful compared with Hugh Gaitskell, the Labour leader, a man he disliked and despised – 'all the limitations of a typical Wykhamist' – as compared (though he did not actually say this) to the broadmindedness and omnicompetence of an Etonian (and member of Pop). He won the 1959 election easily, doubling the Conservative majority.

But it was about this time that Macmillan developed a new weakness: the cult of age. He was now in his late sixties, but almost unconsciously he began to develop the personality of a much older man. Out shooting at the Cavendish estate of Bolton Abbey, he was photographed sporting a pair of antique gaiters not seen on a grouse moor for a generation. He let it be known he only liked vintage Perrier-Jouët, 'an old man's champagne', as he put it. After his first visit to the Kennedys in Washington, he told me, when I asked what it was like: 'Just like when the Borgia brothers took over a respectable north Italian town.' He also said: 'We have to play the wise old Greeks to their virile young Romans.' And he said: 'Kennedy made me feel very old.' Then 'events' started to catch up with him. De Gaulle, who had hated him since Macmillan's days of glory at Algiers in 1943, dealt him a vicious blow by vetoing the British bid to 'join' Europe. In July 1962, Macmillan tried to rejuvenate his Cabinet by sacking seven senior ministers. The thing was botched, creating terrible ill feeling, and the net result was to make him seem, by comparison, old and isolated. Then, next year, came the Profumo scandal, which made him seem ill informed and out of touch, and which was made worse by his own, ill-considered explanation of why he did not know about the goings-on of his ministers: 'I do not move much among young people nowadays.' In short, Macmillan's old-man piece of acting rebounded on him, disastrously. And to top it all, in the autumn of 1963 he suffered from that quintessential old man's affliction, prostate trouble. He had to leave a Cabinet meeting in acute pain, had an immediate operation and resigned. He then exerted himself mightily from his bed in the Edward VII Hospital to ensure that the succession went not to Butler, whom he despised, but to Alec Douglas-Home, another Etonian whom he thought would listen to his advice. He succeeded, and then fell into a deep sleep. He was woken by a telephone engineer at his bedside table. 'What the hell are you doing?', asked Macmillan in the same tone of voice he had used to me nearly twenty years before. 'I'm taking away your red telephone,' said the man. 'You're not Prime Minister any more, you know.'

It was then that Macmillan became aware of the enormity of the mistake he had made. He need not have resigned! He could have had a period of recuperation, then resumed office and won the election the following year. His prostate was only 'a little local difficulty' and he was to live another twenty-three years in reasonably good health. Macmillan's consciousness of his own folly was rubbed in by the fact that Home did not readily listen to his advice, made many mistakes and lost the 1964 election, ushering in Labour for much of the sixties and seventies.

I was conscious of Macmillan being at a loose end in those years, an old, old man (he spent a lot of time and energy perfecting his doddering act) with nothing to do but much to say. A frugal, not to say mean, man, he missed his chauffeur-driven car, because it was free. He often travelled by tube. I sat next to him once on the Circle Line to Westminster. No one else recognised him. I asked how he thought things were going. He nodded his head up and down, as if to express approval. Then he shook it from side to side to indicate despair. He spoke not a word – the public might be listening. But among the elite, or intimates, he was voluble. His words were of varying quality. He wrote his memoirs: six substantial volumes of indescribable dullness and prolixity, spun out to that length because his family publishing firm contrived to make a profit on each. Has any human being ever read them through? He had some consolation in his long exile from power. In 1960 he had been elected Chancellor of Oxford University, beating the academic establishment candidate Sir Oliver Franks. He used his position to take advantage of a rule – he may have invented it – which obliged any of the colleges to entertain him to 'dine-and-sleep' whenever he felt inclined. So he descended regularly on Balliol (his old college), Christ Church and Magdalen – the smaller, poorer colleges saw him less often, and some he ignored completely. On these occasions he would harass the Fellows in the SCR for hours over port. (Not that he drank port: but he would sip his Perrier-Jouët.) The whole of history, ancient, medieval and modern, passed under his reminiscent purview. The older dons gathered round. The younger, left-wing ones grumbled. In the end all were bored. He visited other regular haunts where he felt valued. At the Beefsteak he would take the head of the table, and hold forth on favourite topics: how Lord Curzon missed the premiership in 1923, and his rage thereat; the kind of stiff collars worn by Sir William Joynson-Hicks when he was Home Secretary; the number of copies (40,000) his firm had sold of Morley's three-volume *Life of William Ewart Gladstone*, the first day of publication, and so on. We listened, rarely commented, never interrupted. He was also frequently at Petworth and Cockermouth Castle, seats of his former aide, Wyndham, whom he had made Lord Egremont (restoring an ancient title) in his Resignation Honours; at Garsington, then owned by Sir John Wheeler-Bennett and, above all, at Chatsworth. He had given the Duke a much appreciated junior post, and the Duchess, a Mitford, adored his gossip and stories. But the daughter, Lady Sophie, told me she found 'Uncle Harold' 'a crashing bore'. Between these venues he travelled by rail, using a free pass given to him in perpetuity when he was a director of the Great Western in the 1930s. This entitled him to first-class travel anywhere in the British Isles. All he had to do was to produce the solid gold seal he wore on his waistcoat watch chain. He was the last former director to use this privilege, in the 1980s, and it sometimes puzzled young ticket inspectors. This would provoke from Macmillan a long discourse on the Big Four and its workings half a century before. He had sharp comments on his successors. Wilson: 'a little man over-whelmed by the magnitude of Events'; Heath: 'Pecksniff in too much of a hurry'; Callaghan: 'the mind of a naval petty officer'; Margaret Thatcher's denationalisation policy: 'She is selling the family silver'. He turned down a peerage because his son, Maurice, was an MP with a ministerial future. Then, when Maurice died, he demanded, and got, a hereditary earldom, calling himself 'Earl of Stockton'. He was a bit of a fraud, all through, but I am glad to have known him.

Louis MacNeice (1907–63). It is always interesting to observe how habitual drinkers hold a glass. Asquith, it is recorded, held a port wine glass not between first finger and thumb but between first and second fingers, not using the thumb at all. Bron Waugh drank wine using second and third finger to hold the glass, the first finger to steady it a bit. But this was because he had injured his right hand in the disastrous seconds when the machine gun of his armoured car pumped eleven bullets into his body. Louis MacNeice appeared to grasp his whisky glass or tumbler with his whole right hand as though he held it in a mailed fist, an awkward way of doing things and a bit grim and menacing, though, come to think of it, appropriate to an Ulsterman of Protestant origins, tanking up. He sometimes held his incessant cigarettes between third and fourth, or fourth and little fingers. And he could breathe out a long spout of smoke through only one nostril. Altogether, a fascinating specimen to study in a saloon bar. I used to watch him thus in the BBC pub near Broadcasting House. He was a nice, good man; not talkative – you could see he was the son of a bishop.

Norman Mailer (1923–2007) appeared in Evelyn Waugh's *Diaries* as 'a swarthy Yank pornographer'. My first involvement with him occurred by accident. I had gone to Teddington to interview a politician on Ken Tynan's TV arts programme. Just before transmission – it was a live programme – Tynan came to me in a panic. He said one of his interviewers had not turned up. Could I do Norman Mailer? I agreed. I knew very little about Mailer except that he had written a bestselling war novel. So he had: *The Naked and the Dead*. But I confused him with another American writer who had written a novel about the war, James Jones, author of *From Here to Eternity*. This was more natural than it seems today, for Mailer was not then world-famous as a hellraiser. However, he had not long before done a brief stint in gaol for going for his (second or perhaps third) spouse with a kitchen knife. I did not know this, or, if I did, had forgotten it. My knowledge of James Jones was not extensive either. But I did know that he had spent some time in a 'writers' village', or similar place, run by Mrs Adlai Stevenson, outside Chicago.

That was the topic on which I decided to begin the interview. After preliminaries, I asked: 'Mr Mailer. I would like to ask you about your writing. Did you find it improved, or was helped in any way, by spending some time in this [I did not know the name of it] – this instirtition?' Mailer, suddenly hostile: 'No it did not. Why should it?' Me: 'Well, I thought that was the object of the exercise.' Mailer: 'That's not what the judge said.' Then he added aggressively: 'Are you trying to take the mickey?' At this point I realised something was wrong, and hastily switched the questions to the problems of writing about war. Mailer gradually calmed down. But afterwards, he said: 'Don't ever think you can take liberties with me, Mister Fancypants Englishman.'

I came across Mailer on various occasions over the years, at parties, conferences and the like, but did not warm to him. I found his books needlessly violent, essentially uninteresting, and the one on ancient Egypt, which I was asked to review, grossly ignorant. By the time I focused on him again, in New York, President Clinton was in the White House, and Mailer was on his sixth wife. I found myself next to her at a buffet party. I had just had a harrowing exchange with John Richardson, biographer of Picasso. I was not in the mood for trouble. The lady had a strong Arkansas accent, and was complaining of the media's treatment of Bill Clinton, who of course also came from Arkansas, and whom she knew and admired. She said: 'And the other day, you know what they did, these New York papers – one of them, anyway – they said that Mr Clinton, during his press conference, actually – I don't hardly know how to put this – actually made gas!' I was intrigued by this expression, and said: 'Mrs Norman Mailer the Sixth, do I understand from what you have just said that, during his press conference, President Clinton farted?' This was too much for the lady. '*Aaaaooowooo,*' she wailed, and disappeared into the jovial throng. Some time later, a wizened old gentleman came alongside me, whom I eventually recognised – just – as the fierce war novelist I had once interviewed all those year ago, on ABC. To quote P. G. Wodehouse, he was not exactly disgruntled. But he was far from being gruntled. Before he could start, however, I said: 'Mr Mailer, I fear I distressed your wife by using a word to which she was plainly unaccustomed. I would not for worlds have willingly upset so charming, accomplished and beautiful a creature. Please accept my deepest apologies.' He said: 'Oh. Well. Yeah. Right. That's fine. Well. Right.'

Then he stiffened, and a flicker of the man he had been passed over his features. '*Don't do it again, man.*'

J. P. W. ('Bill') Mallalieu (1908–80) was, of all the MPs I have ever known, the nicest. He was good all through. No envy, no malice, just simple good nature. He and I worked next door to each other at the *NS* when he wrote our weekly parliamentary column, and we had lots of laughs. Oh, how he loved to joke! He was competitive because he was a sportsman – rugger, cricket, tennis, football, anything really – but a good loser. Well, he had to be: he usually lost. He was the only one Bevan liked of his followers: never a cross word between them. Once, at a party, I foolishly encouraged him to have too much to drink. He went off with a woman who was there. Bill, innocent, almost naive, was the victim of a nasty little financial plot, and suffered tortures. The NS lent him money to get out of the jam. But he recovered and was his old jovial self again. He had an enchanting wife and a clever, beautiful daughter, a great rider-to-hounds and life peeress. On form, he could write like an angel. His book about his war, in the Royal Navy, *Very Ordinary Seaman*, is a little masterpiece. He came of old Huguenot stock, and was always known as 'Curly'. But his curls had gone by the time I knew him. God rest the soul of this genial gentleman.

Princess Margaret (1930–2002) attracted a lot of criticism during her lifetime, and since. I always felt sorry for her. What her critics never took into account was that she moved in the world of the rich and well-endowed but never had any money or property. She never had a real home of her own. All the Queen allowed her was a grace-and-favour residence at Kensington Palace. She never gave her sister a London house or a country house. Nothing, in fact. Not even some ancient furniture and pictures. The Queen Mother lived in stupendous luxury in Marlborough House, and in two Scottish castles, with more than forty servants, but gave her younger daughter very little, in money or anything else. Margaret had some good jewels. That's all. People sneered about her house in Mustique. But it was all she owned of her own. And it was given to her by her friend Colin Tennant, not by her family.

Once I was sitting by her at a country house garden party, having a good talk, when a peculiarly obnoxious and pushy social-climbing journalist tried to join us. I froze him out, and he moved away reluctantly. I said: 'One of those days I'll kill him.' She thought for a bit and said: 'If you're serious about killing that awful man, let me know, and I'll come and give you a hand.'

Kingsley Martin (1897–1969) was editor of the *New Statesman* for thirty years and made it the most successful political weekly in the world. He had none of the obvious qualities of an editor, being indecisive, cowardly and ignorant of the technical side of journalism. He was the son of a Nonconformist clergyman who (he told me) 'as he grew older believed more and more in less and less', eventually ending up 'with a passionate faith in nothing'. What Kingsley believed, in politics and in general, was never clear, but he reflected the muddled uncertainties of large numbers of educated middle-class people, hence the success of the paper under his editorship.

He had a handsome, decayed, woebegone face, a fine torso and wobbly legs. In moments of despair at the state of the world or the paper he could emit what was known as 'Kingsley's dying camel noise'. He had many cronies at the Savile Club (chiefly unimportant people at the BBC) and would return from lunch there on Monday full of prognostications about the immediate future. He might have been one of those men who still in those days carried placards: 'The End of the World is Nigh'. Instead he edited, with huge success, a weekly specialising in pessimism. Kingsley was very mean. When, at the end of 1956, I told him I was getting married, he moaned: 'O, o, o, o – you'll be expecting a rise in salary!' After much moaning he gave me one, another £100 a year. He, Leonard Woolf and G. D. H. Cole must have been the three most parsimonious men of the time, specialising in finding cheap curry joints. But Kingsley could be very generous by stealth. He was fascinated by sexual deviation but frightened by sex itself in any form, and had obviously experienced very little of it. When he came to Paris, where I was the NS correspondent, he demanded to be taken to lesbian nightclubs, but immediately he got inside he became timid and asked to leave. John Freeman and Norman MacKenzie used deliberately to read in Kingsley's hearing bits from the *News of the World* about schoolgirls being whipped or spanked. This always brought him out of his lair. No one knew whether he was actually married to Dorothy Woodman, a once pretty, now colossal woman, known to the office as 'the Bandung Cow'. She was an expert on Asia, a vegetarian and car fancier. When I dined with them, *à trois*, an enormous Persian cat jumped on to the table straight in front of my place and eyed me malevolently. 'Oh, I can see he adores you,' said Dorothy.

After Kingsley retired in 1960 he was unhappy and restless. He took a big mansion flat overlooking Westminster Cathedral, and would stand in front of the window, watching the monsignori, etc., go in and out, muttering: 'I don't understand it.' Harold Wilson offered him a knighthood but he turned it down. He expected a peerage, so he could toddle around the Lords with other extinct volcanoes of the left. He always referred to Wilson, in conse-quence, as 'mean'. He wrote a volume of autobiography, *Father Figures*, about his childhood and youth, which was good. His second volume, *Editor*, was no good, and one he planned about the post-war period was never written – couldn't face the uneasy memories. Few remember him now but I do, vividly. His favourite term of praise for a good article was 'crackerjack'.

Groucho Marx (1890–1977) came to be interviewed in the old basement Studio Nine at Associated Rediffusion TV. I enjoyed doing it for he talked well and was easy to get going. His complaint was that union restrictions and the high cost of filming had made really high-class slapstick comedy very difficult. He described to me exactly how they had rehearsed and filmed the famous cabin scene in *A Night at the Opera*, and how many days it had taken. 'There is only one way to get results of that quality: endless rehearsals and many, many re-takes.' Exactly the same point was made later to me by Ernie Wise, about his acts with Eric Morecambe, who he said was a comic perfectionist who insisted on unlimited rehearsal time. Groucho said to me: 'With genius and a lot of luck you can get tragedy fairly cheaply. But comedy is always expensive, and slapstick needs Big Money.' He said: 'You know, Paul, from your own experience, that a good cartoonist is worth twenty good reporters. In the movies a master of comedy is worth more than any of the straight actors, because he is much rarer.' He said he thought he would have been no good without his brothers. 'On your own out there, and told, "Make 'em laugh" – it's an awesome thought. I said to Louis B. Mayer when he was arguing about money, "You try it, Mr Mayer, just you try it for once."'

Reggie Maudling (1917–79) was a big, nice, roly-poly man, sometimes described as 'looking like an unmade bed'. Exceptionally quick and clever at school and university, he had learned to move through life easily. When he stood for the party leadership, he made no effort to put together a team and to campaign systematically so Heath, the 'Professional Politician', won easily. After that, he more or less gave up. He wanted, as he put it, 'a little pot of gold for my old age', and so joined up with the crooked architect John Poulson, and was misled in his schemes. Reggie was a great friend of Hugh Fraser, and we were both staying at Eilean Aigas on the Sunday the Poulson scandal first became public. I remember the menacing headlines in the *Sunday Times*. We went for a picnic up the glen, and Hugh asked me to 'stick close to Reggie and keep his mind off it with your jokes'. So I did: hard work. His wife, a sweet, comfortable lady, with simple, friendly tastes, was stricken, too. It was a gruesome day, everyone avoiding the subject which occupied all our minds.

I recall, too, talking to Reggie at his rumpled London flat, not long before he died. He is the only politician I met whom I never heard say a malicious or even a critical word about another politician. We went over every conceivable topic – Suez, Profumo, the antics of George Brown, etc. – until I said: 'Reggie, is there no one you dislike?' He thought for a minute, then said, 'Well, I'm not so fond of that chap Dennis Skinner.' Then he corrected himself: 'But he's not so bad, really. He told me he's very fond of gardening.'

Gavin Maxwell (1914–69) was one of the ablest writers I have known and the most unhappy. He came from the Scots border gentry baronets on one side, a duke on the other, and spent much of his life living in remote parts of the Highlands. I first met him in 1957 when he came to the *New Statesman*, bringing his otter, Teko, with him. It promptly bit the finger of our literary editor, Janet Adam Smith. She was obviously in great pain but did not make a sound, having been brought up to be hardy and stoical in misfortune. Personally, I thought his otter, imperfectly trained and with very strong jaws, a confounded menace. It was later the hero of his worldwide bestseller, *Ring of Bright Water*. He had a genius for titles. *Harpoon at a Venture* told about his unsuccessful shark fishing off the west Scottish coast; *God Protect Me from My Friends* was about the murdered Sicilian hero Salvatore Giuliano; and *Raven Seek Thy Brother* was autobiographical. He invented a new kind of book, partly about himself, partly about the places and animals he loved. He married the daughter of Lascelles, the courtier, but the marriage was a flop. He was homosexual; liked teenage boys. They always let him down in the end. His affair with Kathleen Raine, the poetess, ended in a cursing. He was extravagant, got through all his considerable earnings, and his beloved house burned down. His disasters were nearly all his own fault. But he could, and often did, write like an angel. I found him difficult but worthwhile. He knew a vast amount about the wild life of Scotland, particularly birds, partly from experience but also through intuition and empathy. He passed on much of what he learned to his pupil John Lister-Kaye, who became a friend of mine. Maxwell said to me: 'Never hesitate to shoot a heron. It will eat twice its body weight in salmon every day it lives, if it can.' And: 'Don't spend the winter in the Highlands, unless you must. It breeds melancholy and alcoholism.' And: 'Highlanders are poets and it is against their deepest instincts to tell you the truth.'

Robert Maxwell (1923–91) was the only man I ever met who genuinely radiated evil. I thought, the first time I met him, in 1955, 'This is a thoroughly bad man.' He was big, about six foot two, and heavy. He had a large head, and enormous face, all the features being to scale. His eyes glittered darkly, his hair shone with black oiliness, his voice was deep and could be very loud. He had a habit, when walking along, of dropping anything for which he had no further use – a tissue, a newspaper, a letter and envelope, a wrapper – for others to pick up. In 1955 he already had a bad reputation for his part in the collapse of Simpkin, Marshall, a firm of distributors in the print trade. Harold Lever, a lawyer-businessman and a fellow Jew, very experienced and astute in City matters, told me: 'Never have anything to do with him. He is a crook.' He called himself 'Captain Robert Maxwell MC'. The MC was genuine (Germany, 1945) but awarded in unusual circumstances. His colonel asked for a volunteer to lead an assault party against a strongly entrenched position. Maxwell asked: 'Is there an MC in it?' Colonel (taken aback): 'Well, I daresay. So far as I'm concerned, there is.' 'Then I'll do it.' Harold Lever thought he should have been banned from further office as a board member of a publicly quoted company. But nothing was done. People were scared of him. He could be terrifying, face to face. When he came up to me at a party, I used to say to him: 'I don't want to talk to you, Mr Maxwell. Go away, Mr Maxwell.' Maxwell was brilliant at doing deals, but had no idea of how to run a company efficiently. I don't think any of his companies even made a routine profit. It was all one-off stuff. Looking good in the balance sheet but moonshine to the practised eye. His plan to launch an evening paper as a rival to the *Evening Standard* was unsound and the project was doomed before it began. He gave a huge launch party which I attended, but left after half an hour, appalled, and met Maxwell just arriving. He was greatly offended at my leaving so soon, and cursed me: 'You will regret this, you swine.'

Soon after I interviewed him on TV and examined him closely about the way in which all his lines of ownership vanished into a Liechtenstein mist. He refused to answer some questions and evaded others, and gradually got angry. After we finished he strode from the set in a rage. A man waiting in the ante-room stood up: 'Mr Maxwell, sir, may I have a word with you?' 'Who the hell are you?' 'I'm one of your editors, sir – the *Daily Mirror*.' 'Bugger off. I'll talk to you later.'

The Mirror Group was in decline before he took over – that is why he was able to acquire it, cheap – but he had no idea how to improve its performance and the position deteriorated fast. The share price fell and that is when he began to raid the pension fund to keep it up. His fellow trustees were too frightened of him to inquire into what was happening, and get satisfactory answers. Any press criticism was met by the threat or service of libel writs.

His eventual thefts were colossal and impoverished what was generally regarded as one of the best pension funds in the country. Many people were badly hit. It was a shocking business and reflected badly on the City, the legal profession and many of his colleagues. His exit from the scene of his triumphs and frauds was Grand Guignol. He arose from his flat in the heart of the *Mirror* building off Holborn Circus, took a lift to the roof, climbed into his helicopter which took him to Heathrow, got into his private plane there, which flew him to Gibraltar. There he went aboard his yacht, the *Ghislaine* (called after his daughter), and ordered it to sea. By this time the boat's fax machine was humming with unanswered and increasingly peremptory queries about the state of the pension fund. He fell into the sea during the night and his body was never recovered. The *Mirror* greeted his death with an adulatory front page, THE MAN WHO SAVED THE MIRROR, but soon changed its tune when the staff realised their pensions had gone up the Maxwell creek.

George Melly (1928–2007) was an amiable jazz or blues singer of a kind I don't appreciate but was widely regarded as excellent. He also formed a team with the artist Wally Fawkes to produce the Flook strip and other cartoons. Melly supplied the ideas and captions. They worked for me at the *New Statesman* but I had to get rid of them as Melly's jokes, so the readers thought, were not funny enough or were obscene. Three things interested me about Melly. First, the awfulness of popular music. Amplification made the musical noise, in which he worked for so many hours each day, so loud that he went permanently deaf. Second, his wife. In the sixties, she used to wear black leather outfits, and I called her the 'Martian Barmaid'. Third, his curious relationship with Peregrine Worsthorne. In a book of essays by different hands, called *The World of the Public School*, Perry claimed he was seduced by Melly at Stowe. Melly hotly denied this claim. He said he never had sex with Perry, and that, anyway, Perry was three years older than he was, so could hardly have been seduced by him. Perry was never able to clean up this mystery. How Melly, an educated and resourceful man, could bear to lead the life he did, in hot, noisy jazz-and nightclubs, with stupid people and brassy girls, was another mystery. But he seemed to enjoy it, and certainly lots of people enjoyed him.

Pierre Mendès-France (1907–82) was the first of my political heroes. He was the only outstanding politician of the Fourth Republic whom I regarded as incorruptible, a view shared by General de Gaulle. He had a Norman constituency famed for its dairy cattle and drank only milk. He was Jewish and when he made his investiture speech as Prime Minister in 1954 the Communist leader, Jacques Duclos, screamed out at him, 'Youpin' ('Yid'). The Catholic party (MRP) led by Georges Bidault also hated him and effectively destroyed his government in 1955. But Mendès-France, his success and his failure, effectively prepared the way for De Gaulle in 1958, and so to the remaking of France. He had a saying: '*Gouverner, c'est choisir.*' He was stiff-necked like an Old Testament Hebrew and his countless friends and admirers found him impossible to work with. He certainly was a difficult man to interview. He would say: 'That's not the right question.' Or: 'Before I answer you, *permittez-moi* to deal with the question at the back of your mind.' Or: 'I will answer that by putting a question to you.' You always felt you were with a great man, though. He had the heaviest five o'clock shadow I have ever seen. There is an undistinguished statue of him in the Luxembourg Gardens. No good biography of him has been, or is likely to be, written.

Dom Mintoff (b. 1916) was Prime Minister of Malta and head of the Labour Party there. He took me on a tour of all the Labour clubs. I have never seen such enthusiasm. At that time his great enemy was the Catholic Archbishop of Malta, Monsignor Gonzi. When I wrote an article in the *New Statesman* supporting Mintoff and criticising the archbishop's behaviour, Gonzi publicly burned the offending issue of the paper in front of a cheering crowd of people. Later, for mysterious reasons, Mintoff and Gonzi had a sudden reconciliation, and became close friends and allies. Mintoff had an orange tree in his garden. He gave me a basket of fruit from it. They looked very ugly and unpromising. But when I got them home we found them the most delicious oranges we had ever tasted.

Nancy Mitford (1904–73) was very kind to me, when I lived in Paris, inviting me to her nice little house across a courtyard in the rue Monsieur ('Gentleman Street' as she called it). She gave little lunch and dinner parties, cooked by her admirable *bonne à tout faire*, Marie. After dinner we played charades. I recall John Sutro giving a stunning imitation of George III going mad. Other guests were Peter Quennell, Evelyn Waugh, Diana Cooper and Harold Acton, and sometimes Yanks like Katharine Graham who owned the *Washington Post* and Claire Booth Luce; though Nancy had no real love for Americans.

She was tall, slender, elegant, with a clean, highly audible voice – the 'Mitford Voice'. She was a dangerous mixture of irrepressible fun and jokes, sparing none, and aristocratic hauteur, with a strict insistence on good manners (as defined by her). You could easily get into trouble with her if you did or said the wrong thing. Her system of U, which for a time in the mid-fifties made her the most famous writer in England, was very personal. I told her it was nonsense to say 'writing paper' was U and 'notepaper' non-U when they meant different things. Strictly speaking writing paper meant the double-folded kind for a letter, notepaper a single, often small, sheet for something shorter. She replied, 'I can see you haven't been properly brought up.' Her great, grand, tiresome Paris society friend, Louise de Vilmorin, who was Duff Cooper's mistress, used to say correctly, 'Chaque famille à ses propres usages.' This was true of England as well as France. Evelyn Waugh agreed with Louise, though he hated her fiercely (as he hated anything belonging to 'Cooper'). But Nancy took no notice. She was very obstinate and her mind, once made up, never changed.

She was wonderful to be with: endless jokes and laughter ('shrieks') and wild, illogical and unsystematic remarks, plenty of empathy and intuition. She could be loving, and also very cold. She was one of the worst pickers of men I have met. Her husband, Peter Rodd ('Prod'), was a shit, a wastrel and a thief. She could never quite get him out of her life. He used to come to Gentleman Street, when he thought Nancy would not be in, get Marie to admit him, then steal any cash he found. Nancy, as a Mitford, did not believe in cheques and banks, but in cash ('running-away money'). She kept wodges of high-denomination francs, pound notes or dollars hidden away. But he was ingenious at finding them. She told me she thought of the wheeze of sewing a big wad of notes in the bottom hem of her drawing-room curtains. But he even got on to that, and cut them out with his penknife. Eventually Marie was told not to admit him (he was Basil Seal in Evelyn Waugh's comic novels).

Gaston Palewski, 'the Colonel', was even worse, if possible. He was the quintessential Gallic womaniser, talkative, culture-smart, clever, full of emphatic assertions on every possible topic, mendacious, unscrupulous, unfaithful and in his own way treacherous. He preyed on Nancy emotionally for years, and eventually when his ship came home and De Gaulle, returning to power, gave him

the magnificent French Embassy in Rome and a huge entertain-
ment allowance, he dropped Nancy and married a rich widowed
duchess. Nancy never got over it. At the same time she was
afflicted by a mysterious malady, which the French doctors never
diagnosed, let alone cured. By this time she had moved to Versailles,
where she was cut off from friends and depended on letters. I
used to write to her from London with gossip, to cheer her up.
She became very difficult because of her pain, and the apparent
hopelessness of alleviating it or curing it. It struck me as
monstrously unfair that she, who had given so much pleasure to
her friends and the public, and inspired much laughter, should
have met such a sad fate. I was writing a letter to her, sitting by
the swimming pool at Eilean Aigas, when I heard the news, on a
pocket radio, that she had died.

François Mitterrand (1916–96) loved plots, plots-within-plots and
counter-plots. Mendès-France said: *'Le pauvre Mitterrand, il a le
goût de policier.'* The weird tale of the fake assassination he plotted
against himself, in the boulevard de l'Observatoire, is an oddity,
even by the Byzantine standards of French *affaires politiques*. He
was also involved in *l'affaire des piastres, l'affaire des ballets roses*
and *l'affaire des fuites*. He had some rum private affairs of his own,
too. During the Second World War he worked for both sides. And
there was the usual Balzacian business with a wife, a mistress
and an illegitimate daughter. The three glass pyramids he had
built in the courtyard of the Louvre symbolised, in descending
order of size, himself, his mistress and his wife. Margaret Thatcher,
who had dealings with him, summed him up to me: 'I gather he
is a typical Frenchman.'

Walter Monckton (1891–1965) was a foxy lawyer whose career
touched events at a number of fascinating points. He could tell

you a lot if he chose. An Harrovian, and a wicket-keeper, he played in the famous match against Eton in 1910, when Field Marshal Lord Alexander also distinguished himself. He always kept in with the rich and powerful and turned down a scholarship to Hertford in order to take a commoner's place at Balliol among the intellectual toffs. He made a lot of money at the Bar, advised Indian maharajahs for princely sums and ran the Prince of Wales's legal office, continuing to give him good (unheeded) advice up to and beyond his catastrophe. Though he was almost blind in one eye he contrived to get into the First World War and won an MC, and in the Second he was busy all over the world. He earned huge sums in 1945–51, both in India and at home and the Dominians, and in 1951 Churchill gave him Oliver Stanley's old seat in Bristol and the Ministry of Labour. Monckton was a wonderful conciliator and go-between, an apostle of moderation, an admirable man of sense. Eden put him into Defence but he opposed his Suez policy and in October 1956 was shifted to a neutral job as Paymaster-General. During the Suez intervention, Nye Bevan used to joke: 'Walter is the only man in the government who inspires moral respect and they don't know whether to wear him as a jockstrap or a gas-mask.'

Nobody knew what Monckton's real opinions were, except on cricket, the only subject on which he could talk without looking over his shoulder to see who was listening. On his political retirement in 1957 he became a City grandee as Chairman of the Midland Bank and the Iraq Petroleum Company, but the post he valued was President of the MCC. People thought he was a Jew but he pointed out that his forebear had been Vicar of Brenchley (which supplied his title) as far back as 1650. He was the Tory equivalent of Lord Goodman as a fixer but the genuine article with none of Arnold's 'jots and tittles' and other legal waffle. He told me, 'The things I fix stay fixed.'

Iain Moncreiffe of that Ilk (1919–85). A little man, with a soft, delightful voice, he knew more personal history than any man I ever met. He lived in Perthshire, in a pretty, comfortable house, and put me and my driver up when I was doing my *National Trust Book of British Castles*. I think he was lonely, though he knew everyone. His sister, grander and richer than he was, lived nearby and he was scared of her, and spoke of her in awed tones. He was very hospitable, too much so for my taste, as every evening I had to write down notes of up to half a dozen castles seen during the day. My driver was an eighteen-year-old girl, tough and resourceful, daughter of a regular army NCO, but naive and simple. The Ilk needed a companion to drink whisky with him and listen to his anecdotage. I left the two of them together, Iain happy as a child, the girl with her eyes popping out of her head, and I went to bed. When I came down in the morning, they were both stretched out on the floor, fully dressed, dead to the world.

Jean Monnet (1888–1979) would disapprove of the way the European Union has evolved. He was connected with *Réalités* when I worked for it in the early fifties. He had worked in America, and had the greatest possible admiration for US ideals and methods. He always stressed three points about building a united Europe. First, it must be constructed with America, not against it. Second, it must have the minimum regulations, and only a tiny number of bureaucrats. It must be essentially voluntary and a consensus. Third, a cultural and poetic side was essential. 'We must have the writers with us, and the artists, and the musicians. Otherwise we are sure to fail.'

The Reverend Sun Myung Moon (b. 1920) was by far the most important figure for many years in Korea, where his Unification Church had millions of members in the south. I twice flew to

Seoul to speak at one of his conferences and each time demanded and got my top fee, $50,000 (plus expenses). On the second occasion I had a family lunch with the Rev. Moon, Mrs Moon, the young Moons and some top aides. The Rev. Moon said he didn't like women rulers. I said Mrs Thatcher had done pretty well in Britain. He said, yes, but she has some weaknesses. Such as what? No sense of humour. I told the story of how she had shattered the all-male Institute of Economic Affairs dinner by saying: 'The cock may crow, but it's the hen that lays the eggs.' Moon received this in silence, the others likewise. There was a pause. Suddenly Mrs Moon, who hitherto had not said one word, got the joke. She burst into loud and prolonged peals of laughter. She roared. She was, if I may put it so, over the moon. And slowly Rev. Moon began to laugh, too. Not very convincingly or energetically, but he did. Then others joined in. Soon they were all laughing, but the happiest of all was Mrs Moon. When I told this story to Mrs Thatcher, later, she said: 'Sorry. I don't see the joke.'

Malcolm Muggeridge (1903–90) was the first writer in the twentieth century to bring the Royal Family back into the arena of journalistic criticism. He did this with a piece called 'Royal Soap Opera' which appeared in the *New Statesman* in 1957. I still remember Kingsley Martin coming into my little office with the typescript in his hand: 'I say! Malcolm has written an absolute crackerjack!' It was a huge success with our readers, but when it was republished all over the world, including the *Saturday Evening Post* in America, it caused sparks. A social-climbing journalist in the *New York Times* London office complained to the Committee of the Garrick Club and Malcolm, needlessly, it seemed to me, resigned. But he was often in hot water. As the one successful editor of *Punch* in the twentieth century, he was an embarrassment to Bradbury Agnew, who owned it then, for attacking

Churchill, as well as Nehru and other untouchables. After five years he gave it up, again in disgust. The BBC once suspended him, but after he became one of their superstars, he found himself an untouchable there, to his amusement.

I took great delight in Malcolm's company and counted myself extremely fortunate to be a friend and confidant of his for many years: really from the mid-fifties to his death in 1990, though in the last decade he was frail and then suffered from Alzheimer's. He always gave me kindly and excellent advice. 'Don't go on a lecture tour of America. The money is tempting but the amount of work involved, the bruising of the spirit, the dulling of the senses – the sheer horror of it all – is too much to bear.' 'Never get too close to newspaper proprietors, or rich men generally – despite yourself you will be corrupted by their values.' 'Always put religion before money. Indeed, put everything before money.' 'Pay bills by return of post, keep right up to date with your income tax. Never have an overdraft. Pay off your mortgage. Arrange your affairs so that you don't have to worry about money – or sin for it. How? By doing without, dear boy.' He gave up, in this order, smoking, drinking, sex, meat and – a long time after – TV. He asked everybody to do the same. 'Appearing on TV is the most corrupting thing of all. And very addictive. It has done me inconceivable harm and caused me much unhappiness. Cut it out of your life if you can.' 'Never let them give you a chauffeur-driven car. It is an incomparable luxury. That's the trouble. You get used to it. Then in the end, they always take it away from you. That's when you really miss it. So never get used to it in the first place.' 'The great thing in life is, as you get older, to learn to do without things – especially luxuries you have come to regard as essentials. Then, if your income falls, you needn't worry. All you really need is a little freehold house. Once you've got that you are sitting pretty. You don't need any of the other things, really. Simple food, your old clothes. Books – that's all. And a good, loving wife – as I've got Kitty and you have Marigold.'

Malcolm had piercing blue eyes, a high complexion, plenty of white hair and a good constitution kept fit by long, daily walks. His voice was amazing, not easily described though easy to imitate, a curious mixture of south London, thirties upper-class, Haileybury drawl and BBC pastiche. It was the key to his enormous TV success. In the end he found the Catholic Church and shut off the din of the world, ending his days in a pretty cottage in Robertsbridge, Sussex, along a track through the fields and woods. A life which was both an epitome of our times and exemplary.

As a legacy, he left some funny TV documentaries, a brilliant piece of instant history, *The Thirties* (still well worth reading), two volumes of autobiography (of mixed interest), a book about the horror of Stalinism, *Winter in Moscow*, and an unpublished *roman à clef* about journalism, which the *Manchester Guardian* had suppressed by law. There are some scintillating drawings of him by Vicky.

Rupert Murdoch (b. 1931) was within half an hour of losing his entire empire in 1990 during the credit crisis. He had overborrowed. He was saved by a young woman from Citibank. A small bank in Philadelphia was calling in its loan, and its chairman would not relent until the girl got the Chairman of the Fed to persuade him. The experience should have shaken Murdoch, given him religion, or a conscience, but it did nothing of the sort. He became worse, morally. When I first knew him he was almost human. He came down to Iver to lunch and I took him for a walk in the woods, where he got himself covered in mud. Afterwards, he read the *Sunday Times*, which he owned, and got so angry he scrumpled it all up in a ball and thrust it in the fire, nearly setting the chimney ablaze. Thereafter he got more and more horrible until

I ceased to see him. Oddly, his mother, whom I met in Australia, and had dinner with, was charming, and a good, sensible woman, very much a lady. Murdoch was the outstanding example, in my acquaintance, of a man corrupted by power.

'Jock' Murray (1884–1967) gave excellent parties in the 1950s and 1960s in the big drawing room on the first floor of his famous publishing house in Albemarle Street. He published highly individual books which could only have come from Murray's. At the parties were usually to be found Osbert Lancaster, John Betjeman, Doris Langley Moore, the great Byron expert, Sir Philip Magnus, the biographer, and Rose Macaulay. Magnus had a bad case of halitosis. He would pivot himself around on his heels in slow circles, so you got a whiff of his poisonous breath at regular intervals, like the flashing of a lighthouse. Jock had a jolly German wife, and was in every respect the ideal publisher – sincere, honest, attentive, generous, perceptive and encouraging; a perfect gentleman always.

Colonel Nasser (1918–70), the Egyptian dictator, was a good example of the futility and stupidity of Arab nationalism. Everything he did failed. His two wars against Israel. His union of Arab states. His intervention in Aden and Yemen. He ruined the Nile with the High Dam and so changed the climate of Nubia for the worse. He impoverished Egypt. He turned Cairo from a beautiful and historic city into a giant grey-columned and dust-infested megalopolis of squatters and refugees. He began the persecution and expulsion of the Copts, educated Christians and descendants of the original Egyptians, and so the destruction of the country's culture, ancient and modern. He spent colossal sums of government money on weapons his troops did not know how to use, and at the same time underfunded the Cairo Museum, one of the world's greatest, which fell into decay. Yet he remained immensely popular to his dying day *because he made the right verbal noises.* Oddly enough, in one visit I made to Israel, I had a driver, a Jewish refugee from Iraq, who looked exactly like Nasser. But this man, though only a humble chauffeur, talked admirable sense about the Middle East. The physical resemblance of these two men was an ironic comment on the whole Jewish-Arab conflict – what nonsense it all was, and is! Nasser made only one remark worth recording: 'The trouble with Jews and Arabs is that they lack a common enemy.'

Jawaharlal Nehru (1889–1964) I met through Kingsley Martin, who treated him as if he were God. The Pandit, as he was known, took this as his due. He came from the highest possible Brahmin caste, and it is a tribute to the strength and resistance of the caste system that he never had any doubt about his superiority over other people. He moved in a kind of hermetically sealed bubble of arrogance and issued his commands with all the confidence of a *Roi Soleil*. In Indian crowds he often forced his way through by whacking people with the sturdy stick he always carried. He introduced me to his daughter, then rather shy, who afterwards became Prime Minister in her turn. In many ways he was a typical Harrovian, and once found himself at the annual sing-song, sitting next to Winston Churchill – they both loved these Harrow songs, and sang them lustily. He told me that he had dedicated his life to fighting imperialism. But he was an imperialist himself – in Kashmir, where he used armed force to impose Indian rule against the majority, in Goa, which he invaded and occupied, though most Goans liked rule by Portugal, and in the hill country, where he put down resistance by the tribesmen ruthlessly. He never lifted a finger to help the Tibetans, victims of Chinese imperialism. As an 'international statesman', he was shifty, inconsistent, mean-minded, mendacious and hypocritical. On the other hand, one had to remember he spent sixteen years in the gaols of British India. To some extent he had his revenge on the Raj by having an affair with the last Vicereine, Lady Mountbatten. He was good-looking, and had learned to handle well-born English ladies in his idle youth when he spent his time in 'watering places'– Cheltenham, Tunbridge Wells and Bath. Altogether an odd hybrid, waiting for a biographer of genius.

Harold Nicolson (1886–1968) was a small, quiet man who told admirable stories about the great, the famous and the notorious, in a low but clear voice. I often lunched with him at the Beefsteak in the 1950s, and heard them. He had a better repertoire of unpublished anecdotes than anyone else. His *Diaries* are not first-class, though readable, because they are self-conscious: he wrote them with a view to eventual publication, as a legacy for his heirs. Some of his anecdotage survives in the trio of volumes he wrote about diplomacy, especially *Peacemaking* and *Curzon: The Last Phase*. Indeed, he revelled in Curzoniana, teaching the chambermaids at the Paris embassy how to do their job, and how, when Foreign Secretary, he was discovered sweeping the staircarpet with a dustpan just before a big reception. How he counted the blooms sent by the posh flower shop in Berkeley Square to make sure he was getting good value. And how he arranged a posthumous frisson for his second wife, who had more or less left him. After his death she visited the family tomb at Keddleston and found his coffin on its slab. Next to it was his first wife's coffin, much decayed. Then, a white patch on another slab caught her eye. It was a small card. Written on it, in Curzon's unmistakable handwriting, were the words 'Reserved for the second Lady Curzon'.

Nicolson told me many stories about Churchill. One went: 'During the First War, Churchill worked closely at one time with

Sir Basil Thompson [1861–1939], a former colonial official and prison governor, who was Assistant Commissioner at Scotland Yard from 1913, in charge of security. He dealt with suffragettes, Irish rebels and, from 1914, German agents. From 1919 he was Director of Intelligence. He was highly successful at getting arrests, which he often made personally, and which supplied him with material for his riveting book, *Queer People* (1922). Sometime in the thirties [Nicolson was vague about the exact date] Sir Basil was arrested for indecent exposure in Hyde Park. His friends went to Churchill to see if there was anything he could do to get the case quashed, Sir Basil being hitherto of unblemished record and the son of the Archbishop of York. Churchill, vastly intrigued, questioned them closely about the circumstances, and finally summed up: "Sir Basil Thompson, a distinguished public servant, aged seventy-five, veering on seventy-six, divesting himself of his clothes in Hyde Park, at eight o'clock on a January evening, temperature well below zero. *Makes yer proud to be an Englishman!*" He refused to intervene, however, and Thompson was duly fined the going rate. £5.'

David Niven (1910–83), a notorious success with women, was once asked by Prince Rainier: 'Who gave you the best blow job?' Niven replied: 'Oh, there's absolutely no doubt about that', and was starting to reply, 'It was Grace—' when he suddenly realised who he was talking to and finished, 'Gracie Fields'. Ken Tynan, who said he had it from Niven himself, told the story at a party in his Mount Street flat. Noël Coward added: 'And it's absolutely true. It was a speciality of Rochdale girls. They called it the Gradely Gobble.'

Richard Nixon (1913–94) led a busy life after his enforced resignation. He lived mainly in New York as he said it was 'the fast-track city'. He wrote books and kept in touch with people all over the world. His detailed knowledge of American domestic politics always was, and remained, exhaustive. He taught me a great deal. In return, I taught him history. He greatly admired my *Modern Times*, and often wrote to me. He used to send us a Christmas garland to hang on the front door every year. I have rarely met a man so anxious, right to the end, to acquire knowledge. He was much more interested in learning than in talking about himself. He lacked the ego obsession characteristic of the professional politician. I last saw him on a famous visit he paid to the Tory Philosophy Group, held at Jonathan Aitken's house in Westminster. Nixon was over eighty. He had just returned from a 'working holiday' in Moscow, where he had met all the leading figures in the disintegrating Soviet regime. The talk he gave us, without notes, revealed an astonishing grasp of what was going on, and who was doing what. Merely to get the names right would have taxed most people – Nixon then answered questions for forty minutes. It was a virtuoso perform-ance by a tireless and penetrating old man which held us spell-bound. Three weeks later he was dead.

Joshua Nkomo (1917–99), leader of the African nationalists in what was then Southern Rhodesia, was under house arrest when I went to see him in a remote place near the Bechuanaland border. I was allowed to take a TV crew with me, which indi-cates that the white supremacist regime was not as severe as its enemies claimed. I was told (1) to give him a bottle of Johnnie Walker Red Label whisky, (2) but not until after the interview was over. Good advice. His 'house' was just a two-room hut, very primitive. He struck me as a delightful man, too good for African politics. After the interview, I presented him with the Scotch. He was very grateful but immediately retired to the inner room from which a glug-glug-glug noise could be heard.

When he reappeared, his eyes were going round in circles. So we left to return to Bulawayo.

Sir Sidney Nolan (1917–92), Australian painter, was a *doppelgänger* to me in the mid-1980s. I was in Australia to get material for a little book on Consolidated Gold Fields to celebrate its centenary. He had been asked by the company to paint pictures of its properties. He and I visited them all. At one mine, the manager arranged the date of Nolan's visit but at the last minute there was a sudden crisis and he was called away. He forgot to tell the assistant manager. The latter was rung, on the day, by the receptionist. 'There's a bloke here called Sid Nolan. Says he's a painter. What do I do with him?' The assistant manager, a busy man, replied: 'Use your head, girl. He says he's a painter. *Send him to the paint shop.*'

The Duke of Norfolk (1908–75) I met while doing an abortive TV series on stately homes. He was the 16th Duke and his names were Bernard Marmaduke. Duke Bernard knew more about royal ceremony than any other person in history. He ran the Coronation in 1953. He showed me round Arundel Castle. He was short, strawberry-faced, peppery, ignorant about most things and obstinate. I asked him: 'Duke, if you had not been a duke, what would you like to have been?' He looked at me in bewilderment. 'But I've always been a duke. It's never occurred to me to be anything else.' Then he reflected. 'I think I would like to have been a butler. I know a lot about butling.'

Nuri as-Said (1888–1958) was the last effective and sensible ruler of Iraq. He ran the country in the late 1940s and 1950s, with British help. When I first visited Iraq in 1951, as the guest of the RAF, who flew me from Gibraltar to their big base at Habbaniya, in the Kurdish country, things were still going well. Nuri had set up the Iraq Development Board, which used the growing oil revenues for constructive purposes, under a long-term plan. Roads were being built, electricity brought to the small towns and villages, water pipes laid down, schools and hospitals set up, and industry created. If these activities had continued, Iraq would now, half a century later, be among the richest countries in the world. But by 1957, when I went to Iraq again, as a journalist, the scene was darkening. I saw Nuri, who told me: 'Iraq is not a real country. It is an artificial creation, put together in a hurry by the British to meet an emergency. You cannot run it by constitutional means, kind words and English-style laws. You need to be tough and resolute. But the British will not allow me to do what is necessary, and the result will be disastrous.' But he would not let me quote him. Everything he said was strictly off the record. I thought he was being far too pessimistic. So did our embassy. But he was right. A year later, he, the King, most senior members of the Royal Family, his cabinet and a large number of his followers were all murdered. That was the beginning of Iraq's long and endless *via dolorosa*, which continues.

Julius Nyerere (1922–94) was the first of the great black African humbugs. He was an intellectual, had translated Shakespeare, etc., and appealed strongly to Western liberals who all said how marvellous he was. Hence Tanzania, under his long rule, received more aid per capita than any other territory in the world. It was all wasted and when he died the country was a total wreck and probably the poorest in Africa (next to Liberia and Sierra Leone, of course). He said to me: 'In the long run it will be the Africans who will teach the whites about statesmanship.'

Sir Maurice Oldfield (1915–81). When I was editor of the *New Statesman* I was given a briefing by this man on two occasions.

I did not know his exact position but it was clear he was a spook. In fact he was then the Deputy to 'C', head of the Secret Intelligence Service. We had a mutual friend in my Oxford tutor A. J. P. Taylor. Oldfield was the son of a Derbyshire farmer, came from an enormous family and spoke with a slight Derbyshire accent. His face looked like a turnip but he was a clever man (his speciality was thirteenth-century English history and he could have become a top academic had he chosen). I recall his saying: 'Never trust the Foreign Office. They have a culture of betrayal.' Oldfield expected to be made head of the SIS in 1968. Instead Harold Wilson, advised by Colonel Wigg, appointed a Foreign Office man called Sir John Rennie. This turned out to be a grand and uncomfortable error, culminating in 1973 in a scandal when one of Rennie's sons was arrested for alleged involvement in the importation of heroin from Hong Kong and the German magazine *Stern*, publicising the story, revealed his position. He had to retire the next year. Oldfield was head of the SIS 1973–8, and afterwards Mrs Thatcher gave him a secret job in Ulster. But he had to be pulled out in 1980 after he had a homosexual affair. He admitted he had lied about being queer, and his positive vetting certificate was withdrawn after prolonged interrogation. He died the next year under a cloud. AJP called him 'The Basil Thompson of our time'.

Charles Onions (1873–1965), bibliographer and editor of the enormous *Oxford English Dictionary*, was librarian of Magdalen when I was up. He told me that he came from a family of bellows-makers and that his mother's family were locksmiths: 'I am the first not to make my living by using my hands.' He said he had 'great satisfaction' in writing the last entry in the *OED*, 'Zyxt', an old Kentish world. 'What does it mean, Dr Onions?' 'I've forgotten. Oh no I haven't. It's part of the verb "to see".' 'I see, Dr Onions.'

'Ha Ha!' He had at least ten children. He was known, mysteriously, as 'Champagne Charlie'. When I finished Final Honours Schools, I took my detested copy of Stubbs's *Charters* and burned it on the library steps. In a minute Onions came hurrying out, closely followed by his crony, old Tolkien (or 'Young Tolkien' as Onions, who was nearly eighty, called him). He said: 'I say, stop that. Stop that! Mustn't burn library books.' 'It's not a library book, Dr Onions. It's my own copy of Stubbs.' 'Oh, that's all right, then.' Tolkien said: 'I'm all in favour of a bit of book-burning myself. Far too many books in the world.' In those days he was unknown outside academia. Since then one hundred million copies of his fairy stories have been sold round the world.

George Orwell (1903–50) I never met, though I might have done, and I often kick myself for not having arranged to talk with one of the most significant figures of the twentieth century so that I could make up my own mind about him. I discussed him often with Kingsley Martin, who remained uneasy in his mind about his refusal to publish Orwell's article on Spain, exposing what the Stalinists were doing in Barcelona. Malcolm Muggeridge told me that Orwell detested Martin, much more than he hated Victor Gollancz, who had likewise refused to publish Orwell's anti-Stalinist *Homage to Catalonia*, snapped up by Fred Warburg of Secker & Warburg. Orwell said that Martin was 'corrupt', and looked it, and that he could not bear to see his face or be in the same room with him. I see what he meant about Martin's face, but Orwell's judgement is unfair. He could be harsh. There was a policeman and a severe judge inside Orwell, as well as many other archetypes.

Orwell was the finest essayist of his generation, the last of the great English essayists. He was not equipped to be a novelist, though he could write fictional parables, like *Animal Farm* and

Nineteen Eighty-Four. He was severely inhibited, 'the most inhibited man I ever came across', his second wife, Sonia, told me. This comes out in his letters: he could not unbend and adopt a conversational style. Evelyn Waugh, who admired him greatly as a writer, said to me that Orwell had the makings of a saint but could not have acquired supernatural grace to become one without joining the Catholic Church, and there was never any chance of that: he simply could not believe. Malcolm Muggeridge thought Orwell might have become a saint even so, but this was more a wish than an informed prophecy. What Orwell did achieve was to create himself as a credible moralist in an age of shallow, false or positively evil moral systems – a man who weighed the implication of what he wrote on the scales of divine justice. Seeing it all *sub specie aeternitatis*, he was a serious writer, in a way no one else of his generation contrived to become. Hence young writers can learn from him, not just in a literary sense but in a moral sense – what to strive for and what to avoid. I discussed him with Cyril Connolly, who had been at prep school and Eton with Orwell. He said: 'I could not be at ease in his presence. He made me feel guilty of an unknown crime. Just guilty, in general. Like a Kafka character.' 'Well, Cyril, wasn't it true, weren't you guilty?' 'Of course. But who was Orwell to bring the unspoken charge? He wasn't God, was he? Or perhaps he was – reincarnated again. He was the nearest thing to God we came across in those days.'

Inhibited as he was, Orwell tended to use, in letters and speeches, the clichés of the public schoolboy of the 1920s. Stephen Spender told me that, in conversation with Orwell, the subject of his first wife came up. Orwell said: 'She wasn't a bad old stick.' When he told this to Mary McCarthy, who had no understanding of obsolete male English expressions – to call his wife 'not a bad old stick' was as near to an expression of love a man like Orwell could articulate – she exploded in anger. 'My God! What a horrible thing to say about her! I always had a suspicion that Orwell was at heart a fascist. Saying *that* proves it!'

John Osborne (1929–94) was a playwright with a touch of genius. He could create great theatrical moments. But his work was marred by megalomaniac arrogance and an unwillingness to accept criticism, however constructive or helpful. He mellowed as he got older, especially after he married his last wife. I liked to hear him talk: good imitations of actors and well-told anecdotes about theatrical incidents.

He came well out of an episode at Buckingham Palace in July 1994. The Queen gave a big every party for more than eight hundred people, of all sorts. All the public rooms at the Palace were open and the guests could wander at will. The band of the Irish Guards played. Good champagne and eats. The librarian had put interesting MSS and drawings into showcases. The Queen tried to have a word with everyone, and many other members of her family were on parade. There were little tables where you could sit and talk and eat, and around one I found myself part of a group of playwrights – Arnold Wesker, Harold Pinter, John Osborne and one or two younger ones. Here is my verbatim recollection of what transpired, written down the following day:

Osborne (in an expansive mood): Is not this delightful? On my way here I said to Helen, 'We are in for a dreadful evening. It will be a bore. We shall know nobody. We must contrive to leave the room as soon as we can politely do so.' And now, here we are, and I am enjoying myself hugely. Music, wine, sitting round this table. They say that writers are quarrelsome, but here we are, on the best of terms, just having a good time. So God Bless the Queen, say I.

Me (aside): This will not last.

Wesker: I agree with John. However, might I take this opportunity, Harold, to remind you – you can scarcely have forgotten – that on the last occasion you dined at my house, you ruined the evening for us all by being gratuitously rude to the principal guest?

(Horrid pause.)

Pinter (taken aback, being more accustomed to opening the offensive than being on the receiving end of an unprovoked salvo): Have a care what you say, Wesker.

Wesker: Ruined the evening for all of us. Moreover, your motive for going for my friend was simply that he was rich, and an American.

Me (hastily and not entirely accurately): No, Arnold, I don't feel that what you say can be entirely right. I have known Harold for many years and I can't say I have ever known him to be rude to anyone. Indeed, I'd go so far as to claim that he is constitutionally incapable of being rude.

Pinter (triumphantly): There you are! Paul is quite right. I am constitutionally incapable of being rude. So shut your f— gob, Wesker!

Osborne: There, there, children – enough of this. We can't have the Queen coming round and discovering us at odds. [Imitating Queen's voice] I thought I'd find my playwrights like a little nest of singing birds so what is all this squawking? Stop it at once *or I'll have you thrown to the corgis.*

Osborne's end was tragic-comic. He had a lot of elaborate work done on his teeth – implants, etc. It cost £20,000. Shortly afterwards he was taken ill, fatally, as it turned out. His last words were bitter: 'What a bloody waste of money!'

Camilla Parker Bowles (b. 1947) had many merits but the chief of them was that she was funny. Not to all, of course. Princess Diana said to me: 'I hear she has people in fits. But she was no joke to me.' Her ability to make people laugh was her prime hold over Prince Charles. She was thus in the long tradition of funny royal mistresses, which include Anne Boleyn, Nell Gwyn, Georgina, Lady Jersey, 'Skittles', Lillie Langtry and Lady Porchester. After she married Prince Charles and became Duchess of Cornwall she made fewer jokes, said a friend, and Camilla added: 'Because the Cornish have no sense of humour.' But this itself might have been a joke. Her sister, known as 'the Sergeant Major', was even funnier.

Pope Paul VI (1897–1978) was known to his predecessor, John XXIII, as 'Hamleto' because he was indecisive. In fact, during his long pontificate he took a number of foolish decisions, or perhaps was persuaded into them by liberal progressives in the Vatican, which have plagued the Church ever since, though some were reversed by the Polish and German popes. I did not like the Montini Pope. He had an unattractive face, with dark, uninteresting eyes overshadowed by black eyebrows: a face which did not reflect the light. His movements were fidgety and he had a habit of looking over his shoulder. He introduced a lot of petty new rules, many of which made no sense. He hated splendour, tradition, colour, the beauty of ancient ritual and vestments. He forbade the cardinals from wearing their magnificent red hats, with their fascinating and complex tassels – a form of apparel which went back to the formation of the College of Cardinals in the twelfth century. Why such destruction of a surely harmless splash of colour? It was during his pontificate that many orders of nuns were told to 'modernise' their habits, so wonderfully picturesque garments, going back to the Middle Ages in most cases, were abandoned and replaced by pointless and characterless plain dresses or skirts and blouses which had no historical significance. In my youth the streets of Rome were made vivid and poignant by these holy figures in their enormous headdresses and sweeping skirts. Now, nobody takes any notice of the nuns. There are far fewer of them anyway, for the 'reforms' introduced by Paul VI and his henchmen discouraged recruitment. Alas, alas! He was one of those people who are always, from infancy, judged to be 'delicate', and who go on living for ever, niggling at their plain food, refusing wine, taking no strenuous exercise, valetudinarians who dose themselves endlessly and cling to life with tiresome tenacity. No doubt he was a good man in his fashion – I never heard of anything wicked he did – but he lit no candles in the hearts of ordinary men and women, as a true pope should.

Pablo Picasso (1881–1973) was probably the most evil man I ever actually came across. He told me he was not a genius but a clown. I was told, however, 'If you publish that he will sue you.' While he was painting *Guernica*, two of his women, whom he had deliberately set upon each other, were fighting on the floor of his studio, to his delight. He was the richest painter who ever lived, and did more harm to art than all the Goths and Vandals, the Puritan iconoclasts and the totalitarian thugs combined.

General Augusto Pinochet (1915–2006) was perhaps the single most misjudged figure of the twentieth century. He was invited to take power by an overwhelming vote of both houses of the Chilean Congress, at a time when the country was being invaded by international revolutionaries, 20,000 of whom had already arrived, when armed gangs were taking over towns and factories, and the inflation rate, the world's highest, was running at 20,000 per cent a year. He shot all the gunmen he could get his hands on, and then turned the country round. Instead of becoming another Cuba, over nineteen years Chile became easily the richest country in Latin America – and has remained so. The changes in Chilean agriculture are particularly remarkable and are reflected in the country's worldwide food exports. But, of course, by preventing the Communisation of Chile, Pinochet made himself a marked man in Moscow. His demonisation was the last major triumph of the Soviet propaganda machine before the Soviet Union itself collapsed in ruin. I doubt if the lies so successfully spread about Pinochet will ever be corrected.

Pinochet gave a tea party for Marigold and myself at the Ministry of Defence in Santiago. He had then retired from the presidency but was still in charge of the armed forces. Tea is the most important entertaining meal in Chile, and is like high tea in the north of England. Pinochet was in a spotless white uniform, and had invited some of his young officers to meet us – they wore smart blue. The Chileans are the most well-mannered, civilised, educated and culture-conscious of the Latin Americans, and are wonderful hosts. But the repast had the unexpected Chilean touch. It began with peach ice cream, went on to croque-monsieur, then to seafood salad, and if they had suddenly brought in a steaming-hot steak and kidney pudding I would not have been surprised. We all had a jolly time and Pinochet and Marigold got on well, discussing terrorism (she was then running the British-Irish Association and was a leading expert on the IRA).

Pinochet gave Britain invaluable help in the Falklands War, help which saved hundreds, perhaps thousands, of British lives. That makes our treatment of him when a Spanish magistrate served a writ on him in London all the more shameful. I complained bitterly to Tony Blair, then Prime Minister, but he said it was not his province, but Jack Straw's, as Home Secretary – and, anyway, it was a judicial not a political matter. This was manifestly untrue, as was later admitted, when Pinochet was allowed to go back to Chile. Nothing has ever made me more ashamed of my country.

George Plimpton (1927–2007) I first met in Paris in 1952, when he was putting together the enterprise which became the *Paris Review*. He was still in charge of the magazine more than fifty years later, when I last saw him, on Lake Como, at a literary gathering in 2006. The great feature of the *Paris Review* was long interviews with writers about their work, a subject which fascinated George (something of a frustrated creative writer himself). He eventually published seven volumes of these interviews, most of which he conducted himself – a valuable source for the study of twentieth-century literature. The survival of the *Paris Review* for more than half a century is almost unique in such publications, and was entirely due to George's persistence and courage (helped financially, in its later stages, by Drue Heinz, whose enthusiastic backing George secured). George as a person was almost as keen on sport as on literature, and wrote about it with skill and success. He also had a passionate interest in fireworks. But the *Paris Review* was his lifework. He had five main characteristics. (1) Enormous charm, of the particular kind possessed by East Coast WASPs, of assured background, ample means and unshakable self-confidence. He could usually bed any woman he set a mind to, without ever arousing envy in men. (2) Total lack of malice, so rare among those who spend their lives among writers. (3) The manners of an old-fashioned, upper-class Yankee gent. (4) Single-mindedness in running his paper. Nothing – sex, politics, society, travel, the theatre, even sport – was ever allowed to divert his energies and attention from getting the next issue out. (5) A real concern for writers, however selfish, disgusting, ungrateful, messy and idle they might be. He was a hard-working and patient guardian angel to them, and I did not envy him his life of drudgery and self-sacrifice in the cause. However, many years of successful bonking was his consolation.

James Pope-Hennessy (1916–74) came to a fearful end after a lifetime of self-abuse. When I first knew him he was almost terrifyingly good-looking, in a sinister, ninetyish way. His brother, John P-H, was the Great Panjandrum of art scholarship, ran the V&A and was known to scared acolytes as 'the Pope'. Their mother, 'the Dame', was Una Pope-Hennessy, author of the first modern life of Dickens. 'Jamesie' was clever and his life of Queen Mary is the best of royal biographies. But he took drugs, drank a lot, and regularly consorted with rough trade. Worse, he invited them back to his house. They read in a gossip column that he had negotiated a big advance for his next book, assumed it had already been handed over, in cash, and stashed at his house, off Holland Park Avenue. So they jumped him and tortured him to death in a vain attempt to get him to tell where his non-existent cash was hidden. A warning to all promiscuous homosexuals – not heeded, of course. My best memory of Jamesie is his saying, *à propos* of his 'cruising ground', 'A bum in the hand is worth two in Shepherd's Bush.'

Karl Popper (1902–94) was one of the most influential political philosophers of the twentieth century. His book *The Open Society and Its Enemies* was the most effective frontal attack on the whole philosophy of totalitarian dictatorship, tracing it back to its Greek roots. I read it in my second year at Oxford when it was new, then reread it in the seventies, and this time it really went home. It helped to shape my twentieth-century history, *Modern Times*. After this appeared, out of the blue, Popper wrote me a fan letter, the most gratifying I ever received. He was a difficult man. He was the hero, or anti-hero, of the famous clash with Wittgenstein which occurred in King's College, Cambridge, in 1946, an incident which lasted only ten minutes but was the subject of a book, *Wittgenstein's Poker* (2001). What actually happened – whether Wittgenstein in fact threatened Popper with a poker – is a matter of dispute. All the evidence about the occasion is conflicting. Usually Witters got away with his tantrums, but this time he was up against a master tantrumo. Later Popper wrote an essay about Wittgenstein's *Tractatus Logico-Philosophicus*, demolishing it, to his satisfaction anyway. He said to me: 'Don't trouble yourself about him and his book. It is not worth the effort. You will find there is nothing at the end.' Me: 'I believe you are right. But the effort is exhilarating.' 'Well: there is something in that.' Popper's book on scientific method also had a profound influence on me, not just in my understanding of science but in my whole approach to the question of proof. I learned from him that in taking up a position it is vital to look for the evidence against it with the same care and enthusiasm you bring to totting up the evidence for it. And I have always tried to do that. But it requires a great effort of will. Popper lived at Penn. I invited him to lunch. 'Where will we have lunch?' 'In the dining room, of course.' 'Can you give me an absolute guarantee that no one has smoked in that room for at least six weeks?' 'Well, no. I don't think I can.' 'Then I'm not coming.'

Anthony Powell (1905–2000) had a military bearing and might have become a regular officer like his father. He lived in an early nineteenth-century house in Somerset which had once belonged to a mill-owner. It was imposing and might have been agreeable but was musty, dusty and dead – nothing had been moved or changed for years. He and his wife, Lady Violet (Frank Longford's sister), were both snobs, though harmless ones. More seriously, they were both genealogical fanatics, and would spend hours working out 'connections'. His genealogical mania was more boring than hers because it had a tiresome Welsh dimension. I used to think Tony was merely 'Waugh-and-water', but gradually became fond of his novels and saw the point. Malcolm Muggeridge, when editor of *Punch*, made it a lively journal people actually read, and appointed Tony literary editor, a job he enjoyed. Then Mugg went and his successor, a self-important nonentity (forget his name), sacked Tony. I spent that evening with him, trying to give him comfort; he became very drunk and sorry for himself. But he got over it and was really better off living deep in the countryside and receiving visitors. There was a gentle streak of malice in him. The last time we went down there (Marigold knew them much better than I did), I told him we enjoyed living in Notting Hill, as so many others did. 'It's nice being in walking distance of your friends.' 'And enemies?' he asked.

J. B. Priestley (1894–1984) was the best essayist and writer of 'middles' of his day. When I took over as editor of the *New Statesman* in 1964 I found he had become estranged, owing to a misunderstanding with my predecessor, John Freeman – no doubt Priestley's fault. For he was a paranoid prima donna, always looking for insults where none was intended. I wanted him to write for the paper again, and I remembered my mother's dictum, 'Yorkshiremen love flattery. Lay it on as thick as you like.' So I wrote him the most effusive letter I have ever composed, and it worked. His reply began: 'I have always thought you showed unusual powers of perception.' He not only wrote for me, but an annual visit to Kissing Tree House, his big mansion near Stratford, also became a fixture for Marigold and myself. He lived there in some style, with an excellent cook and a wine cellar conducted by his wife, Jacquetta Hawkes, the archaeologist, who had learned her vintages from her one-time lover. Priestley ran his little bar concealed by false bookshelves in his big library, in which he mixed strong martinis and pink gins. Jacquetta was very much the lady and changed her clothes at least four times a day: morning outfit, smart lunch garb, tea-gown and evening dress. She had been divorced by Professor Hawkes, who cited Jack as co-respondent. In those days the press was forbidden by law to publish the evidence in divorce cases. All they could do was print the judge's final summing up and his verdict. This gave great power to the judges, who could assassinate one of the parties if they chose to abuse their power. This happened to Jack. The judge said, among many other hostile remarks: 'I am told the co-respondent is a writer of fiction. And having listened to his evidence, I can well believe it.' Thereafter, Jack hated judges and often inveighed against them.

Jack told me a lot about himself and his career, much of which I have put in my entry on him in the *DNB*. His novel *The Good Companions* was one of the great bestsellers of the twentieth century. It came out in July 1929, just before the Wall Street Crash. Heinemann were daunted by its length, over 250,000 words, and thought themselves daring to print a first run of 10,000 copies. By the end of August, 7,500 had gone. But the gathering gloom pushed its sales miraculously. By Christmas, the publishers were delivering 5,000 copies a day by van to bookshops. He was also, in the thirties, a highly successful playwright, at one time having three hits running concurrently. 'I averaged £30,000 a year from my plays in the 1930s,' he told me. 'That was real money then, with income tax only two bob in the pound.' He loved to play croquet on his excellent lawn, and, in between strokes, to tell me exactly how much money he had handed over in income tax. He spoke pure English very well but with a marked Yorkshire accent he never lost. His voice was low and rumbling and he was a superlative broadcaster. In 1940 his Sunday evening talks, beautifully composed verbal essays, rivalled Churchill's in popularity. He had served through all the horrors of the Western Front in the First World War but never talked about it. However, once, when we were having breakfast, Jack in a brown woolly dressing gown, he offered Marigold a slice of bread to accompany the vast array of fried and scrambled and poached eggs, bacon and kippers, kidneys and mushrooms, on the sideboard. She said: 'Oh, I never eat bread.' He pondered this enormity and said: 'I can see you never served in the trenches.'

His publishers used to give dinners on his birthday from eighty onwards. I often spoke for a few minutes and gave the toast on these occasions. I used to sit next to the delectable Peggy Ashcroft, and she would hold my hand under the table. He died shortly before his ninetieth birthday, saying: 'I have had good value from my annuities, but I resent still having to pay income tax at my age.' He was proud of his origins. He showed me a photo, taken on the steps of Kissing Tree House, of himself, Harold Wilson, Graham Sutherland, Henry Moore and Len Hutton. 'Look at that. What talent, eh? And all Yorkshiremen.'

V. S. Pritchett (1900–97), unlike other important critics of his day, Raymond Mortimer, Edmund Wilson, Desmond MacCarthy, Cyril Connolly, Philip Toynbee and Lionel Trilling, was of humble origins and never went to university. But in some ways he was the best of the lot, with a huge range born of hard-grind reading. Unlike the others, he understood the lower middle-class and the industrious poor, his knowledge being reflected in his often brilliant short stories. He knew parts of Europe as well, having – again, unlike the other critics – tramped it. He walked all over hot, dusty Spain, something even Hilaire Belloc found beyond him.

In the thirties he did the main literary feature in the *New Statesman*, 'Books in General', for a salary of four pounds a week. In the winter of 1939–40, with a growing family, he found he could not manage and screwed up his courage to ask Kingsley Martin for a raise. 'God heavens, VS, don't you know there's a war on?' 'Well, yes, Kingsley, I do, but – .' 'And thanks to wise government regulations, the price of everything is controlled to prevent profiteering. So you can't complain about rising prices.' And so on. Eventually, after much argument, which Pritchett found almost unbearably painful, Kingsley said: 'Very well, then, if you insist. You may have – another pound a week.'

Pritchett, because of his background and training – his first job had been in the leather business – was totally without the bohemian instincts of the literary class. He always paid his bills promptly, never borrowed money, drank little, rose early and worked long, regular hours. In old age, he said to me: 'People say take it easy, VS. But every morning, I have a compulsion to drag myself, groaning and cursing, up the steep stairs to my study at the top of the house, and start putting yet more words on paper.' He lived into his nineties, and wrote to the end.

The Queen Mother (1900–2002), widow of George VI, always known in royal circles as Queen Elizabeth to distinguish her from the sovereign, known as the Queen. She spent much of her childhood in Glamis Castle, where King Duncan was murdered by Macbeth, and there was a steely side to her. She had married the Duke of York with reluctance, knowing his fragility, but became fiercely loyal to him, and when Edward VIII's obsession with Wallis Simpson made her husband King she thought it would be the death of him, and so turned on the Windsors, persecuting them for the rest of their lives – and beyond. But she never tried to stop George VI from smoking, which was actually the weakness that killed him. She came from a different age: there were eight courses at her wedding breakfast. She kept up lavish standards at her various houses as a widow, never bothering about money. I was given a vignette by one of her old chums: sitting up in bed watching racing on the telly, a box of Black Magic chocs in one hand, a drink in the other. Her male staff tended to be homosexuals, and she was said to have phoned down, after a long day: 'If any of you old queens can spare the time, there's another old queen up here who is still waiting for her large gin and tonic.' She occupied Clarence House, off the Mall; Royal Lodge in Windsor Great Park; Birkhall, near Balmoral; and the Castle of Mey, overlooking the Pentland Firth. She formed a collection of modernish pictures, which I have seen. Not bad, but too many pipers, as you'd expect.

Kathleen Raine (1908–2003) occasionally published poems in the *New Statesman*. I liked her. But you could see, from miles away, that she was trouble. She had an affair with Gavin Maxwell, who eventually ended it. In revenge, she solemnly cursed him from under a rowan tree, as used to be done by witches. In due course his otter died, his boyfriend left him and his house burned down.

Simon Raven (1927–2001). I once was with him on a Greek cruise. Despite the heat (it was May) he wore uncompromisingly English clothes of his class and age: a Harris tweed jacket, cavalry twill trousers, a club tie (Leander), a waistcoat with brass buttons and brown brogue shoes. He had a panama hat. He sweated and he puffed and panted but he never took his jacket off. He followed the guided tours with their glib academic lecturers (this was a prim Hellenic cruise) most assiduously, and he usually had a relevant volume, in the original Greek, in his hand – Pausanias, or Herodotus. He believed in the pagan gods. His face was red, with purple blotches. He drank a lot of ouzo, and retsina, he was amiable but never intimate, detached, *sui generis*. I found him repellent, physically, and cannot believe that he slept with as many men and women, boys and girls, as he claimed. His novels are racy, libidinous, striking in a crude way, but lack depth of character; the people in them are types, at best archetypes. Seeing him on this cruise, I would not have given him six more months to live. In fact he managed ten years. He owed his survival to his publisher, Anthony Blond, who paid him a regular stipend *not* to live in London. He chose Deal in Kent. Finally he entered Sutton's Hospital, an almshouse for indigent old gentlemen in Charterhouse Square. There is a good biography of him, *The Captain*. I remember him for one of his *obiter dicta*, which he pronounced to me in a low but solemn voice: 'Never fornicate with a girl and a youth on successive days. It is an affront to the gods.'

John Raymond (1922–65) was assistant literary editor of the *New Statesman* and a rising critic when I first knew him. He was one of the best-read men I have ever met and had a fine book collection at his ground-floor flat, 57 Redcliffe Gardens. He was at Westminster, but was forced to leave at the age of sixteen in 1939. Both his parents were actors. His father, Cyril Raymond, was a top-rank supporting actor, never out of a part. His mother, Iris Hoey, was a West End star in the twenties, but somehow fizzled out. When war broke out in September 1939, the government, terrified of mass air raids, shut down all the theatres, and both John's parents were suddenly unemployed. As they, like most actors, never saved a penny, John was removed from Westminster and put to work as a trainee manager at Sainsbury's. All prospect of his going to Oxford suddenly vanished. John never got over this blow. A huge sense of inferiority festered within him, and this was one factor which led to drinking. Another was doubts about his sexuality. Though he had girlfriends, he also went cruising every evening in Soho. He taught me a great deal about literature, introduced me to many writers, put me on to countless books and took me to literary parties when I first came to London. He and Maurice Richardson ensured that one or the other got a card for every publisher's party, and took each other – and me. So in a short time, in 1955–6, I met everyone in 'the circuit'.

He was always up early. Occasionally I used to spend the night in his spare room, and heard him, from six onwards, drilling his toy soldiers. He had about a thousand, some of them real collector's pieces. Many had names, and he would talk to them. 'Now then, Ainsworth – late on parade again? When are you going to take soldiering seriously?' 'Mr Mountain!' 'Sir.' 'Your cap badge is crooked. You are a disgrace to the Royal Fusiliers!' 'Sorry, Captain Stanley!' 'Well, Sergeant, any defaulters?' 'No, Major Pearson. But Private Opie 'as done a bunk.' 'Done a bunk, Sergeant?' 'Yes, sir. Scarpered. Vamooshed. Gorn absent wivvout leave, Major.' 'Oh, that's bad, Sergeant. Woman trouble, I suppose?' 'Wivvout any bleedin' doubt, sir' 'Oh dear!', etc. Sometimes they had early morning mock battles, for John had large numbers of Prussian, Napoleonic and Indian soldiers, as well as units from the Red Army, the French Foreign Legion, the Kuomintang and Japan. He had a military band in Grenadier uniform, and a complete field hospital and a large engineering section, with elaborate equipment. Some of his soldiers he had had from the age of ten, but he was continually buying new ones.

John often went to the theatre, and occasionally wrote notices. He knew all the famous actors and sometimes took me to tea with old stagers like Athene Seyler and Margaret Rutherford. He belonged to half a dozen clubs, including the Reform, the St James, the Savile, the RAC and Brooks's. He got me into the Beefsteak. He also belonged to countless afternoon drinking clubs, such as the Colony, the Mountjoy and the Albion. He was an habitué of the Caves, the French and Fitzrovia, as well as many Chelsea places such as the Ring of Bells. He worked very hard from early in the morning, but from lunchtime on he was in and out of pubs, clubs and theatres. He went to see *The Boy Friend* fifteen times, and was asked to leave for joining in the choruses. He liked the cinema, especially French gangster movies such as *Du rififi chez les hommes* and *Touchez pas au grisbi*. He sat in the Curzon cinema with a big cigar in one hand and an Eskimo Gervais in the other, alternately puffing and licking. He and I used to go on Friday lunchtime expeditions to Brighton, which we began with a bottle of champagne at Henekey's, progressed to a fish lunch at English's, a game of clock golf on the Front, then a tour of the second-hand bookshops, of which Brighton then had ten. Back by a late train, dining on board the Pullman. We also went for weekends in Paris, staying at the Louisianne and going the rounds of the cafés and dens. I then still had many friends and naughty girls in the city. John was superb company. His conversation was witty and rich, his anecdotage enormous but never oppressive, and he was immensely tolerant. He looked a bit like Winston Churchill, a bit like a large baby. But his drinking slowly but inexorably increased, and his character changed, from amiability mounting into rage. After I married and had children I saw less of him, and there came a point when I found his company distasteful and dropped him. He lost his job, his work fell off and his last years were sad. He was heartbroken when all his toy soldiers were stolen. He died of kidney failure, complicated by drink. He published two volumes of collected literary criticism, both worth reading, *England's on the Anvil* and – I forget.

Ronald Reagan (1911–2000) impressed me the first time I saw him, when he was Governor of California. He impressed me again, as a campaigner, when I watched him early in 1980, months before he got the Republican nomination. I wrote Margaret Thatcher a long letter from Washington (where I was a visiting professor at the AEI) saying he was sure to get the nomination and likely to win the presidency by a handsome majority, and that she ought to make her mark with him now, as they had a lot in common and could make a formidable partnership. She wrote back: 'This is not at all the line I am getting from the embassy. They say Reagan has not a hope and that Carter will be re-elected easily. But,' she added, 'I like what you tell me and will do what you say.' In fact they formed one of the great Anglo-American partnerships in history. They had in common (1) Very clear views on two or three central points of policy, which were right and which they pushed with all their strength and with unyielding persistence. (2) Immense willpower on the things they thought mattered. Will is more important than any other factor in politics. (3) A strong feeling for certain gut issues which they shared with a large number of ordinary people at all levels of society. They could be very divisive – Thatcher particularly – but each knew that a majority – perhaps not a large majority, but enough – was with them. So each won elections convincingly. Reagan won two with big majorities, Thatcher three, and would have won a fourth, easily, had her party allowed her.

In addition to the strength he showed with Thatcher, Reagan had a power of communication which, in my experience, was unique. He could get across simple messages with unrivalled force, and ease. It was very difficult to dislike him if you had any kind of personal contact, even just TV. It was not charm, because that is always a bit calculated and therefore suspect. It was a form of friendship, sealed by jokes. He essentially communicated by jokes, especially by that quintessential American form of joke, the one-liner. This was invented by Benjamin Franklin, and honed to perfection by Mark Twain. Reagan had about four thousand one-liners, which he knew by heart and which he could produce to fit any possible public occasion. And, in this, his chosen territory, he had a first-rate mind and a reliable instinct. It was intuition backed by training, experience, but also, I emphasise, by brains. I became aware of this when I heard him say in Washington: 'I'm not too worried about the deficit – it's big enough to take care of itself.' This was a case of an intuitive grasp of economic essentials, for it was true, and proved by events to be so. It also got a big laugh, both at the time he said it, and later, when people turned it over in their minds. Of course Reagan also had all the skills of an experienced and highly professional actor, including the invaluable ability to appear totally at his ease, even in the most stressful confrontation. Nothing is more likely to upset your opponent. This, too, I saw, when Reagan was at the Irish Club in New York with Jimmy Carter at the beginning of the campaign. This should have been home ground for Carter, but Reagan took it over with one remark. After a long – too long – statement by Carter, repeating things people had heard him say many times, and whose unnecessary vehemence betrayed his nervousness, Reagan simply said: 'There you go again.' The timing and tone of voice were perfect, and he got a big laugh from the audience, all of whom (I imagine) were lifelong Democrats.

The first time I met Reagan, he looked at his cue card which he took from his left-hand jacket pocket, and said, 'Good to see you again, Paul.' I laughed and he laughed, and we both laughed together. Why, exactly? It didn't matter. We had achieved close contact. A second time was more formal – black tie, etc., with a mike, photographers and all the trimmings of presidential ritual. We shook hands and I looked at his smiling, handsome face. He said: 'Don't look at me – look at the cameras.' There spoke the old pro – so I did, and I have a photo of it. But there was one thing I learned about Reagan, and which must be understood to grasp the nature of his power. He was ruthless, and especially in his amiability. He was friendly with all but intimate with none.

Nobody got really close to the inner Reagan, not even Nancy, I think. Thus, as president, he could discard an old associate, and friend, without any damage to himself, or heartbreak, or even momentary distress, exactly according to the needs of his presidency. At a certain level, he was ice-cold. This was one of the secrets of his eight-year presidency, among the most successful, at home and abroad, in US history.

Vanessa Redgrave (b. 1937) sometimes came to see me when I edited the *New Statesman* in the 1960s. I thought her a glorious girl, and an excellent actress. Of course, her political ideas were dotty. She came to one of our Sunday lunches at Iver, together with her husband, a film director called Richardson. Each arrived in a separate chauffeur-driven Rolls-Royce, a characteristic showbiz procedure, it seemed to me. The lunch was marked by a magisterial rebuke, delivered by Elizabeth Jane Howard, to Mary Kenny, for saying that Jane Austen 'was obviously a lesbian'. Then Vanessa abruptly dragged back the spotlight on to herself by announcing, 'To keep anyone in prison is disgraceful. All the prisons ought to be opened *now*. And all the prisoners released *immediately*.'

Lord Reith (1889–1971) was the most dissatisfied man I ever met. He felt he had made a hash of his career, and that at every decisive moment he had made the wrong decision, been the victim of malice or been cheated out of his due. But what was his due? What did he really want to be? He did not know. He told me: 'I want to be *stretched*. I feel I have never been *stretched*.' And he spread out his arms as wide as they would go. He was a very physical man. He was six foot six and seemed taller, an elongated pyramid on a tiny base. A deep indented gash on his forehead (a Great War scar) gave him an agonised look. His eyes were fierce. He was a huge success at the BBC, 1922–38, and became one of the most influential, feared and admired men in the country, and then threw it all away by switching to Imperial Airways. He had a bad war, as MP, peer and minister in secondary posts, finally dismissed by Churchill. He envied Churchill his power. Reith held all kinds of jobs but none satisfied him after the BBC, and even that eventually bored him. He was an Old Testament figure and should have been a prophet. He would have flourished in the Reformation. He did a vast amount of flying in those days and he told me his height was a torment to him. But then everything was. Of his sayings, I recall: 'Life is a conspiracy against great men.' 'The House of Commons is a torture chamber. The House of Lords is a tomb.' 'Never desire something which the politicians are in a position to deny you.' 'Ambition is the worst of all self-inflicted wounds. Both chronic and fatal.' 'No one who is any good can possibly be happy in this world.'

Paul Reynaud (1878–1966) had been Prime Minister when France collapsed in 1940. After resigning, he tried to drive to the South of France with his mistress, Madame de Portes. She was ultra right-wing and his evil angel. In the crowded traffic – everyone was fleeing from the Panzers – Reynaud had to brake suddenly. A huge trunk flew off the back seat and literally took off Madame de Portes's head. He mourned her for the rest of his life. In the early 1950s I saw him almost every day, in the summer, when I had a swim in the Piscine Déligny, a giant houseboat pool moored near the Assemblée Nationale. He was a little man with a skinny figure. He always wore a women's white-rubber bathing cap. I asked: 'Is he very proud of his hair?' 'No, no. Nothing to do with that. The cap belonged to Madame de Portes. He wears it in memory of her.'

Maurice Richardson (1900–78) was a bohemian writer of the old school. He was very strong and could knock people down when he felt like it. The night before my wedding, he attended the bachelor dinner party given by John Raymond in a private room at the Reform Club. Henry Fairlie made a speech in which he classed Maurice, unlike the rest of us, as belonging to 'the Old Generation'. Maurice brooded on this and decided it was an insult. Afterwards we took taxis to the Savile, and as we debouched on to the pavement Maurice said to Fairlie, 'You are an impudent little whippersnapper. Take that.' He knocked him flat. Fairlie lay on his back on the pavement, pleading: 'I have a hole in my heart. Don't hit me again.' One of the car drivers phoned the police and said there was a fight going on outside the Savile Club. By a misassociation of ideas, the police went to the Savage Club and arrested Maurice Bowra, who was standing outside shouting.

Maurice was an expert on fountain pens and used to write a column on the subject for *Lilliput*. He was known to the girls at the Parker Pen centre in the Haymarket as 'Old Nibby'.

Sir Ralph Richardson (1902–83). He was the best all-round actor of his time. He would do anything within reason and was never out of a part. 'I don't believe in resting,' he told me. Indeed, he was always acting. Sitting next to him at the Beefsteak, I was treated to his white solidarity role. 'Those unfortunate settlers in Rhodesia. My heart bleeds for them. By Gad, they fought for us in the war. They are our blood brothers, our comrades, our kith and kin. Must we abandon them in their hour of need? Never!' And his eyes flashed, he laid down his knife and fork, and joined his hands over his breast. I then put the case of the poor unfortunate blacks, their country stolen, the cruelty inflicted on them, etc. Suddenly, he saw the opportunity to play another part: the man with an open mind, the thinking person open to reason and judicious argument. 'Ah, these points you make must be weighed. They are substantial. They deserve cogitation. There are serious moral issues here. Yes, yes. You've convinced me, I may have been mistaken. You've convinced me, my dear sir.' And his face would assume an expression of benignant disinterested wisdom – an amazing performance. Richardson rode around on an enormous motorbike, specially built for him. But in other respects he was abstemious. He amazed the theatre world by leaving £1.25 million when he died, a huge sum in those days, especially for an actor.

Helena Rubinstein (1870–1965) was a very plain woman, not even a *jolie laide* but not without a certain sinister glamour. She had a wonderful *appartement* on the Ile St-Louis, where I had tea with her. She offered me a job of a rather indeterminate kind as a companion-assistant. I had to give her 'ideas and encouragement'. But I already had a job. She spent her life trying to improve the appearance of women's faces but had no great success with her own. There was something Dickensian about her – that is, if you can imagine a Dickens character of entirely French or cosmopolitan fabrication. Such weird, rich, commercially successful women were to be found in those days. Not now. Or rather, since plastic surgery has become physically safe and aesthetically sophisticated – and common – they are less noticeable.

Robert Runcie, Archbishop of Canterbury (1921–2000) was a decent man but he sometimes did, or said, silly things. On one such occasion, I wrote a *Daily Mail* 'Page Eight' rebuking him. Now the *Mail* people were good to me: they always treated my copy as sacrosanct and never changed a word without my express permission. But of course they put on their own headlines, and I never saw a page proof. On this occasion, I was alarmed to see on Page Eight in large letters: '"Runcie, in the name of God, Go!" by Paul Johnson'. The next day, as it happened, I went to a big lunch at Ten Downing Street. The first person who came up to me was Dr Runcie, beaming: 'You see,' he said, 'I'm still here!'

Bertrand Russell (1872–1970) was a clever man, devoid of wisdom and with poor judgement. He once told me that writing his *Principia Mathematica*, published in 1903 when he was thirty, had exhausted or worn down his brain, which had never been the same since. That may be so, but he certainly had a good mind when I first met him, in 1955, when he was over eighty. I thought his *History of Western Philosophy*, published in 1945 when he was seventy-three, and which I read in my first year at Oxford, was superb. I learned a lot from it. He did some good stuff for us when I first joined the *New Statesman*, including his 'Open Letter' on A-bombs, which brought the famous reply from Nikita Khrushchev. But he also struck me as frivolous and even silly. I was present when the meeting of intellectuals which led to the Campaign for Nuclear Disarmament was held at Kingsley Martin's flat in the Adelphi. So was Russell. So were Denis Healey and J. B. Priestley and one or two others. The occasion was notable for a row. Healey said, after we had been talking for an hour or so, 'We must be realistic about this.' Whereupon, Priestley became angry: 'Realistic? Realistic. For nearly half a century I have heard people say about these issues, "We must be realistic." And what is the result of all this *realism*? Two world wars and fifty million dead, and now the prospect of a third in which the entire human race will go up in smoke. Realistic? To hell with it!' Russell's glee at this outburst was remarkable. He was sitting on a big pouffe, holding his knees, and he rocked from side to side and roared with laughter. The fury of Jolly Jack and the consternation of Healey were matters of intense amusement to him. Eventually, Kingsley Martin rebuked his hilarity but Russell contrived to giggle.

'I knew this would happen,' he said. 'Oh, the folly and fury of wise men gathered together! Ha, ha, ha!'

A decade later, in 1968, he was persuaded by Kingsley Amis to sign a letter to *The Times* protesting about the Soviet invasion of Czechoslovakia. There were various famous names on it but Russell's was the most important. Kingsley asked me to negotiate its appearance with the letters editor of *The Times*. I knew very well that one of Amis's motives was personal vanity. He wanted the superimposition on the letter of the tag 'From Mr Kingsley Amis and Others', for it was then *The Times'* practice to proceed in such cases alphabetically, and his name was the first. But it seemed to me, and *The Times* letters editor agreed, that it would attract more notice, and it would be more appropriate, to put 'From Earl Russell OM and Others'. So that is what was done. Amis, of course, was furious, but did not like to say so. Russell was furious too, rang me up and accused me of deceit, dishonesty and double-dealing. 'You have given the impression, quite deliberately, that the letter was my idea and initiative, whereas if you had followed the alphabetical rule it would have been clear I was a mere signatory.' 'Well, Lord Russell,' I said, '*The Times* man and I acted for the best. We thought the letter would have the most impact with your name at the head. And as you presumably want the letter to be effective, you cannot reasonably object. It is not logical, Lord Russell, and you of all people ought to be on the side of being logical.' There was a growl of rage from the other end of the phone. 'Logical fiddlesticks!' said Russell, and slammed down the receiver.

'Bobbity' Salisbury (1893–1972) was for years regarded as the *éminence grise* of the Tories. He had been Eden's number two at the FO and resigned with him in 1938; then worked under Churchill throughout the war, led the Lords 1945 onwards, and sat in the Cabinet 1951–7. He turned down the Viceroyalty of India in 1943 – otherwise, he, not the silly Mountbatten, would have been the last Viceroy, and history might have been different. But not much. He backed Eden over Suez (but with many misgivings, as he later told me), and then, when Eden resigned and declined to advise about his successor, Salisbury (he had become Marquess in 1947) took on the job and recommended Macmillan. He said everyone in the Cabinet, bar one, 'preferred Mac to Rab'. But he did not like Macmillan much: never had him to Hatfield – 'Windbag. Stories too long, and frequent.' Like all Cecils, 'Bobbity', as he was universally known, was always resigning or threatening to. In March 1957, he quit over the minor point of Archbishop Makarios's release from detention. This raised not a ripple – one of the most ineffective resignations of modern times. From that point, Bobbity ceased to be the *éminence grise*, and became a mere ranter on the Lords back benches. The House of Cecil has not had much clout since.

Sir Malcolm Sargent (1895–1967) was a superb conductor, particularly of choral music. He was a Lincoln man, tall, with a handsome, monkey face, jet-black Brilliantined hair brushed back without a parting, and long bony but sensitive fingers. I first met him when he brought his orchestra, the Liverpool Philharmonic, to Stonyhurst during the war. He was affable, extrovert, proud of his ascent to fame from humble origins (his father had been a coalman, his mother a gardener's daughter). His musical training at Peterborough Cathedral had been thorough and he was a superb organist who could play anything at sight. He had intermittent bad health, and his beloved daughter died of polio in 1944, just before I met him. His face, I noticed, had a haunted look. But he easily got back his zest for life. He was hugely successful with women (of all ages) and a tremendous ballroom dancer. He was a bit of a snob, and greatly valued his friendship with Princess Margaret and, especially, the Queen Mother. He talked to me a lot about music at the Beefsteak, and also about his social triumphs. One lunchtime, when the club was crowded, we were sitting in the middle of the table and he began: 'The Queen Mother said to me the other day . . .' I stopped him. 'Malcolm, there's so much noise I can hardly hear you. And others might like to hear the story. Can't you speak louder?' So he did. But by chance, there was a sudden hush in the talk. So everyone was amazed to hear Malcolm shout in a loud voice: 'THE QUEEN MOTHER SAID TO ME THE OTHER DAY.' Then he stopped, appalled. There was a pause, and a general laugh. He threw down his napkin and ran from the club.

Jean-Paul Sartre (1905–80), unlike most intellectuals especially left-wing ones, was generous. Once, lunching with my girlfriend Jackie at the Brasserie Lipp on the boulevard St-Germain, we found Sartre at the next table. Although I did not know him very well, he insisted on taking up our bill and paying it with his own. He was always doing that kind of thing. Indeed, his generosity eventually got him deeply into debt with his publisher, and I think he was virtually penniless when he died. His funeral was the biggest of its kind in Paris since the death of Victor Hugo in the 1880s. Since then the City of Paris has renamed the Place Saint-Germain the Place Jean-Paul Sartre and Simone de Beauvoir – a touch vulgar, as well as clumsy.

Hugh Scanlon (1913–2004) was for many years head of the Amalgamated Union of Engineering Workers (later the AUEW), whose endless strikes, work to rules and go-slows effectively destroyed the West Midlands car industry. During his time of glory I often had to debate with him on TV. I have never met anyone of such impenetrable stupidity. Across his dense and dreary mug floated a fog of ignorance and prejudice, lacerated from time to time by flashes of pseudo-Marxist ideology, half remembered from wartime adult education lectures. He had a flat, almost toneless North Midlands accent which gave even his most fatuous remarks a grim folklorish poetry. His favourite maxim was 'Freedom is conforming to majority opinion'. There was no evil in the man: just brainless chaos. In due course he was promoted to the House of Lords, for services to our foreign competitors (as I used to tell him), and he attended it on every possible occasion in order to collect his maximum dues and expenses. He lived, thus ennobled, for many years, in preternatural idiocy, dying as ignorant as the day he was born.

Arthur Scargill (b. 1938), boss of the miners' union, I crossed swords with many times on TV in the decades when the unions rode high, 1960–80. I found it impossible to have a serious argument with him, as his approach was essentially revolutionary. I found him the most temperamentally destructive man I ever met. In my view, he played a big part in destroying both the British coal-mining industry and his own union, once the most powerful in Britain. And he helped to destroy the power of the unions as a whole by challenging Margaret Thatcher's government in the 1980s to a stand-up fight, which he lost. Several people lost their lives in this violent battle and Scargill should have been held to account. Instead, he dwindled into insignificance. He did not seem like a Yorkshireman to me – more Irish. I am glad to have met him, though: he gave me an idea of what Britain would be like under a totalitarian government of the left.

Arthur M. Schlesinger, Jr (1917–2007) was America's most prominent historian in the 1960s and 1970s. Rather as Virgil was court historian to Augustus Caesar, or Macaulay to the Whigs, Schlesinger was court historian to the Kennedys. He was even closer because he actually held an official position in the J. F. Kennedy administration and had an office in the White House. He went on missions abroad. In 1961, after the Bay of Pigs fiasco, Kennedy sent him to Europe, Britain in particular, to talk to prominent media and academic people and give the (favourably slanted) inside story. I invited him to our Sunday lunch at Iver and made sure other people like Perry Worsthorne, Hugh Thomas and Colin Welch were there. He was very plausible and effective. The previous year I had seen Fidel Castro in Cuba and he had given me a magnificent box of Monte Cristo cigars (I had to pay for it by listening to a private two-hour harangue by that monster of uncontrolled verbiage). Offering Schlesinger a cigar, I waited till he had taken it out of its aluminium case, lit it and was puffing luxuriously before I told him who had given me the box. He took it in his stride. He said: 'This is not a Communist cigar. It is a good cigar. And a cigar remains good, if it's good in the first place, whatever its provenance.' He was never at a loss for a word. He always wrote fast and well. His account of the Kennedy administration was written in record time and is first-class of its kind. His life of Robert Kennedy ditto. Fortunately for his reputation he was not called upon to write about that slob and reprobate Edward Kennedy. He knew everyone who mattered in politics and academic history on both sides of the Atlantic and was a first-class example of an Anglo-American establishment figure – the equivalent of our Roy Jenkins in many ways. His books made him rich, he was probably the best paid professor in America, and he always stayed at the best hotels and ate in the best restaurants. As it happened, his finest book was his first, in my opinion, written before he became involved with Kennedy's Washington, *The Age of Jackson*, wrong-headed in some ways, but a ripping yarn. Like many small men, he adored tall women, and had a splendidly lofty wife, Alexandra. He lived to be ninety, and had a long, faithful, fulfilled and, so far as I could see, happy life. Was there a snag?

Jean Sibelius (1865–1957). I was taken to see him in 1949 at his lonely house in Järvenpää. He seemed very old. He took out a box of cigars which, he said, had been sent to him by the President of Cuba, Batista. They seemed very luxurious. Should I take one? He might grudge it if I did, be offended if I didn't. I took one, and that was evidently the right choice. He said: 'It is a good thing for a young man to learn to smoke expensive cigars.'

Bob Silvers (b. 1935) effectively created the *New York Review of Books* and ran it for many years. I first met him in Paris in 1952 when he was in the American army working as a clerk at the Fontainebleau HQ of General Eisenhower, and later of General Ridgway. As soon as his day's clerking was done he would get a lift by military truck to central Paris, or use public transport, so that he could be sitting at his table at Les Deux Magots, or the Café de Flore, by 6.30 p.m. I used to laugh at his enthusiasm for Left Bank literary culture, which totally dominated his life. I compared him to Stuart Preston, known as the Sergeant, who was on Eisenhower's staff from 1942 and made himself a notable figure in London intellectual society – later immortalised by Evelyn Waugh as 'the Loot' in *Unconditional Surrender*, the last volume of his Sword of Honour trilogy. But Preston did nothing very much after the war, whereas Silvers became a great power among the Anglo-American intelligentsia, and made his magazine feared, honoured and universally read among English-speaking cultural nobs. Nancy Mitford said to me once, in the sixties: 'Isn't Bob Silvers sweet? He's written me such a nice letter saying he's been forced to carry a nasty review of my book in his paper, and apologises profusely. Did you ever?' I said: 'Darling Mrs Rodd, what I like about you, after many years in the literary racket, is your pristine innocence. Not a word goes into his paper which Bob does not personally control.'

Wallis Simpson, Duchess of Windsor (1896–1986) took a lot of secrets with her into the grave. Her baptism had to be delayed because the doctors were unsure of her sex for a time. Hence the name bestowed on her when she was born, Wallis. She was known as Wally, like Wally Hammond, the famous Gloucestershire batsman. A photo exists showing her as a teenager, with masculine-style (women's) clothes, brisk hair-do (not Eton crop) and monocle. She sometimes smoked cigars at this time. She was reputed to be able to perform 'the Baltimore clinch' whereby her vaginal muscles could grip a man's penis when it entered her, and retain it inside until the sex act was complete. As Edward VIII was afflicted by premature ejaculation, this was the source of her power over him. Baltimore, the place of her origin, was the fastest growing seaport in eighteenth-century America because of its trade with China, round the Horn. Thereby a Cantonese strain entered the town's citizenry and the term 'Baltimore Chinese' came into use. Wallis was an example. When Evelyn Waugh was asked: 'Why did the Duke of Windsor prefer her to his throne?' he answered: 'Oriental tricks, old man, Oriental tricks.' On the other hand, she is reported to have said, more than once, 'I never allow a man to touch me below the Mason-Dixon line.' Some said she never had sex with any of her husbands. But who can possibly know? The Paris couturiers loved her. She was devoted to high fashion and her body was the perfect object for them to work on. Balenciaga thought the world of her. When Dior died, there were two prie-dieus put out in front of the rest of the congregation. One was occupied by Jean Cocteau, the other by the Duchess of Windsor.

I saw the Windsors occasionally in Paris. After a dinner at Mrs Margaret Biddle's they played bridge. When they went down badly she rebuked the Duke for a key mistake: 'I shoulda thought you of all people could be relied on to play the King.' So it was reported to me. But I didn't actually hear her say it.

C. P. Snow (1905–80). He was both a scientist and a novelist, and for a brief time, when he promoted the notion of the Two Cultures, was one of the most famous people in England. His legacy is the phrase he coined, 'The Corridors of Power'. I always thought him, in his public persona, a bit of a fraud. At the *New Statesman*, I had to sub-edit, or, rather, rewrite, one of his more ponderous pieces, and discovered he did not know the difference between 'production' and 'productivity'. My efforts to explain it to him were unavailing. His novels, about struggles for power in Whitehall and Oxbridge, seemed to me unreadable, and are now unread, though they had a big vogue in the fifties. When Wilson came to office in 1964, Snow was one of the intellectuals he brought into government, as number two to Frank Cousins, the union boss. These two boobies formed a mutual admiration society. Snow referred to Cousins as 'a man of massive character'. Cousins classed Snow, 'the most formidable mind of our age'. He told me: 'I sat in the gallery of the Lords the other day and heard Charles speak, and I thought to myself, with wonder, that amazing man is my *under-secretary!*' The combination was yet another of Wilson's bright ideas, which ended in total failure, and produced nothing.

Personally, Charles Snow was a man of infinite kindness, always going to great trouble to help people. Physically, he was repellent. He had begun to look old at forty, and he had tiny, almost life-less hands, uncomfortable to shake. He came from Leicester and was proud of it. He gave suppers of local products, brilliantly coloured orange cheese and Melton pies. I once hurt him by chucking a party he gave in order, at short notice, to dine with Beaverbrook at Cherkley Court, something I had never done before. He could not understand the attraction, shook his head and said, 'Your loss'. For all his display of worldliness, he was curiously naive about the way the world actually worked.

He and his wife, Pamela Hansford Johnson, were the ruling couple of literary London in the fifties. She was an incomparably better writer and novelist than he was, much more intelligent and shrewd. But she was bitter. The climax of her emotional life had been her brief affair with the Welsh rotter, Dylan Thomas, never consummated, quickly forgotten by him but remembered by her all her life. I believe he got quite a lot of money out of her.

John Sparrow (1906–92) was a clever barrister who flourished in Oxford after the Second World War and was Warden of All Souls 1952–77. Although he had many of the instincts of a scholar, and an inquisitive nose, he lacked purpose and perseverance, and did nothing with his life. But there were one or two things for which he will be remembered. First was discovering the notebooks of Geoffrey Madan in the London Library and editing and publishing them – a real treasury of wit and curious facts and quotes. Second was his close reading of D. H. Lawrence's *Lady Chatterley's Lover*, which led to his discovery that the gamekeeper had not merely seduced her ladyship but sodomised her. If he had discovered it in time to give evidence at the trial, the jury would undoubtedly have convicted Penguin Books. As it was, by the time he proved his case in an *Encounter* article, it was too late. Sparrow was unusual in his generation, in that he was forcefully reactionary. He could be formidable in argument. He was dark, with straight, glossy hair, rather handsome in his way but homosexual (though not practising). He could be funny (e.g. during the Suez Crisis in 1956 he said 'London is a hot bed with cold feet'). But he gradually took to drink, and after his retirement in 1977 hit the bottle hard. He dined at All Souls every night, got drunk and abusive and behaved as if he was still Master (thought he was, indeed). So he was banned from the premises. A sad end to a life of missed opportunities. Yet he is remembered, whereas most Wardens of All Souls are forgotten. I recall his saying to me: 'Beware fashionable dons, the kind you see at London parties. They are all bad men.'

Stephen Spender (1909–95) was already old when I got to know him. We met at Drue Heinz's villa overlooking Lake Como. We immediately became friends. At Como I spent many happy hours in conversation with him, with the blue, blue lake below, and the shadows deepening on the massive limestone cliffs opposite, the skies above changing every minute. He was the perfect person to be with. His experiences went back to the early twenties for he was invited by Lady Ottoline Morrell to Garsington when still in his teens and from then onwards met everyone in the literary world. So he could tell you about Lawrence and Joyce, Barrie and Conrad, Hemingway and Fitzgerald as well as everyone since then. But he never monopolised the conversation. He drew you in, asked your opinions, listened carefully, laughed and made it clear he delighted in your company. He knew the value of pauses, too. Many of his stories involved Auden, always casting Auden in a superior light, himself in a humble one. He was a very modest man. Of course, some might say he had a lot to be modest about. Evelyn Waugh wrote: 'To see him fumbling with our rich and delicate language is to experience all the horror of seeing a Sèvres vase in the hands of a chimpanzee.' But Stephen made no great claims for himself. I often asked him to read or recite one of his poems, and enjoyed hearing him. But chiefly I liked him talking about the great men and women he had met.

He had a lot of gentlemanly instincts: rectitude, respect for people's feelings, tact, sensitivity. He could spot when people were downcast, and cheer them up, or were painfully shy, and would encourage them to talk. I never saw him cross, petty, malicious or intolerant – though some of his stories had bite, especially about people he had learned from experience to fear or distrust – Lucien Freud, for example. I was once asked to come to his rescue. A hostile American had written a book which misused earlier writings of Stephen's to present an inaccurate and damaging picture. He was dreadfully upset and helpless, not knowing what to do about it. I wrote a piece in the *Spectator* exposing the book's faults, and as a result the plan for an English edition was dropped. Stephen was profoundly grateful.

He had always been good-looking, but in old age he became positively handsome, indeed beautiful, like a classical god. What is more, his new son-in-law, Barry Humphries, being rich and fond of new clothes, had made many elegant suits for Stephen who, for the first time in his life, was expensively and superbly dressed. He became these grand outfits and was a figure of elegance at London parties. I have a photo of Stephen and Andrew Devonshire, another well-set-up and beautifully dressed man, of comparable age, chatting together, two English gents of the Old School – the last two, really, now alas both gone.

Norman St John-Stevas (b. 1929) was literally a colourful figure on the political and literary scene (he edited the *Collected Works* of Walter Bagehot) for many years, having a face composed of red, blue and purple hues. At the famous Victorian fancy-dress ball given by the Longfords at Strawberry Hill (Frank went as Albert, Elizabeth as Queen Victoria; I as Sir Robert Peel), Stevas raised eyebrows by going as Pope Pio Nono. On close inspection, the white papal robes were seen to be authentic, made for and worn by an actual pope. I believe they belonged to Pius XII. But Stevas's glowing mug was in notable contrast to the pale aesthetic features of old Pacelli.

Arianna Stassinopoulos (b. 1950) was one of the very tall, clever ladies Bernard Levin worshipped. He loved to be seen with her. She once gave a dinner party to which we were invited. She had somehow discovered it was my birthday, and produced an elaborate cake she had baked and decorated herself. I scarcely knew the other guests and found it a little embarrassing. But as Marigold said, it showed kind intentions. Or did it? Soon after, she departed for the United States and other worlds to conquer, where her fortunes were mixed.

Adlai Stevenson (1900–65) was a successful Governor of Illinois who twice ran as Democratic presidential candidate against Ike, and was twice heavily defeated. He insisted on elaborate make-up when he appeared on TV. When I interviewed him on *This Week* in 1961, live, we had an absurd row, and he became angry – so angry he rushed out of the studio. He went straight off to see Harold Macmillan at Number Ten without taking his make-up off. I often wondered what old Harold thought.

Michael Stewart (1906–90) was a good example of the ephemeral nature of political fame. His father, a science teacher, died when he was four and his mother, also a teacher, brought him up. He was clever, industrious and incorrigibly dull. He got scholarships to Christ's Hospital and St John's, Oxford, where he got a first. He had a good war in Intelligence and Education (captain) and won the safe Labour seat in Fulham in 1945, holding it for a quarter century; then a life peerage. He was always on the front bench and, under Harold Wilson, was twice Foreign Secretary, as well as doing Education and Economic Affairs. He was known in the trade as 'a safe pair of hands' or 'a steady hand on the tiller'. His one moment of splendour came in the year 1968 when he returned to the Oxford Union (where he had been president) to fight, and win, a TV debate defending American policy in Vietnam. He was a good debater; nothing else, and in five years in both houses of parliament he never made a memorable speech. For a time he had a connection with the *New Statesman*, which treated him generously, giving him good pay, space and publicity. He proved notably ungrateful. 'Not just a cold fish,' said a colleague, 'but one with a nasty bite.' In my dealings with him, I found him curiously inert and lifeless. It was like negotiating with a dead man. In the end, of course, he did die, and was instantly and totally forgotten.

John Strachey (1901–63) was the son of the *Spectator* editor John St Loe Strachey. He was introduced to me by Bob Boothby when I first came to London in 1955. He had been at Magdalen but never took his degree. He boxed the political compass all his life: first Tory, then Labour MP, then PPS to Mosley when he was a member of the MacDonald government in 1929, then followed Mosley into the wilderness, became a member of his New Party, but left it when Mosley became anti-Soviet. Then he was a Communist and a power in the Left Book Club, wielding more authority than anyone except Victor Gollancz himself. Then, under the influence of Keynes, and shocked by the Nazi–Soviet pact, he left the CP, writing his resignation letter to the *New Statesman* in April 1940. He went into the RAF and rejoined Labour in time to win a seat in 1945 and join the Attlee government. Minister of Food from 1946, he was the object of the most vicious, sustained and unfair press campaign, chiefly carried out by Beaverbrook's *Daily Express*, I can ever remember.

He was the creator of the disastrous scheme to grow ground-nuts in Tanganyika, or at any rate got the blame for it. He also had a disastrous relationship with Klaus Fuchs, who was unmasked as a spy in 1950. He said to me: 'I am accident-prone. What does that say about me?' Me: 'Something about judgement?' 'You may be right.' Kingsley Martin thought the world of him. 'John Strachey is the cleverest man in England.' He published his articles more frequently and at greater length than, in my view, they merited. Harold Wilson also valued him and would certainly have included him in his 1964 government. But Strachey died in summer 1963. He was an agreeable man to be with and told me good stories, e.g. how, in 1929, Ramsay MacDonald, Prime Minister, having no car of his own, and there being no official car provided in those days, used to walk to the end of Downing Street and hail a taxi when he wanted to go anywhere. And how Mosley, confronted by a choice between New Party business and the chance to seduce a woman, would toss a coin.

Sukarno (1901–70), the dictator of Indonesia, was clever at coming up with neologisms. But he could do nothing else. He whipped up hatred against the Chinese minority, killed many of them, locked up others and drove the rest into exile. But the Chinese were the commercial middlemen who ran the buses and trucks and brought the goods to market. As a result of Sukarno's anti-Chinese pogroms, when I was in Java, the food rotted in the countryside and the cities were starving. In Jakarta there was nothing to eat except blackened bananas. Sukarno said to me: 'The most dangerous people in this country are the Boy Scouts. The Boy Scout Movement is the most evil organisation in the world.' Of course, Sukarno came to a sticky end; as was only proper.

Hannen Swaffer (1879–1962) arrived in my tiny office at the *New Statesman* in 1957 and filled it with smoke. He was not only the Spirit of Old Fleet Street but an old-fashioned smoker. That is, he never took the fag out of his mouth until it was a stub and he was ready to replace it with another. The ash just fell down the front of whatever he was wearing. He sported an old three-piece suit, high stiff collar, black silk stock, a big black felt hat with a wide brim, and white socks. His yellow-grey-white hair came down to his shoulders. Northcliffe called him 'the Poet' because of his long hair, and made him editor of the *Daily Dispatch* in 1910. He had also edited two other dailies or Sundays, written gossip columns, been Beaverbrook's theatre critic in the *Express*, and was called 'The Pope of Fleet Street'. He came to offer me general advice about journalism, 'having spotted you as a likely lad'. This was: 'Never trust newspaper owners. They are a disgusting lot. Never call editors sir. Always be polite to the subs. Never swear at copy-takers. Treat advertisers like dirt. Use as few adjectives and adverbs as possible. Respect Fowler always. Read and remember Quiller-Couch on writing prose. Treat actors like servants. If you're given champagne for lunch they want something from you they shouldn't get. Finally, abandon journalism before it abandons you.'

'Swaff' had a musty, dusty flat high up in a building without a lift, but with magnificent views over Trafalgar Square and down Whitehall: 'So I'll have a grandstand seat when the Revolution comes.'

A. J. P. Taylor (1906–90) got me my scholarship to Magdalen. He came to pick me up from my room to take me to the committee of dons interviewing the potential scholarship lads. Present were Bruce McFarlane, 'Tom' Stevens, C. S. Lewis and Gilbert Ryle. It was a jovial occasion, none of the political correctness which has now spoiled Oxford life. They did not care about my social, political, educational or religious background, only – is he bright? Has he ideas, imagination, a thirst for knowledge? Will he add lustre to the college? During the discussion a big row broke out between AJP and Lewis over the existence of God, the possibility of an afterlife and theodicy. Ryle joined in, aggressively, and I intervened as an irenic force (surprisingly), and made jokes. That got me the scholarship.

AJP was a good tutor. He gave you exactly an hour, one-to-one, every week, and a useful hour it was, for he set good essay subjects, listened carefully to what you read, made useful and informative comments, broadened the topic into a general historical discussion, and provided good lists of further reading. Then, he had a big wen on his forehead. In 1948, during the long vac., he went to the Soviet-arranged International Conference of Intellectuals at Wroclaw in Poland, where he distinguished himself. He made a fierce, unscripted speech, denouncing the conference as a Soviet fraud, and its sponsors and arrangers, and many of those attending, as Stalinist stooges. This was true, but no one had dared to say it before, or contrived to use such a perfect platform to say it from. Kingsley Martin, who was present, wrote a famous piece in the *New Statesman* showing how AJP had decisively weakened Stalin's grip on Western left-wing intellectuals, and writing that the big wen on Taylor's forehead 'blazed forth as a symbol of dogged English John Bull courage'. Taylor took huge offence, and when he returned to college in October, the wen had been removed by surgery.

Taylor had four marriages. His first wife, Margaret, spent all her money on Dylan Thomas. Then he married Tony Crosland's sister. Then he remarried Margaret. Finally, he married a Hungarian lefty. His first two wives caused him uneasiness and misery partly because AJP had a streak of cowardice which prevented him voicing his real thoughts on emotional issues. His real marriage was to Beaverbrook, first as valued and well-paid contributor (AJP was tremendously keen on money, and had an avaricious streak), then as friend and guest at Cherkley Court, then as biographer, and finally as boss of the Beaverbrook Library. But even this ended in disillusionment, for AJP decided he had wasted a lot of his life with the Beaver, and the library was disbanded and eventually sold by the Beaver's heirs. He tended to have much-loved heroes who disappointed him. His supposed friend, Sir Lewis Namier, advised the Prime Minister (Macmillan) that AJP should not be appointed Regius Professor of Modern History at Oxford unless he agreed to give up his newspaper and TV work. AJP refused, so was not appointed. He never spoke to Namier again.

AJP was a powerful lecturer, as well as a first-class tutor. He deliberately had his weekly lectures at 9 a.m. in Magdalen College Hall – no one else did it so early – but filled the hall nonetheless. The House Bursar protested, saying the college servants had difficulty in clearing the place for breakfast in time. AJP said: 'This college was founded by Waynflete to promote knowledge, not to cater to gluttony.' His lectures were mainly attended by men, whereas C. S. Lewis, who could also pack the hall but started at 10 a.m., got mainly women. AJP's lectures were marvellous to listen to but afterwards you couldn't remember anything he said. His TV 'talking head' programmes, also delivered straight, without notes, though wonderful broadcasts, attracting huge ratings, suffered from exactly the same fault. I don't know whether his books survive or not: I am certainly not tempted to reread any of them. But already four biographies of him have appeared, and he evidently remains a figure of interest.

He came from Southport, where his father was a successful retired Manchester cotton-broker. Southport is the quintessentially suburban town of the north, wholly middle class, with a National Museum of Lawnmowers. It is on the opposite side of the Ribble Estuary to Lytham, where I lived, and we used to laugh at it, for the tide came up close on our side but not on theirs, except once a month at high tide, the only time when you could bathe comfortably at Southport. But when I made a joke about this to AJP he was not amused. His sense of humour was unreliable and sometimes non-existent.

But he helped me to learn to write English. 'Keep your sentences short. Just occasionally put a longer one in. Strong verbs. Few adjectives. Forget about adverbs unless essential to the meaning. Short quotations, if any. Beware subjunctives. Forget about optatives. Never tell anecdotes unless they're really good, apt and short. Don't read Carlyle – he's catching. Gibbon the same. Don't despise popular historians like Trevelyan, Arthur Bryant and Neale – you can learn tricks from them. All writing is a series of tricks – don't kid yourself it's anything else. The great thing is to master all the best tricks of others, then invent some of your own. Be realistic about yourself, don't get cocky but take a proper pride in your skills. And always work hard. Nothing is ever accomplished without a lot of sheer hard work. Now push off, I'm busy.'

Elizabeth Taylor (b. 1932), the film actress, and her then husband Richard Burton (1925–84) had recently made the movie *Antony and Cleopatra* when I saw them, dining at La Méditerranée in Paris. This was one of my favourites, specialising in seafood. It had beautiful murals painted by Christian Bérard in return for free food, all dishes accompanied by his invariable sauce béarnaise. Taylor was ravishing with intense violet eyes, Burton hugely handsome but already becoming brutish with drink. They arrived in a huge limo, after us, were attentively served and had finished their meal and left before we had been served our main course.

'That is the reward of fame,' I said to Marigold. Naturally, it all ended in tears before bedtime.

I met Burton once, and he was sober. He said: 'Elizabeth's tits have the great and rare merit of being firm and soft at the same time. I can't say more than that, can I?'

Denis Thatcher (1915–2003) was a shrewd fellow, a typical Harrovian, a successful businessman, and an all-round clubman before he became the perfect prime ministerial consort. Margaret was much more dependent on him than most people realised – indeed, without him she would not have been a great Prime Minister. He saved her life. Her habit of spending half the night working on her next day's speech was irksome to him. He would make her come to bed, if he could. On the night of the Brighton Conference IRA bomb, he had been long in bed while she was working in the sitting room of the suite. He said, 'Oh, give it a rest, Margaret. *You're not writing the Bible, you know.*' This made her laugh, and so she joined him, thus avoiding death, for the IRA device blew the sitting room to pieces, while the bedroom was unscathed.

He employed lovely, out-of-date terms in his jokes, which had the flavour of use but were not really hackneyed. Anyway, they always made me laugh. In Rome, at a big party – *la tutta Roma* – I spotted a furtive little figure, with two bodyguards. 'Isn't it Andreotti?' I asked Denis. 'Yes, it is. *He'll soon be in the slammer.*' (He was, but only briefly, his friends in high places protecting him from charges of Mafia involvement.) At Mark Birley's ultra-smart Italian restaurant in Mayfair, where we were all three guests of Maurice Saatchi, Mrs Thatcher praised the food: 'Absolutely delicious!' Denis, who had carefully studied the menu: 'So it should be, dear. They're charging like the Light Brigade!' He hated under-done beef. In Warsaw, for the opening of a new hotel, the Bristol, restored by Olga Polizzi, I sat next to Denis. When the waiter plonked a vast plate of pink-red meat in front of him, Denis acted swiftly. 'Here! I say! Yes, you! Speaka da English? Good. Now, take this plate, and give it back to the chef, with my compliments, and say I want it cooked. Cooked! Understand? COOK-ED. Eh? Got it? That's a good fellow.' He turned to me: 'I could almost hear it mooing!' I pointed out that the bill of fare said 'Roast wild boar'. 'That's a detail. It's the principle of the thing that matters. Continentals will do anything to save a bit of fuel.'

Margaret never got over Denis's death. Some years later, I escorted her to Italy to stay with Carla Powell at her villa in the Sabine Hills. Margaret was becoming forgetful. In the evening she would look at her watch and say: 'I ought to be getting home. They don't always look after Denis properly.'

Margaret Thatcher (b. 1925) was up at Oxford with me, a Somerville girl, reputed to be brainy and industrious. She moved in Conservative Club circles, regarded as bad form in my college, Magdalen. I once asked her to go on to the river with me but she said she had just had her hair done and did not want to get it 'tousled'. Her hair was very important to her always. In 1975, after she had become Leader of the Conservative Party, we were both invited to address the Institute of Directors, at their annual gathering in the Albert Hall. The dressing rooms are in the basement, where we foregathered. A staircase there heads straight up to the back of the platform, and is the only access to it for speakers. Unfortunately a powerful column of air rushes up the staircase, or down it, or sometimes both. Mrs T spotted this immediately and panicked. 'It will ruin my hair-do.' So I said: 'Margaret, what we will do is this. I will go first and spread myself out. You crouch behind me and keep in step. Once you are at the top of the stairs you will be OK.' So that is what we did, and it worked perfectly.

We both made good speeches, and were wildly applauded, and she said: 'Can't wait for the election. And get that swine Callaghan out.'

I liked Mrs T and admired her. I saw her as the saviour of the country, like Churchill in 1940. And, of course, she did save the country. I helped her all I could, in every respect – ideas, speeches, encouragement, praising her to the skies in the *Daily Mail* and other papers, and beating the drum for her in the US.

The trouble with Mrs T was that she was nearly always serious. She tended to lecture rather than speak and went slowly, emphasising nearly every word. I occasionally tried to give her lessons in elocution, particularly on the art of emphasis (she often picked on the wrong word) but there was never enough time. She was, however, an apt pupil. You never had to tell her anything twice, and if she respected you she would listen, sometimes taking a little book out of her handbag and making notes. One day I said to her: 'Government can do all kinds of things, and does. But three things it *must* do, because no one else can do them. These are: external defence, internal order, and running an honest currency. These should occupy most of the attention, energy and resources of the government. Of course in practice governments do many things but the more of them it does, the more likely it will do the three essential things badly. All three suffer, but the one which tends to suffer more is currency – in other words, inflation.' She was much impressed by this, and wrote it all down. Some years later when we were discussing how she ran her government, she said: 'Listen, Paul. Let me tell you something important. Governments do all kinds of things, but there are *three* things it *must* do . . .' Then it all came. I laughed. 'I told you that.' 'You told me? Nonsense! I have always known it.' This happened on various occasions – and I got my own maxims back in the form of a lecture. That was her style. She reminded me of the exchange between Coleridge and Lamb: 'Charles, have you ever heard me lecture?' 'I have never heard you do anything else.'

The thing to grasp about Mrs T is that she was the Eternal Scholarship Girl. She loved learning, swotting things up, being tested, passing with honours. When she first became Prime Minister, she knew little about defence, foreign affairs and many other key subjects. She gradually acquired an encyclopaedic grasp of all of them. She always mastered her briefs, if necessary sitting up all night. She had no poetry, little imagination, and none of the Churchillian romanticism. But, unlike him, she did not go off at tangents, waste time, indulge in fantasies or allow space in her mind for incipient megalomania, always liable to infect great leaders. I could not see any evidence of the corruption of power. Unfortunately she did not have, close to her, people prepared to contradict her flatly or even shout her down – people she respected. Heseltine never opposed her openly, face to face: he just plotted and schemed secretly. The same with Howe, until right at the end. All her Cabinet enemies were cowards.

Another conversation I had with Mrs T right at the beginning. I said: 'There are four marks of a great leader. First, simplicity. You need to have just two or three big, simple ideas in which you believe body and soul. Second, will. This is the most important of all. You must have enormous will, and put it behind those ideas. If they are right – and they must be right – then you have great-ness. Third, you must have persistence, another name for courage – the courage to go on and on and on pushing your big ideas, particularly when the odds against them are overwhelming. Fourth, you must have the ability to get your ideas across to the public.' Mrs T: 'I agree with all that.' 'Now: what are your big, simple ideas?' Mrs T: 'First, reduce expenditure and taxation, which means reducing the role of the state. Second, a limited state, therefore, but within its limitations the state must be master – overwhelmingly strong. That means, in our present situation, breaking the unions. They destroyed the last three governments – Wilson in 1968–70, Heath in 1974, Callaghan in 1979. Now they must be destroyed in turn. Third, government must clear the space so that gifted and energetic individuals can realise their potentials. That means reducing the public sector to almost zero, and taking away all the needless restrictions on enterprise. Fourth, the rule of law must be upheld always, everywhere and at any cost.'

She added: 'As for getting my ideas across to the public, I am not so sure. Perhaps that's where I need help.' She was right. On the other facts in great leadership, she and Reagan were equal – and she was much his superior in acquiring knowledge and turning it to account. But he could communicate in ways which she never grasped. And she had no one to help her. From first to last she lacked a Minister of Information of genius. That was really all her rule lacked, and it was fatal, particularly over the Poll Tax, the issue which finished her.

Mrs T was not a deeply calculating, far-sighted and consciously planning politician. But she was lucky. Lucky in her constituency: solid, loyal, devoted, near central London, a source of confidence in her. Lucky in her parliamentary career – no mishaps, good minor jobs. Lucky in Keith Joseph's courage failing him, so that she suddenly became the candidate of the right against the tottering Heath: she could never have become Tory leader, and so Prime Minister, otherwise. Lucky in office. First, she knew she had to smash the unions. But how? The miners and the print unions played straight into her hands, by behaving idiotically and violently, putting the nation solidly behind her. Second, the Argentine junta gave her a matchless opportunity to become a national leader, and to display the courage to fight, and win a dangerous, long-distance war. That was luck – to show what she was made of – so she became 'the Iron Lady'. (Another piece of luck: the Russians coined that phrase, with the object of damaging her. It stuck, to her immense benefit – like Vicky's unintentional gift of Supermac to Macmillan.) Third, she stumbled on the magic formula of dena-tionalisation. But she had the intuition she was on to a winner, and it became a central plank in her platform and was imitated all over the world as 'Thatcherism'. This was a good example of Victor Hugo's dictum: 'Nothing is more powerful than an idea whose time has come.' And Mrs T was a leader whose time had come.

Her fall need not have happened, and would not have happened had she been left to herself. Her instinct was to fight. But on this issue, the influence of Denis Thatcher was decisive. He thought her time to retire had come, and he was adamant: 'It's not fair. But nothing in life is fair. You've had a good run for your money. Now you must go willingly, gracefully and immediately. You owe it to me, apart from anything else. I've had enough. And so have you, really. You'll be grateful to me afterwards.' Of course Denis detected that she was not the woman she had been. She had worked almost unbelievably hard for nearly twelve years – only he knew how hard – and she had damaged herself. He thought it wise, in her own interests, to go there and then. He wanted her to have a long and dignified retirement.

I certainly did not agree with Denis Thatcher at the time. But now I think perhaps he was right. He probably detected signs of the retreat of mental power which later afflicted her. It fascinated me that when her memory began to go, what remained as essen-tial to her was not her position as an all-powerful Prime Minister, but her role as Denis's wife. With her at Carla Powell's, near Rome in spring 2007, she never mentioned her years at Number Ten, though was quite willing to talk about them when I brought the subject up.

Margaret Thatcher was the first and only woman I ever heard

use the masculine word 'wet' as a term of contemptuous criticism. This was a White's Bar adjective, going back to the time of Suez in 1956, I think. Mrs T picked it up, probably from Quintin Hailsham, and used it with great effect against her enemies in the party and especially within the Cabinet. In her parlance, the opposite of 'wet' was not 'dry' but 'one of us'.

Dylan Thomas (1914–53) and his wife Caitlin spent part of 1946–7 at Magdalen College as the guest of Margaret Taylor, wife of my tutor. A. J. P. Taylor hated them both, particularly Dylan, but Margaret, who claimed to be Celtic, and who wrote poetry, longed to be a patroness, which was probably why she gave all that money to Thomas. In return, she had some superficial fawning, but much sneering and abuse behind her back, some of which surfaced when Thomas's *Collected Letters* were published in 1985.

The Taylors had a college house, Holywell Ford, on the banks of the Cherwell, where I went for my tutorials with AJP. In the garden was a wooden structure, almost on the river, where the Thomases lived for a time. There is some confusion as to whether this was a summer house or a wooden caravan. My recollection is of a summer house, rather ramshackle. But there was also a caravan for a time. In the summer term of 1947 (I think) I watched Thomas at work. He sat in a canvas folding chair, with his papers on a picnic table, outside the summer house. He wrote a bit, then went inside for a bottle of beer – Bass, probably. He drank it, then walked to the Cherwell bank and hurled the empty bottle into the river. Then he wrote a bit more. Another expedition to the summer house produced a second bottle of Bass. That too was emptied and thrown into the river. More writing followed, then a large bottle of beer, holding a quart but half-emptied, was fetched. That was disposed of too. Then the writing was abandoned, and Thomas went into the summer house for good.

At the time I don't recall anyone remarking on the Taylor ménage, or the Thomases' role in it: people were polite in those days and tended to mind their own business. AJP thought Dylan Thomas a scrounger, a liar and thoroughly dishonest. So he was. He was also careless, and forgot which lies he had told. He sometimes gave a poetry reading, and said: 'This is a little poem I put together yesterday when I was feeling a little sad' – and read out something written a year or two – or more – before, and already published. So far as I could tell, he had no trace of a Welsh accent. All Welsh and Scots in those days tried to speak with an Oxford accent, if they were ambitious. Opinions differ about the merit of his poetry. What cannot be denied is that he was the greatest, and most prolific, writer of begging letters of the twentieth century. If the time he spent penning these mendacious and depressing epistles had been devoted instead to poetry, his *oeuvre* would have been twice as large.

Roy Thomson (1894–1976) was a Canadian newspaper owner who came to England when he acquired the *Sunday Times*. This belonged to Lord Kemsley, head of one branch of the Berry family. The other branch, headed by Lord Camrose, owner of the *Daily Telegraph*, felt Kemsley had a moral duty to sell the paper to them, as it was the natural Sunday complement to the six-day morning *Telegraph*. But Kemsley hated the other Berrys and sold his paper to Thomson to spite them. I used to hear all about this family row from Pam Berry, who naturally took the *Telegraph* side. This sale was the beginning of the end for the Berrys of both sides, for it led the *Telegraph* Berrys to set up the *Sunday Telegraph*, which never made money and weakened the group as a whole. Nothing whatsoever now survives of this once-powerful and prosperous twin empire, all the titles being in alien hands.

Thomson was a curious roly-poly-like little man, with a big head and enormously thick spectacles. He could hardly see at all, and surveyed the dim portion of the world within the short radius of his eyesight with suspicion and often with bewilderment. He visited Russia and was escorted on a tour of Moscow by his underlings. After his return, I met him at a reception, and asked for his impression. All he said was 'Those guys have no catsup. How can they get through life without catsup? Workers' paradise – huh!' He was a philistine and revelled in it. He called editorial copy 'The stuff you put between the advertisements'. He was obstinate. At the 1963 party to celebrate fifty years of the *NS*, among the hundreds of guests was Thomson, and John Freeman asked me to look after him. Gazing around him myopically, he said: 'These new hotels are big but they have no class.' Me: 'This isn't a new hotel, Lord Thomson. It's the fiftieth anniversary party of the *New Statesman*.' 'Aw no, young man, you're mistaken. This is the opening party of a new hotel. I've been to this kind of event before, and they're all the same. Let's see if they've got good burgers. And a nice dollop of catsup.'

James Thurber (1894–1961) was a good example of the limitations of comedy, the most difficult of all the arts to practise, either in word or line. His drawings, and his comedy set pieces, like 'The Night the Bed Fell on Father', were probably the best things ever to appear in the *New Yorker*. But they all came out of the capital of experience. He could not add to his capital or invent new experience. Nor did he have the skill or self-restraint to spin it out, dilute it. So he lived on capital and one day it was all spent. By then he was going blind anyway, and was drinking too much. When I saw him he was a sad figure. Comics are like boxers. Just as boxers have to stash their money and get out before they are punch-drunk, so comics must beware of becoming joke-drunk. They rarely are, alas.

Professor Richard Titmuss (1907–73). A funny little man, son of a man who failed at farming, then haulage. He looked after his mother all his life. Completely self-educated, he began as a clerk, never sat an exam, or held any academic position until, in 1950, he was elected to the Chair of Social Administration at the LSE. He owed this to his *Problems of Social Policy*, which has some claim to be considered the most boring 'important' book of the twentieth century. He was the great guru of the 1950s Labour Party, 'the High Priest of the Welfare State' as Edmund Leach called him. He certainly had a clerical aura, and all his writing had a strong moral flavour, though he was an atheist. He wrote a book about selfishness, called *The Gift Relationship*, about the sale of blood. He appealed strongly to Hugh Gaitskell, based on a shared belief that 'the Gentleman in Whitehall knows best'. But Wilson dropped him immediately he became leader, and in 1968 fobbed him off with a non-job as Deputy Chairman of the Supplementary Benefits Commission. He said to me: 'Government must have a policy about everything which is physically controllable. If we could control the weather, we would have to have a weather policy.'

Sir Henry Tizard (1885–1959). Military scientist, who had a tremendous battle with Lindemann ('The Prof.') during the war, for Churchill's ear. Tizard got on very well with senior civil servants but could not abide politicians, especially mavericks like Churchill. So he lost, and eagerly accepted the invitation of the Magdalen dons to become college president. But he was soon bored and did not last long. He took a brief fancy to me and invited me to tea, when he told me some of his troubles. (I was not yet eighteen.) I asked him: 'What are those rolled-up things over there – carpets?' 'No, tapestries.' They were in fact very valuable, had been in storage during the war, and had not yet been rehung. He strode over to one, and gave it a kick. Clouds of dust arose. Liking the effect he gave it another kick, then another, saying: 'Oxford is full of moulding, rotten old things like this, relics of the past!' He went on kicking in a kind of frenzy, perhaps seeing the rolled tapestries as 'The Prof.' (who was then on the other side of Oxford at Christ Church). Seeing he was becoming breathless, I said: 'Would you like me to give you a hand, kicking those things?' My voice suddenly brought him to himself, with a start. 'No! No!' he said, 'Certainly not. What an absurd idea. Good day to you!' And he showed me out. I never saw him again.

Arnold Toynbee (1889–1975) and his son **Philip Toynbee** (1916–81). It is extraordinary to think that when I first went up to Oxford in 1946 many people regarded Arnold Toynbee as the world's greatest living historian. The first six volumes of his *A Short History* appeared that year. It was immediately denounced by Hugh Trevor-Roper, and many other academics (especially Peter Geyl, who wrote a superb essay about it) as a pretentious fraud. But, considering its length (four more volumes appeared in 1957, then two more in 1961, and a condensation the same year; an illustrated version came out in 1972), its expense and the repellent nature of much of its writing, it is impressive how many copies were sold, especially of the abridgement. But how many were actually read? I dipped into it a lot but whenever I came across an event I knew about, Toynbee always got it slightly, sometimes profoundly, wrong. I complained about this to A. L. Rowse, who said: 'He is certainly all wrong about Queen Elizabeth. The only book he seems to have read is Lytton Strachey's *Elizabeth and Essex*. I read some of it because it was attacked so ferociously by Hugh Roper. As Hugh is wrong about so many things I thought he might be wrong about this too. But I fear he is right. Not that Arnold will mind, as he is the most insufferably conceited man in creation.' Rowse related to me a conversation between Churchill and Attlee at the Commons. Churchill: 'Have you read this man Toynbee?' 'A bit.' 'What do you think of it?' 'Nothing.' 'Same here.' 'Who do you think is our best historian?' 'Arthur Bryant.' 'So do I.' Rowse laughed: 'And why not? He is good. Though not as good as me.'

By all accounts, Toynbee was an obsessive worker. The only time I met him, he said to me: 'Make a plan for each workday. Never lose a minute. People waste a lot of time over meals. I don't. Napoleon never spent more than ten minutes over a meal, if he could help it. I do the same. Walking is good, because you see and learn things. All other sports and exercise are a waste of time and energy.' He leaned towards me confidentially (we were at a Chatham House party): 'You can waste a lot of time, too, on – er – well – sex. There again, Napoleon is an example. He believed copulation should never take more than ten minutes.' I thought he was a grandiose booby but I remembered what he said about Napoleon – another count against the monster.

Toynbee's austerity and work obsession must have made life with him hell. He married a daughter of the great Gilbert Murray, but the marriage did not last. They had three sons, of whom I knew Philip, for many years chief literary critic of the *Observer*. When Philip was in his sixties, he sent his father, still alive but pretty old, a long, itemised bill, coming to (I think) about £80,000, and headed 'For Ruining My Childhood'. He meant it seriously, too, though naturally Arnold did not pay up. Philip was tall, like his father, and handsome in a rough and primitive way. As a boy he had been a Communist, along with Esmond Romilly, who married the CP Mitford girl, Jessica. They ran away from school, Philip from Rugby, Romilly from Wellington. Philip was, so he said, the first Communist President of the Oxford Union. But in the war he was a captain. When I knew him he was famous for founding, with Ben Nicolson (Harold's son) a 'progressive' lunch club, at Bertorelli's. I was never invited to one of their 'do's', being part of a rival gang. In any case, I was always careful never to sit next to Philip at a meal as he was liable to get horribly drunk and vomit all over you. As a critic he was erratic. He made a fool of himself over Colin Wilson's *The Outsider*, which he hailed as a masterpiece and helped to make into an ephemeral bestseller. But his work was gradually taken over by his religiosity. He attacked my *History of Christianity* for not devoting enough attention to mysticism. He certainly did not make that mistake himself. All his energies went into a gigantic poem, *Pantaloon*, never published in full. So he became a famous bore, like his father, though in a different way.

Hugh Trevor-Roper (1916–2004). When I first knew him in 1946 he was a dashing, highly fashionable 'Student' (or Fellow) of Christ Church. He was one of the Censors of disciplinary officers, which gave him great social power, for the college was crowded with rich or aristocratic undergraduates. In return for privileged treatment (i.e. allowing them to have cars) Roper would be invited to their parents' homes for weekends or their London parties. He had established his reputation as a historian by publishing successfully, just before the war, his biography of Archbishop Laud. Then he had had a good war, culminating in being given the official task, with all facilities, of establishing what happened to Hitler in 1945. He produced *The Last Days of Hitler*, a tremendous critical and commercial success which made him a great deal of money. He used to hunt with the Cottesmore, dine at Blenheim, and do all the other ultra-fashionable things open to a pushy, social-climbing academic.

But Roper was always looking for more, and for a self-enhancing row. He hated medieval (as opposed to early modern) historians. He hated Magdalen. This meant he particularly hated the Stubbs

Society, the highly influential club of historians, both dons and undergraduates, which was run from Magdalen and consisted mainly of medievalists. Bruce MacFarlane and his pupils were particular targets. I was treasurer of the Stubbs in 1947 and due to become secretary and then president. Roper never came to meetings but at the crucial end-of-term one he arranged secretly to be present with a carefully drilled gang of his followers, and voted all the medieval people out of office. This coup, planned exactly like the Communist takeover of trades unions, was exactly to Roper's conspiratorial tastes and succeeded brilliantly. I was cross at the time but then forgot all about it. Twenty years later, when I was editor of the *New Statesman*, we published a review of a foolish book which Roper had published on the Middle Ages, the text of lectures he had given at Sussex University. It was critical but fair, but it was written by Bruce McFarlane. It was arranged by the literary editor and I knew nothing about it until I saw it on the page at the printer when I was putting the paper to press. Next week, at the Beefsteak Club, Roper came over to me and said in a loud voice: 'You have waited twenty years for your revenge, and now you have taken it, you red-haired, papist swine.' I did not know what he was talking about, but he was gone before I could ask him to elaborate. A member said: 'What's the matter with that chap?' Another said: 'Oh, that's Trevor-Roper. He's always pursuing some vendetta or other. Take no notice.' I realised later he was referring to the Stubbs Society business, which he assumed I remembered as well as he did. I told the story at London parties, and made people laugh. It got back to Roper and he realised he had made a mistake.

He prospered socially – for a time. He married Field Marshal Haig's daughter, Zandra. He was made Regius Professor of Modern History by Harold Macmillan – and in return he organised the campaign to get Macmillan elected Chancellor of Oxford University.

He begged Margaret Thatcher to make him a life peer. She agreed and he became Lord Dacre, an ancient title to which he believed he had a claim. Then things began to go wrong. There were no children. He failed to write the big book which was to establish his reputation for posterity. Zandra told me: 'The attic in our house is full of boxes containing Hugh's unfinished manuscripts. Plenty of Chapter Ones. No Chapter Twos.' He could not have been easy to live with, and Zandra became increasingly waspish and critical of him, to his intense discomfort; though when she died he missed her and became very lonely. He was probably bullied by Rupert Murdoch, owner of the *Sunday Times*, which paid him a generous retainer, to authenticate, after insufficient scrutiny, a German manuscript purporting to be Hitler's secret diaries. This almost immediately turned out to be an obvious forgery. Roper's reputation as a contemporary historian crashed, and all his many enemies turned on him. Worst of all, he began to go blind.

At the time of the Hitler diaries fiasco, I wrote him a sympathetic letter, telling him not to take it too much to heart. He was grateful, and wrote: 'It is incidents like these which reveal who your real friends are, if you are lucky enough to have any.' From that point we were on very good terms and had some excellent talks. He came once or twice to my house, but his increasing loss of sight made it difficult for him to go out. He was a stricken figure, and I felt sorry for him.

Roper is well worth a short, spirited, perceptive and well-informed biography.

Ken Tynan (1927–80) I first set eyes on early in October 1946 when I arrived at Magdalen with my regulation school trunk, and found the Lodge in commotion. Tynan had half a dozen trunks, and was ordering around the porters: 'Have a care with that, my man. It is freighted with golden shirts!' He was dressed in his favourite plum-coloured suit, made (I later learned) from billiard cloth, and dyed, with a spectacular mauve shirt and shocking pink tie. His fair hair was long, and floated. His face was epicene. His voice, accent and cultivated stammer were straight from the 1890s. He had come up the previous year, had learned all the tricks and was determined that his second year would make him not only the most talked-about man in Oxford but a national figure. Most of the other undergraduates had been in the war – colonels, wing commanders, RN lieutenants and the like – and simply goggled. *Brideshead Revisited* had come out the previous year and was in everybody's hands. It was clear Tynan intended to bring it all back. Alas, the grip of the Attlee Terror was too strong for that. Mile-long queues outside the Oxford Cake Shop (the only one that had decent stuff for tea parties), snoek and whale meat on the college menu, shortage of drink (and its price!) and general depression were too strong even for valiant Ken. Also, he didn't have the money. He was always borrowing ten-bob notes. He used to get engaged to a different girl every week (often Catholics from Cherwell Edge), he spoke at the Union, made a success of the Experimental Theatre Club, rival to the dowdy OUDS, and figured largely in *Isis* and *Cherwell*. But it was all an act. In his third year, bullied by his tutor, C. S. Lewis (a tremendous nagger, amid all his virtues and gifts), he rather gave up, and went down subdued, with a second.

Tynan was shocked to discover he was illegitimate, his father being Mayor of Warrington, Sir Peter Peacock (from whom he got his middle name), a card who ran two families. He never met his half-siblings. His first patron was James Agate, the *Sunday Times* theatre critic, who was then all-powerful, for he did cinema for the *Tatler* and books for the *Express* as well. Agate had responded to his invitation to come and see Tynan perform *Hamlet* at his school, King Edward's, Birmingham. Agate was enthusiastic, but disappointed to find that his new young friend was not homosexual. Far from it. Tynan was keen on girls – very keen – but his interest was spanking and caning. He told me: 'You'd be surprised how many girls are willing to be spanked. Almost all, in fact. Quite a lot will let you cane them, which really hurts, but only on condition you allow them their "revenge". I don't like being caned – very painful. For corporal punishment the best girls, I find, are rabbis' daughters. They have a strong sense of the *need* for punishment, which increases the sexual pleasure.' He told me he got regularly a journal called the *Spanking Times*, and liked to open it up and read it during a train journey. 'How the other passengers stare, especially the women.' Ken was a great exhibitionist. It was his strongest characteristic – to be noticed. Disapproval was as important to him as approval.

Tynan at Oxford was as fully adult as he would ever be. He lived to be fifty-three, and changed less in those thirty years or so than any of his contemporaries. He did not 'mature'. He became older, more set in his ways and more obstinate. But emotionally, intellectually, aesthetically, he remained as he was at eighteen. When I first knew him, he was desperate to meet stage personalities – Margaret Lockwood, James Mason, Joan Greenwood, for instance. It struck me even then as a bit childish. But it got worse, especially after he first went to Hollywood, and dug himself in there, where he found many of similar tastes. This passion for mixing with celebrities marks his letters and diaries, and spoils them, in my view.

Ken went on to have a certain success in life. He was an excellent theatre critic of the *Observer*, perhaps the best thing he did. He wrote some wonderful profiles of showbiz people for the *New Yorker*. He was literary adviser to the new National Theatre but was completely outfoxed by Laurence Olivier, much more a man of the world, especially the theatre world. He turned out to be no good at acting, not much good at directing and no good at film-making because he could not inspire the money-men with confidence. His one commercial success was *Oh! Calcutta*, but he mismanaged the financial side of it. It destroyed whatever reputation he had as a serious person, and this was not compensated by sudden wealth. In fact, he was always and increasingly in debt, and died owing a lot. The burden of debt made his last decade very difficult.

He was also increasingly ill, as emphysema tightened its grip. I never knew anyone more dependent on cigarette smoking than Ken. It was not just an incorrigible habit but also a physical pleasure. He sucked in the smoke, with all the power of his lungs, and exhaled it with luxurious ecstasy. He was a human smoking machine. I begged him to give it up, as it was clear it would kill him. He said: 'No possibility. I enjoy it more than fucking. It is more necessary to me than masturbation. It makes my enjoyment of spanking seem very feeble by comparison. And I can do it any time or all the time if I want. It is worth dying for.'

Tynan's first wife I didn't know much. His second wife, Kathleen, a Canadian, was one of the most beautiful creatures I have ever seen.

The trouble with Tynan was that he lacked any religious impulse whatsoever, and felt he had no need of spiritual and moral guidance. He would not talk to me about such matters. All he had in life was the make-believe of the London theatre and the Hollywood movie. Its stars were his angels, good and bad. When I think of him, I shiver, slightly.

Hedley Verity (1905–43), killed in Sicily serving as a captain in the British Army, was the most graceful sportsman (cricketer) I have ever seen. A left-hand slow bowler for Yorkshire and England, he moved on the wicket with all the grace and deliberation of a ballet dancer of the highest class. All his limbs and every bone and muscle, from his toes to his wrists and fingers, were part of the dance as he moved up to the wicket to bowl, and each ball had a different dance script. It was showmanship, of course, but also serious cricket for Verity was a difficult bowler to play at any time, and if the sun came out after rain, so that the pitch became 'sticky', he was unplayable – quite capable of taking all the wickets and skittling out a good side in an afternoon – something he did on three occasions. No one bowls with this kind of visual style and balletic showmanship now, and I am very glad to have seen it, when I was a boy, and thought cricket more important than anything else on earth.

Louise de Vilmorin (1902–69) was much talked about in the fifties. I met her at Nancy Rodd's. She was (fairly) pretty, very soignée, *gratinée* all over, as Diana Cooper put it, and undoubtedly clever. She was Duff Cooper's last regular mistress, tolerated by Lady Diana but not much liked by Cooper's White's Club chums. When she came over to London all the hostesses, like Pam Berry, gave parties for her. Evelyn Waugh held her in great detestation. To suck up to Waugh, Mrs Rodd would refer to her as 'the Head Girl Frog'. But when he was out of earshot, as it were, she would suck up to de Vilmorin. What the source of her power over women was I never learned but it cannot have been healthy. It is notable that this category of woman does not exist in Paris now.

Evelyn Waugh (1903–66) used to write me postcards occasionally – for instance, after I had written an article on the opening of the Second Vatican Council: 'I see your vision of the future church – coloured cardinals, distributing contraceptives to the faithful.' I first met him in the summer of 1948 at Oxford, where he came to give a talk at the Old Palace, to the Catholic undergraduates. He had recently returned from Hollywood, where he had been much taken by Forest Lawn Crematorium, and had gathered material for the last of his fictional satires, *The Loved One*. He was very funny indeed, and afterwards, over drinks provided by Monsignor Val Elwes, the Catholic chaplain, he was friendly and affable. He was short, rather red-faced, and at a distance his loud checks made him look like a bookie. Close to, he had the appearance of an ageing faun, and could sometimes look diabolical. His eyes were his most powerful feature, penetrating and full of expression, blazing at times, always radiating emotion and great intelligence. His way with words could be startling. Words, spoken but especially written, were the most important thing in life for him. His handwriting, nearly always with an old-fashioned nibbed pen, and ink, was beautiful, clean and elegant. He loved getting letters in the morning, and would answer them right away. His diaries were written in the evening. Hence the contrast between the two thick volumes of his letters, and his diaries: the first is sober, the second liable to convey a whiff of alcohol.

Like the ancient Hebrews, Waugh saw words as related to God. 'In the Beginning was the Word, and the Word was with God, and the Word was God' – this opening of St John's Gospel was sober truth to Waugh. His conversion to Catholicism was the most important event of his life. He had a real grasp of Catholic theology, unlike Graham Greene, who never understood it. Sin – the Devil – Hell – were real to him. In Paris, Nancy Mitford told me, in considerable awe, that when she rebuked him for being verbally cruel to a harmless American guest in her house in the rue Monsieur, and said: 'I don't know how you can reconcile being so beastly with your supposed Christian charity and Catholic faith in the teaching of Jesus', he replied with deadly seriousness: "Nancy, I may be as bad as you say – but, believe me, were it not for my religion, *I would scarcely be a human being.*'" The last seven words were delivered with terrifying emphasis. He felt that only by, as it were, holding the Crucifix in front of his face could he prevent Satan entering his body and possessing it. The Council and its enactments, and especially the sacrilegious (as he saw it) changes in the liturgy, came as a devastating blow to him. He had joined the Church precisely because it was unchanging and – lo! – it had suddenly changed. Courage, fidelity and loyalty he placed above all other virtues, and as he first said to me: 'I have spent my life learning with bitterness that cowardice, treachery and disloyalty are the order of the day, and one constantly rewarded and encouraged by society.' He said: 'The changes to the Church have knocked the stuffing out of me, and living is a penance.' He had all his teeth, which had been troubling him, taken out, without anaesthetic, and false ones made. But he could not wear them, and ate less and less. But he had a good death, suddenly without suffering, after mass and Communion, on Easter Sunday.

His novels are full of hidden treasures, for he often put people into them, usually in revenge for real or imaginary acts of hospitality. Once, at Inverness Airport, waiting for the London plane, which was late, I had a long talk about Waugh with Lord Lovat ('Shimi' as he was known, Gallic for Simon – as the eldest Fraser, in each generation, was called). Shimi told me: 'Waugh hated me because I got him out of the Commandos. I had to. He was not only useless but a menace. He was not fit to command men. He sneered at them, mocked them, made fun of them. They loathed him. The minute they had gone into action, they would have shot him in the back. This was not just my view. All the senior officers agreed. But I had the job of telling him and sacking him. So he put me in his novel as Trimmer. *I am Trimmer!* It's outrageous, but so it is.' Trimmer is the handsome, fake war hero of the Sword of Honour trilogy. Waugh envied Shimi his height, his looks (he was a sort of upper-class Errol Flynn), his title, his castle, his position as Chief of the Fraser clan, and his unquestionable glamour. Waugh took revenge by turning Shimi into a woman's hairdresser. He would have been pleased to hear our conversation, for it revealed Shimi's fury and showed the blow had hit home.

Victor Weisz, or 'Vicky' (1913–66), was the greatest cartoonist of twentieth-century Britain, with the possible exception of David Low. Low was, I suppose, a more assured draftsman and he got better likenesses in his soft-pencilled portrait drawings. But Vicky had more ideas, was much funnier, and at his best had a scintillating, mad invention which recalled Gilray. He was immensely productive, and each week, when he brought in his *New Statesman* cartoon (promptly at 12 p.m. on Monday), he would give us five or six from which to choose. (He was also drawing five cartoons a week for the *Mirror*, then the *Evening Standard*.) He was always highly self-critical, diffident about his work and needed continual reassurance. 'Do you like it?' 'Yes, Vicky, marvellous.' '*Sure* you like it?' 'Yes indeed, Vicky.' Later: '*Quite* sure you like it?' 'Yes, Vicky, now go away.' Later still: 'I don't think you *really* like it?' 'Oh, go to hell, Vicky.' 'You see, I knew you didn't like it all along.' But if one could put up with his neurotic habits, he was delightful company. He had a strong, infallible moral sense, and was the best judge of right and wrong I ever came across. If I ever needed moral advice I would always go to him. I regarded close friendship with him as a great privilege, one of my most precious possessions.

Vicky was of Hungarian-Jewish origin, went to the Berlin School of Art, and became the family breadwinner at fourteen when his father died. He drew for the *12 Uhr Blatt* and published his first anti-Hitler cartoon at fifteen. After the Reichstag fire he escaped to London. Gerald Barry, editor of the *News Chronicle*, took him up and taught him the English sense of humour by getting him to read selections of Shakespeare, Jorrocks, *Alice in Wonderland*, *Punch*, Dickens, Edward Lear, A. A. Milne and even *Wisden*. He studied the scripts of Tommy Handley's *ITMA* radio programme, went to Gilbert and Sullivan, pantomime and music halls, learned true Cockney rhyming slang, watched movies by George Formby, Will Hay and Gracie Fields and, with Maurice Richardson's help, went over the back numbers of *Lilliput* to analyse the photo selection. He grew to love classics like *Gulliver's Travels* and *The Pickwick Papers*, *Three Men in a Boat* and P. G. Wodehouse, and learned to speak English pretty well, so that his captions became almost as good as his drawings.

He told me that when he first came to England, and had a bedsit in Hampstead, he went into a café for a cup of coffee. He was unemployed, almost penniless, depressed and suicidal. The wireless began blaring the 'Horst Wessel Song'. He said to the slatternly waitress, transliterating from the German: 'That song. I cannot hear it [meaning, I cannot bear it].' The waitress, muttering 'Some people need their ears tested!', obligingly turned up the volume. Vicky rushed out into the street in a state of despair: 'I thought England was turning Nazi! It was days before the mistake was explained to me. But then, gradually, I came to understand and love the English – passionately. And to love their sense of humour, and make it my own.' He became the chief cartoonist of the *News Chronicle*, eventually leaving it for the *Mirror*. He described the change as 'like leaving a lady with syphilis and taking up with an honest whore'. But his last, and happiest, job was on the *Evening Standard*, which had Beaverbrook's unique blend of upper-crust sophistication and populism. The Beaver loved him and he sort of loved the Beaver. He told me: 'Beaverbrook phoned me early this morning. He said: "Mr Vicky, the Prime Minister has been complaining to me about your cartoons. You have annoyed him. And, Mr Vicky, the Home Secretary has complained to me about you. You have annoyed *him*. And yesterday the Foreign Secretary complained. He is annoyed. *Very* annoyed. Mr Vicky, I congratulate you. *People have gotta be annoyed!*'"

He and I both shared a favourite politician, Aneurin Bevan. We went with him for a long ramble on the Downs while he rehearsed out loud his famous 'Naked into the Council Chambers of the World' speech, which he delivered to the Brighton Labour Party Conference the next day. Vicky wanted him to tone it down, I to beef it up – and he took my advice. It was the last great speech he made before his death. Vicky did a series of drawings of him while he was making it, transferring them afterwards to a single large page, which we used in the NS to accompany his obituary. He did the same with a page of drawings of Churchill we used when the old man finally died. He gave both the originals to me. I look at these two splendid gifts from Vicky every day of my life.

He married several times. With his habitual melancholy, punctuated by bouts of acute depression, he was a difficult man to live with. He had no children. He told me: 'I will not willingly bring into this horrible world an innocent child.' What finally killed him was giving up smoking. He got through sixty to eighty a day, and knew they were harmful. Eventually, with a gigantic effort, he stopped – successfully. But not smoking hugely deepened his depression. His fourth and last wife, Ingelore, was devoted to him, and he was very dependent on her. She did her best to carry him through difficult periods, but she had a good job in the fashion trade and could not always be in London. The next time she was away, he took more sleeping pills than usual – many more. Did he deliberately kill himself? I shall never be sure. I got the news of his death on Wednesday afternoon, as I was putting the NS to press, and I had to sit down immediately to write his obituary. I blamed myself for not doing more to help him bear his life. So did Ingelore, and continued to do so, killing herself on the ninth anniversary of his death. He took the world too seriously – a mistake which was inevitably fatal. Yet impotent old age, without drawing, would have been worse.

H. G. Wells (1866–1946). I never met Wells, but his ghost haunted the offices of the *New Statesman* in Great Turnstile, in the shape of his raincoat. On a visit, he had left it there in 1945, not long before he died. No one claimed it, and it thus became the Office Raincoat, to be borrowed by anyone caught unprepared by rain. It hung on the back of the door in my little office, at the end of the corridor on the editorial floor. Baroness Budberg, a former mistress of his, was still around in the fifties. I asked her how it was that Wells, who seemed from descriptions and photographs to have been an unprepossessing little man, was so attractive to women. She answered: 'It was because he smelled of honey.' The next morning, when I got to my office, I inspected the raincoat with a fresh eye, or, rather, nose. But all it smelt of was rusty old raincoat.

Rebecca West (1892–1983) was once a beautiful and always a handsome and talented lady with an extraordinary – I would say unique – propensity for quarrelling and provoking rows. The first time I met her, having never hitherto thought about her at all, I found myself, to my astonishment, having an acrimonious dispute with her about a triviality. She carried around with her a faint but distinct whiff of sulphur. How? Why? Her sister, Letitia Fairfield, whom I also knew a bit, was quite different: calm, reasonable and irenic. West's real name was Cicely Isabel Fairfield. Her drunken Irish father detested his family. When she was nine, her mother took her and her two sisters to her home town of Edinburgh, where she got a good schooling at George Watson's Ladies College. She was a well-educated woman and her brain was razor-sharp.

The tragedy of her life was her affair with H. G. Wells in 1913, which led to the unintended birth of a child, Anthony West. She retained a love-hate relationship with Wells, the hate gradually eclipsing the love, until Wells's death in 1946. Apparently, she quarrelled with her son Anthony until her death. She produced a great deal of journalistic and literary work in her life, some of it first-class. Her *Black Lamb and Grey Falcon*, though too long, is the best book ever written about that large stretch of the Balkans once called Yugoslavia. She also had a humdrum marriage, for nearly forty years, with a businessman called Andrews. But the Wells business and its consequences dominated and poisoned her life, just as the affair with Byron did with Claire Claremont. Indeed, there are almost uncanny parallels between the two women, reflected in their letters. It is sad to think how gifted women can be marked for life by youthful folly of the emotions. Rebecca West said to me: 'I have had to fight tremendous battles all my life and have often given way to anger. But then I had good reason.' Well: she would say that, wouldn't she? Letitia Fairfield warned me: 'My sister is an oyster who carries her own grit around with her. Beware!'

2nd Duke of Westminster (1879–1953) was always known as Bendor, after a horse, Bend Or. When I was an officer cadet, during my military service 1949–51 (you did two years in those days – nine months in the ranks, fifteen months in commissioned service) I was stationed at Eaton Hall, near Chester, which was the main training centre for infantry officers. It was the seat of the Grosvenors, who had been there since about 1070. The house had been hugely expanded in Victorian times. In 1939 it had been requisitioned by the government, and at one time had housed the boys of Dartmouth Naval College. Stonyhurst played them at athletics, so I had been there before. I loved it. As a cadet I slept, along with three others, in a big bedroom with a brass plate on the door saying 'State Bedroom, Number Six'. The place was run by guardsmen, mainly Coldstreams, though the adjutant was a Welsh guardsman and very severe. The RSM was Copp, a horrible man with a huge grey face. The NCOs were down on us all but especially Green Jackets, as we had a different drill. So we had a hard time, and the work was very heavy, with a lot to learn by heart. We were exhausted all the time. I rarely went to Chester, but during brief times off I liked to walk round the vast gardens and admire the house and its endless purlieus. They included a station for a small-scale railway, which took the guns out shooting, and an immense clock tower, rather like Big Ben.

One day, when I was among the parterres, a burly figure came by and said: 'Hello there! What are you doing?' He seemed author-itative. I said: 'Nothing. Admiring this place.' 'Do you like it?' 'I love it. I think it's one of the most marvellous places I've ever been.' 'What, you love the house?' 'Yes.' 'And the clock tower?' 'Especially the clock tower.' 'Do you think it's good architecture?' 'Certainly.' 'So do I. But you and I seem to be the only people who do. They will pull it all down when I'm gone.' He walked slowly off. I realised I had been speaking to the Duke. Three years later he died, and they did pull it down – though not the clock tower. Oddly enough I had already met, at Oxford, one of his four wives, Loelia, who had divorced him and then married again, a boulevardier called the Hon. Freddie Cripps, father of my friend Milo Cripps, the bad boy of my time at Oxford. She once gave me a wigging for 'leading poor Milo astray', though I was entirely innocent: rather, he led me astray. Loelia spoke well of Bendor's generosity, 'but I'm glad I'm not still married to the brute'. I rather took to the sad old Duke, born to unimaginable riches, spoilt and selfish, but sharing with me a fondness for a then unregarded and doomed piece of Victoriana.

Huw Wheldon (1916–86) was the Great Panjandrum of BBC TV culture. He came from Prestatyn, a seaside resort in North Wales where we used to go sometimes for holidays, a place of unspeakable tedium. He claimed he did not speak any English until he was seven. His father was a solicitor who worked in Lloyd George's law firm. Both he and Huw had exemplary war careers, the latter, oddly enough, in the Ulster Rifles, a crack regiment. He made his name in the Festival of Britain, and in the BBC, by devising a conker competition for children which attracted 60,000 entries and was a huge success. From 1958 to 1964 he ran *Monitor*, the pioneer TV arts programme. This made him a great power in the land for it was watched by everyone who mattered, and Wheldon's magisterial presentation was absolutely mesmeric. But I noticed at the time, and thought it ominous, that Wheldon gave his seal of approval to everything that was new and original, and to every new arrival on the arts scene, regardless of merit. He became one of the most powerful men in Britain, and at the time his work received high and universal praise. Had he not set the powerful machinery of TV to work in the cause of bringing culture to everyone? Looking back, I see this programme as a milestone on the dusty road to cultural degeneration in Britain, with novelty, and popular success, the sole criteria of value.

After he finished with *Monitor* he went higher and higher up the BBC hierarchy, though he never got the top job. Lord Hill (Charlie Hill, once 'the Radio Doctor') thought he was 'too big for his Welsh boots' and appointed a nonentity, Charles Curran, instead. Wheldon was not happy as a BBC grandee. He told me: 'None of the creative people want to know me now. I have nothing to offer them.' He was covered in honours and honorary degrees, but somehow shrank and became sad. His stories grew longer and longer, and with less and less point, and one tended to avoid his button-holing. But that, alas, is a typical story of fame and its aftermath.

Colonel George Wigg (1900–83) was a tall, ugly, ungainly man with a huge nose and a loud, sergeant major's voice. His origins were humble and he owed everything to the army, where he rose from private to senior NCO, then to colonel. He was in the RAEC and was an autodidact. He loved the army passionately and defended it like a jealous wife. As an MP he always took the army's view in the House, and put it well before party. He believed John Profumo, as War Secretary, had misled the House over the equipment of the British troops sent to Jordan in 1958, after the Iraq coup. Thereafter he pursued Profumo relentlessly and played a part in uncovering the Cliveden scandal and the relationship with Christine Keeler. He told me: 'I am prepared to be sued for libel and go to gaol if necessary.'

Wigg could be very frightening. If angry, he would say: 'I will get you, *believe you me.*' Or: 'I will have your *guts for garters.*' When I just joined the staff of the *New Statesman* in 1955, one of my jobs was to phone Wigg every week to get inside information on defence. I disliked doing this as he was such an awkward fellow. So some weeks I didn't. But he knew my orders, and always phoned himself sooner or later: 'Wigg here. Not a voice you care to hear, eh? Evading duty, eh, Mr Johnson? Now listen here, *scrimshanker*, while I tell you something important.' And so on. However, immediately after the Suez debacle, when I was writing my first book, *The Suez War*, a quickie, done in ten days, he proved very useful. Each evening he would come to my flat in Cadogan Place, having called at 'the War House', as he referred to it, and got the latest 'gen'. Not everything he said stood up but most of it was quite true, and sensational. I put it all in the book, though Arnold Goodman, as the publisher's lawyer, took nearly all of it out as 'a flagrant breach of the Official Secrets Act'. While writing the book, I was also courting Marigold, who was usually in my flat when Wigg called. She made herself scarce, cowering in a corner.

But he spotted her, and called out loudly: 'Has that woman got security clearance?'

Wigg's finest hour was at Tom Driberg's wedding, celebrated at All Saints, Margaret Street, where Tom was a sidesman, with masses of candles, thick clouds of incense, gold vestments and tinkling altar bells. Wigg was an old-fashioned army Anglican, low church, a stickler for the liturgical rules, and who knew the various Acts governing C of E services. He stood upright towards the back of the groom's side, and called out at intervals: 'This is all illegal, you know. *Illegal!* It's against the *law!*' His voice thundering 'Illegal' punctuated the ceremony throughout, enlivening a gruesome occasion.

Wigg was in Number Ten throughout the first Wilson government, 'to prevent anything like the Profumo affair happening in my administration', as Wilson put it. In fact, he engaged in endless battles with Marcia Falkender, Wilson's secretary. Afterwards both contestants went to the House of Lords, both typical of the new kind of peer who took over the Upper House from the sixties. Wigg drew a grubby curtain over his career by getting himself arrested off Oxford Street for importuning women. But I remember him with a certain wry affection. He called the army 'my raddled Old Bag'.

Edmund Wilson (1895–1972) visited Oxford when I was an undergraduate. I was taken over by my tutor, Bruce McFarlane, to A. L. Rowse's rooms in All Souls. I did not really know who Wilson was – had never read him – but realised he was famous and important. He seemed quite small: plump, with a big head and large eyes. His mouth was pursed, prissy and he seemed to disapprove of everything. He said: 'I guess England's finished. You don't seem to have any money or resources [he said '*re*sources']. Everything here is old, decaying, falling down. You haven't even begun to repair London yet, and here in Oxford all of the stonework is beginning to fall off. It's kinda diseased, as though the colleges have leprosy.' He seemed to be delighted by this evidence of decline. None of the dons present contradicted him. It was true that England and Oxford were at a low ebb. The winter of 1947 had been horribly cold and we had not yet recovered from it. Everything was rationed and we were hungry for good, rich food. There were no funds for anything, let alone repairing the stonework. I felt annoyed by what Wilson said, and the failure of my elders to answer him. So I said: 'The delay or cowardice of America in entering the war so late, and then only when you were attacked, put an unfair burden on us. We had to fight the Germans alone, and we are still exhausted by our efforts.' Wilson focused on me, and said in a chilly voice: 'I stand rebuked by the young.'

Many years later in New York, when I was taken to see him by his niece, Norah Sayre, I reminded him of this conversation. But he had forgotten it, and there is no mention in his diary of his visit to Oxford, though it refers to the decay in the stone of the colleges. Wilson's hatred of England and the English was very marked, and is inexplicable to me. I think the roots of it lay very deep in history. He was still in spirit fighting the Revolutionary War, or the War of 1812, even though his opponents were Oxford dons, English literary critics like Raymond Mortimer and writers like Evelyn Waugh. I found it hard to get through this anti-English carapace to the interesting and open-minded man within.

Harold Wilson (1916–95) was a kindly man and, by the standards of politics, a decent man. When I first got to know him in the mid-fifties, he was enormously good company, well informed, witty, full of excellent stories, friendly and generous. I never liked his pipe. But it was essential to him, a little crutch to overcome a certain inner instability and nervousness. It was not true, as Tommy

Balogh said, that 'Harold knows nothing about economics.' He was a mathematician – but then so was Keynes. He knew all about statistics, which was his real profession. But he never gave me the impression that he grasped the essentials of economics, or that he knew how to translate economic aspirations into practical politics. That was the real weakness of his governments. When, in 1951, he and John Freeman and Nye Bevan were discussing the theoretic basis on which they were to resign from the Attlee government, it was Freeman who supplied the central argument – that the scale of rearmament was too large for the available manufacturing capacity, and would merely lead to inflation. This was quite beyond Nye, and Harold could not get its importance. So it was Freeman who invented the principles of Bevanism.

Gaitskell and Wilson stood for the two alternatives open to Labour – either to concentrate on a single, clear and specific policy, which meant splitting the party; or to have a vague, woolly consensus on nothing very much. Harold Wilson always chose the second, though he tried to clothe it in fierce-sounding rhetoric. Hence, when Gaitskell suddenly died at the end of 1963, Wilson was able to reunite the party in a matter of weeks, and to win (just) the 1964 election. But having got to Number Ten, what to do? The idea of 'creative tension', with the competing economic ministries, the Treasury and the DEA under the mad and drunk George Brown, was complete nonsense. Everything went from bad to worse under the first Wilson government, and under the second, which he did not expect and came as a surprise to him. Wilson more or less abdicated and allowed Michael Foot to hand over all power to the unions. Looking back on it, it is amazing to think of the idiocy of those times, with first Brown, then Foot, allowed to do what they pleased, under Wilson's weak rule. The sixties and the seventies were bad times for Britain, and Wilson bore a heavy responsibility for the failures.

But if you forget about his disastrous career as Prime Minister, Wilson was a likeable man. He gave good parties in Downing Street – the only PM of my time who did, recalling the great days of Lady Palmerston's *drums*. All the current celebrities came, so you met people like the Beatles and Sean Connery. Wilson's Kitchen Cabinet of Falkender, Balogh, Wigg, Kaufman, etc., supplied a continual office sitcom of high (and low) comedy, with Arnold Goodman as a supplementary clown on a colossal scale – 'Good job Number Ten has a wide door so he can fit through it', I used to say. There was animal interest, too. Wilson's exceptionally stupid comic dog, a golden Labrador called Paddy. Then there was 'Harold's Old Dad'. Wilson Sr came to life especially at Party Conferences. At Brighton, for instance, he used to sit just inside the main door of the Grand, the Conference hotel, with a little table on which his drink stood. All the sycophants in the government, or those who wished to get into it, would buy the old boy drinks. 'Care for a drink, Mr Wilson?' 'I don't mind if I do.' I never actually saw him drink but when you looked his glass was always empty. So far as I know he was never interested in politics in the tiniest degree, but then flatterers were not to know that.

Wilson was very shrewd about manipulating the honours system, inventing new ministries and pseudo-Departments of State, bringing in prominent outsiders and giving them grand titles, etc. So there was always a lot of *va-et-vient* in Downing Street, which gave the impression that important things were being done. But it was all theatricals, grease paint and stage scenery. I remember Barbara Castle saying to me in the Wilson twilight of 1975–6: 'All he does now is fiddle with the honours list – it's the only thing he has left which he controls.'

But Wilson was, as I have said, kind. He came to see me in hospital. He would do that sort of thing. He noticed when humble typists were in distress, for instance – and would try to cheer them up. And he knew when to go. He was forewarned about Alzheimer's, and went immediately. He had never forgotten being a Boy Scout, and was a great patriot at heart. Queen Elizabeth II said she liked him the most of all her PMs.

Ludwig Wittgenstein (1889–1951) visited Magdalen College in 1948 to take part in a discussion in one of the small lecture rooms. I was not present – knew nothing about it. But at dinner he was brought into Hall by Gilbert Ryle, the philosophy Fellow. I was in the body of the hall with the hoi polloi, sitting between Karl Leyser and John Cooper, both future history dons of distinction and Fellows of All Souls. Suddenly, as the senior members filed in to sit at High Table, Cooper said, in his loud, rasping voice: 'It's Wittgenstein!' I had never heard the name, but I said: 'Good God!' What struck me about the small, slight guest was that he had no tie: wore his shirt open-necked. In those days it was a cardinal offence for an undergraduate to attempt to dine in Hall without a tie. The servants would have refused to admit anyone so antinomian. For someone to sit at High Table thus undressed was inconceivable. Yet here this obviously famous man was, tieless, brazen. And not without a certain air of distinction, either. A year before, at Trinity, Cambridge, Wittgenstein had been involved in a row with Karl Popper, and had reputedly threatened him with a poker. On this evening, too, Wittgenstein's behaviour let to a row, with an elderly philosophy don. No poker was flourished. But the don dropped dead a few days later.

Leonard Woolf (1880–1969) was on the board of the *New Statesman* when John Freeman resigned as editor, and tried to prevent me succeeding him. His grounds were simply that I was a Roman Catholic. He wrote me a letter saying, 'There is nothing personal in this.' But it seemed to me very personal. He did not get his way, and was obliged to resign from the board. But it meant I was a bit inhibited in beginning my editorship, reluctant to make necessary changes for fear of people saying, 'So Leonard was right after all.'

Three things about him struck me. The first was his relationship to his wife, Virginia. Early in my editorship I published a long piece on lesbianism, then hardly discussed at all. It was quite daring in those days, though read now it would strike one as painfully circumspect. I was lunching with Kingsley Martin the week before, and brought a proof, feeling I needed his support. To my dismay, Leonard was there. However, he seemed delighted by my daring, and said: 'My wife was a lesbian, you know.' Afterwards Kingsley, who had been embarrassed, as he always was when sex came up, said: 'Forget what Leonard said about Virginia. Please don't repeat it. Anyway I don't think she was a lesbian. It was just that some women found her attractive.'

The second thing about Woolf was his meanness. This crops up in Virginia Woolf's diaries, where she records having to pay for certain things, at his insistence, out of her earnings. Parsimony was one of the things which drew Leonard and Kingsley together. They both liked Indian restaurants and competed to find the cheapest. Once they took me to lunch to a dingy place in a little block opposite Charing Cross Station, since pulled down. Neither used the word 'cheap'. Kingsley said: 'This restaurant is the best value in London.' Leonard said: 'I know an even better one in Islington.' It was certainly cheap, and nasty. Even so, they bickered over how the bill should be divided between them: 'You had an extra helping of popadoms, Kingsley.'

The third thing was the wrinkles in Leonard's face. They made him look like a crocodile. What caused them – smoking? That was certainly true in W. H. Auden's case. I often wished I could see Auden and Woolf together, to see which had more wrinkles, and vertiginous creases, per square inch of face.

Richard Wright (1908–60) I knew in Paris in the early fifties. He was the first black man I got to know. He had fled there to escape what he called persecution in the US. The French feted him, bought translations of his books in vast numbers, gave him French nationality and made him an honorary citizen of Paris. I loved arguing with him at Les Deux Magots, the Mabillon and the Café Tournon, especially about colonisation. Then came the moment of truth. He was invited to visit the Gold Coast, the most advanced of the British colonies in West Africa. It was an eye-opener, and he came back visibly shaken. 'Man!' he told me, 'Those people are not like us. They are so backward it hurts. Man, they are goddam *savages*!'

His wife was white, pretty, clever and amorous.

Woodrow Wyatt (1918–2007) was married to various women, not all of whom made it into his *Who's Who* entry. He was at various times an MP 1945–55, 1959–70, a publisher of books, a newspaper columnist, an editor-publisher of local newspapers and a TV journalist. He and Richard Dimbleby started *Panorama* in 1955 when I first met him, and later he achieved fame by unmasking the Communist conspiracy in the Electrical Trade Union. This took real courage, of which Woodrow always had plenty. He was also brash, arrogant, pushy, boastful and not always honest. He ran the Tote for many years, the real source of his power and influence. He knew everybody and never hesitated to telephone them if he wanted anything. He said to me: 'If you want anything in this bloody hopeless country, from a dinner invitation to a life peerage, ask for it. And ask, ask and ask again. You always get it in the end. Never be diffident. Never take a back seat. Speak up for yourself. Blow your own trumpet – hard as you can. Take my advice – effrontery always pays.' He always lived above his income and when he died left behind diaries for his widow, Verushka, to flog to the Sunday papers. They are not to be trusted. Woodrow, Bernard Levin and I occasionally held a political *conversazione* over lunch at his house to be recorded and published in the *Sunday Telegraph*. These were a great success. When Mrs Thatcher was Prime Minister he was always phoning her to give unsolicited advice. But he was not often put through, as her aide, Charles Powell, told me. After many applications, she gave him a life peerage in 1987 – 'Baron Wyatt of Weeford'. He was very proud of his wine cellar, and his heavily annotated cellar book. Also of being related to R. E. S. Wyatt, the England cricket captain in the 1930s.

When he lost his seat in the 1970 election, and I phoned to commiserate, he said: 'You are the only one who has bothered to do so. One's many friends are forgetful sods.' He was the social stormtrooper in a rough world.